Albion

of Scotstoun

A Century of Cars, Trucks & Buses

Paul Adams & Roy Milligan

Albion
VEHICLE
PRESERVATION
TRUST

Dedicated to all Albion employees, past and present, whose contributions to design, production, inspection or testing, ensured the well earned reputation of the product where it mattered most, with the customer. A history of Albion would not be complete without recognising the service given by so many individuals, and in many cases generations of families, over the last 100 years.

© Paul Adams & Roy Milligan

First published 1999
Albion Vehicle Preservation Trust
18 Netherdale Drive
Paisley PA1 3DA
Fax: 0141 883 1373
e mail: pauladams_avpt@yahoo.co.uk

Scottish Charity No. 028791

ISBN 0 9535946 0 2

Printed by
Cordfall Ltd
0141 572 0878

Frontispiece: This wartime view is of DYS 23, a WD.CX22, shows it engaged on a haul of part of a marine diesel engine weighing 86 tons between Govan and Dundee. The Scammell at the rear was towed along with the load, but was used as a booster when steep gradients were encountered. The truck belonged to Road Engines and Kerr (Haulage) Ltd., Glasgow, and was one of a small number which were released by the War Department during the Second World War for essential duties.

Contents

Foreword

by Jim Hastie, Chief Executive, Albion Automotive Ltd.

When Albion Motors was established in 1899 in Glasgow, initially as a car factory, it was not suspected that it would develop to become Scotland's most successful motor manufacturing company.

'The Albion', as it is affectionately known to thousands, began to specialise in the production of trucks before the First World War and continued to build them until 1980. It merged with Leyland Motors in 1951 and then became part of the British Leyland combine in 1968.

Albion survived the collapse of the British truck market in the 1980s but almost went into extinction in 1993 as a result of DAF going into receivership.

As one of the founder directors of Albion Automotive, which was formed in late 1993 as an automotive components supplier with plants in Lancashire as well as Glasgow, I am delighted to have played a part in ensuring that the proud history and heritage of 'The Albion' has been maintained.

In October 1998 Albion Automotive was acquired by American Axle and Manufacturing, a Detroit based company whose major customer is General Motors. A key feature in the acquisition was that Albion Automotive would be a wholly owned subsidiary and would continue to trade under the Albion name.

As the Albion centenary approaches and the larger automotive companies continue to accelerate towards globalisation it is comforting to know that the Albion name is already destined to flourish in its hundredth year and to continue beyond the millennium.

I would like to congratulate Paul Adams and Roy Milligan on the tremendous achievement in compiling this book. The meticulous detail will be much appreciated by all who understand the history and tradition of 'The Albion.'

Jim Hastie
February 1999.

Introduction

by the Authors

In the first 70 to 80 years of the twentieth century, the name Albion on the radiator or front panel of a truck or bus was every bit as familiar to the man in the street as the name Volvo or Scania is today. Indeed, the Albion radiator with its sunrise logo was as much a symbol of distinctiveness in the commercial vehicle industry as the Rolls Royce radiator continues to be in the car industry today. And it was not just in Scotland or Britain where the name Albion was a byword for reliability and longevity, but in many countries overseas, where Albion once exported more of its production than any other British manufacturer. It is no surprise, therefore, that the name lives on at South Street, Scotstoun, where Albion Automotive continues to be a successful manufacturer of components to the motor industry, one of the very few names of the British motor industry to have made it to its centenary, and to have survived the disintegration of British Leyland.

In compiling this book we have set out to provide a description and/or an illustration of every significant type of model which the company made, and we believe that we have been largely successful in achieving this aim. Identifying models has not been an easy task. Before 1930 Albions were never referred to in the technical press by their model number, but instead by horse power or payload. Indeed, some early models with 'A' prefixes appear to have had these designations applied retrospectively. When unidentified photographs have come into our possession we have taken as much care as possible to try and correctly identify the model, and we are reasonably confident that the vehicle depicted is a good example of the type. Also post-1930 a very small number of photographs could not be identified with absolute certainty, but again we are confident that the photograph represents the model described.

A small number of models have not been covered, simply because we have been unable to find any technical record or photograph of these types. Similarly, it has not been possible to provide details of every variation of every model, because either they were built in insignificant numbers, or because the variations were minor or too numerous to list. In any case, the amount of research needed to obtain details would have distracted us from the main task of this book. We have also not attempted to include in detail the post 1972 range of Leyland-badged trucks with Bathgate built cabs, nor the mainly export range of Clydesdales and Vikings which emerged around this time. Vehicle policy was being decided elsewhere by now, and we did not consider this range with its higher proportions of bought-in components to be true Albions. In writing the captions, we have tried to be honest in detailing a vehicle's known faults where these have come to light. Not every Albion model was a success, but unreliable operation was an uncommon event, especially in the days when the company was independent.

Readers will notice that technical information is more in-depth for earlier models. This is because the motor vehicle was still evolving during the early decades of this century and each manufacturer had its own engineering solutions to particular problems. We have endeavoured, therefore, to highlight these engineering innovations and differences wherever possible. It is probably reasonable to say that by the 1960s all commercial vehicle manufacturers were producing their own versions of a relatively standard product, which was as much a result of legislation as evolution. By this time virtually every Albion model had a Leyland engine, driving through an Albion 5 or 6 speed gearbox to an Albion double reduction rear axle. It is clear, therefore, that there is only so much that can be said about these models.

It has taken two years of intensive research to complete this book, and along the way some contradictory information has been found. Everything has been checked as far as possible, and with a wide range of knowledgeable people. To the best of our knowledge everything that is written is correct, but if anyone has any comments to make, we should be pleased to hear from them.

We should also like to know the present whereabouts of a number of Albion Motors' photographic albums. Much of the former Albion publicity material has survived, but significant amounts are missing. The Albion Archive at Biggar will not be complete until these documents have been tracked down. We should also welcome information on any Albion vehicles which are not included on our Register of Preserved and Surviving Albions.

Paul Adams and Roy Milligan
Glasgow, March 1999.

Preface

by Ian Maclean, former Albion Engineer, and presently Registrar of the Albion Club and the AVPT

Of all the engineering companies which have functioned in the West of Scotland, Albion Motors was perhaps the most highly respected. A well organised and largely self-sufficient factory, with an Empire-wide chain of service depots and agents, was run by a progressive, far-seeing and beneficent management and experienced engineers, to whom the quality, reliability and reputation of the vehicles they made were their absolute concerns.

The founders, Thomas Blackwood Murray and Norman Osborne Fulton, and, later their friend and fellow director John Francis Henderson, were talented men, each contributing in his own way to the progress of the company. Murray was responsible for design and engineering, and many were the ideas and patents which came from his fertile brain. Fulton was in charge of production in all its aspects, and Henderson's responsibilities included bodywork, spare parts and service. In the former field Henderson must receive credit for the attractive, yet business-like, appearance of Albions up to and even after his death in 1941.

Many and varied indeed were the models which Albion produced, very often tailor-made to a particular customer's requirements. And so to this day there is still confusion among vehicle enthusiasts and transport historians and writers as to which model an Albion might be. This book is intended as guide to the extensive range of vehicles which Scotstoun made and will also, we hope, be seen as a Centenary tribute to the founding friends, whose Albion name is still respected by vehicle people and remembered with fondness and pride by "Albion men".

Two organisations today look after Albion owners, enthusiast and enquirers. The Albion Club is a wing of the Biggar Museum Trust, based in Biggar, Lanarkshire, where Thomas Blackwood Murray originally lived and

where he built and tested the first Albion car. Membership is open to all interested in Albions, whether owners or not, and the normal facilities of a one-make vehicle club including a magazine are of course available. The Albion Vehicle Preservation Trust was formed in 1967 to purchase, garage and rally one of the last Albion heavy coaches, a 1950 Valiant, and in 1991 a 1967 Viking coach doubled the fleet. In a joint arrangement with The Albion Club, the AVPT keeps the Register of Preserved Albions, and has so far collected details of some 680 Albions surviving world-wide.

In their researches for this book the authors were fortunate to find and be assisted by so many people knowledgeable about Albions; a pleasant surprise was the longevity of former Albion employees, another recommendation perhaps for the good working environment within the company! Our appreciation and thanks go to them all.

Ian Maclean
March 1999.

The Founders

Thomas Blackwood Murray.

Thomas Murray was born in 1871 and after secondary education at George Watson's in Edinburgh, graduated with a BSc in electrical engineering from Edinburgh University in 1890. After working on a variety of electrical engineering projects in Edinburgh, he joined Mavor & Coulson of Glasgow in 1893, as manager of the Installations Department where he became involved in electrical applications for the automotive industry. By 1896, Murray was on the move again, joining the new Mo-Car Syndicate to manage the electrical department and where he met Norman Fulton. He served out a three year contract with Mo-Car, resigning in 1899 to form the Albion partnership with Fulton, which he financed with a bank loan secured by his father against Heavyside Farm, the family home near Biggar in Lanarkshire. Murray received a DSc from Edinburgh University in 1917, and remained chairman of Albion until his retirement in 1929 due to illness.

Norman Osborne Fulton.

Norman Fulton received secondary education at Allan Glen's School in Glasgow, thereafter serving his apprenticeship as an engineer, with further studies at the Andersonian College. Fulton worked in the food processing and chemical industries, where he became interested in the organisation of the manufacturing process. He joined the Mo-Car Syndicate in 1896 to work for its founder, his cousin George Johnston, leaving in 1898 to spend a year working as a mechanic for the Pope Manufacturing Company of Connecticut. They had just started building cars but were already familiar with the mass production of bicycles and the use of standardised interchangeable parts. Fulton used this valuable time to communicate with Murray in Glasgow, sending back sketches and some parts for the first Albion. On his return, Fulton put up his half share of the £4,000 required to fund the Albion partnership.

John Francis Henderson.

John Henderson was born in Harrow-on-the-Hill, London, and received his later education at Blair Lodge, Polmont, near Falkirk. Like Murray, he gained a BSc in electrical engineering from Edinburgh University, graduating in 1901. During his studies he spent 18 months working under Lord Kelvin as a Thomson scholar. He later joined Mavor and Coulson where he met Murray, and moved to Albion in 1902 where he was able to provide the additional capital required as the business expanded. The Murray-Fulton partnership was converted to a private limited company in July 1902, with Murray, Fulton and Henderson as joint managing directors. In addition to his management responsibilities, he influenced the look of Albions, and is credited with the more elegant style of radiator introduced from 1923.

This is an extract from a letter written by Thomas Blackwood Murray just after his resignation from the Mo-Car Syndicate and written to his former colleague, Norman Fulton, while he was working in the United States. Had Murray accepted George Johnston's offer to remain and taken over the management of Mo-Car with Fulton, this book would not be celebrating the centenary of Albion.

27th October, 1899.

My Dear Norman,
        Many thanks for your kind letter of 5th inst., which I have just received . . .

        . . . "Le grande ordeal" is over. It took place on Wednesday 25th inst. Mr. Johnston was very decent and I had not to rake up any old sores, so much the better. It could have done no good and would only have embittered feelings on both sides. He wished us success and promised to help us if he could, in fact was most generous. Perhaps Norman we may (if successful) one day be able to help him. He is a real kind man at heart but it beats me completely just how he manages to keep afloat at all. He said he would have preferred to have us both there again, and he even said he would like to go out of it entirely and leave us. I asked him to let me away not later than the end of November.

        About friction clutches, I have been making very full enquiries but I can't find any maker who will guarantee clutches to work under oil. However . . .

                                Yours Faithfully,

                                    T.B. Murray

Chapter 1

The Early Years
1899 to 1919

By the end of the nineteenth century it was clear that the motor car had become a practical reality, but this new technology was still in its infancy and had many engineering challenges to overcome. Albion was fortunate to be established by two men with experience from their days with the Mo-Car Syndicate, one of the earliest of the British manufacturers, and so it was no accident that the Albion Motor Car Company established itself so quickly with a solid and dependable product. Frustrated by a lack of progress at Mo-Car and eager to proceed with new ideas, Murray and Fulton made plans to build their own car. A partnership was formed late in 1899 between Murray and Fulton, and they were then free to concentrate on their own new enterprise, with the design and manufacture of the first vehicle already well under way.

1899 was a significant year for the newly formed Albion partnership, but it also saw the beginnings of Argyll as the Hozier Engineering Company with the Mo-Car Syndicate using the Arrol-Johnston name on their cars. The foundations of the Glasgow trio of famous As were

now in place and although Mo-Car was already producing cars, Albion and Hozier did not turn out their respective first models until the following year. Albion was only one of around 50 Scottish firms who tried their hand at motor manufacture before 1918, and thus had many rivals. England and Europe too had many aspiring car manufacturers whose products competed with Albions, although many of the early manufacturers were in fact merely re-engineering imported chassis. Many were imported from France, greatly assisted by the French practice of building right hand drive cars for their domestic market, while others used that period to design and develop their own unique products. It is perhaps not surprising that the first Albion had more than a passing resemblance to models already on the market, in particular the 1899 Peugeot with its 8hp, rear engined, 2 cylinder configuration. Indeed the overall appearance of the first Albion owed more to the neater proportions and layout of the Peugeot than the heavier looking Arrol-Johnston 4 seater of 1899. However, the 1901 Arrol-Johnston looked

---

Setting the Scene.

The first practical motor car came about in the early 1880s following the efforts of Carl Benz and especially Gottlieb Daimler, at that time working quite independently. In 1884, Daimler patented a small high speed gas engine, followed in 1885 by a single cylinder liquid fuel engine with enclosed crank and flywheel, which was to be the parent of all Daimler and similar engines. Daimler's right hand man, Wilhelm Maybach, had invented the float-feed spray making carburettor in 1893 and although both men had left the Daimler Motoren Gesellschaft shortly after its founding in 1890, the progress made in France by other makers resulted in an alarmed Daimler management inviting Messrs Daimler and Maybach to rejoin the company late in 1894.

The Daimler engine was also used by many others, and in 1894 Panhard and Levassor acquired the manufacturing rights in France, with Emile Levassor subsequently perfecting the engine with the assistance of Daimler himself. In the Paris to Bordeaux race the following year, a Panhard-Levassor car came first, having covered 735 miles in just under 49 hours at an average speed of 14.9 mph, confirming the motor spirit engine as a serious rival to the steam engine.

In 1896, this time in a 1,060 mile race from Paris to Marseilles, a Panhard-Levassor again took first place, with Peugeot, their most serious commercial rival, coming second. Peugeot used Panhard-Levassor engines until 1896, thereafter developing their own 2 cylinder engines mounted horizontally and transversely at the rear and with sliding gear transmission in the style of the Panhard.

By 1896, the partnership of Count de Dion and Georges Bouton had developed the first high speed variant of the Daimler engine, running at 1,500 rpm compared to the 700-900 rpm of the original Daimler version. Further significant developments in the 1890s included the first pneumatic tyres specifically for motor cars and the introduction of the low tension magneto, combining the 1897 and 1898 patents of Bosch and Simms respectively, which at last replaced a variety of less reliable ignition systems. In 1899, other companies which were also to become well known names made their debut, such as F.I.A.T. in Italy, and oil companies, Castrol, and Duckhams in Britain. Home motor manufacturers still to make their appearance over the next decade or so included Austin, Maudslay, Morris-Oxford, Rolls-Royce, Rover, Singer and Vauxhall.

very similar to the Albion dog cart, perhaps as a result of the common factor of Murray and Fulton.

Initially, all of the major components were designed in-house by Murray or under his direction and were unique to Albion, a feature which made them stand out from the competition. The ability of Murray to patent many inventions and other improvements enhanced an early reputation for reliability, enabling the company to successfully compete in what was then a hand built, low volume and fragmented industry. The more important of these patents that are very much part of the early Albion story are described in more detail in Appendix A. The founding of the Albion Motor Car Company coincided with a new century and a new technology and it is easy to dismiss the early models as simple and crude, sold into a market eager for anything motorised. However it soon becomes apparent from a study of the products and their features, that from the outset they were well thought out, designed to be reliable and to give the utmost satisfaction. Many unsolicited testimonials from customers eager to confirm the economy and reliability of their vehicles were evidence of a growing reputation, which soon became a byword in the motor industry, and it did not take Albion long to gain official recognition of their achievements.

In 1901, with production from this fledgling company barely under way, a privately owned 8hp A1 gained a Silver Medal at the Glasgow International Exhibition Trials run by the Automobile Club of Great Britain and Ireland (later to become the RAC), assisted by the Royal Scottish Automobile Club. A further Silver Medal was won by the 12hp A3 in the Automobile Club Reliability Trials in 1903, and then a Gold Medal in the 1905 Reliability Trials, this time by the 16hp A3 model. The 1906 24/30hp A6 four cylinder car also gained honours, winning a Silver Medal in the Royal Automobile Club Vapour Emission Trials of 1907, with the 16hp A3 as runner-up. In 1908, the A6 was awarded the Scottish Cup in the Scottish Automobile Club's Reliability Trials for the lowest fuel consumption per ton mile. Publicity gained from these endorsements of Albion's technical achievements helped sales considerably in the early days, and a measure of the company's success is amply demonstrated by the steady climb in production figures for the years leading up to the 1914-18 War.

The rapid growth of the company could not have been sustained without the initial sale and repeat sales of these early vehicles, often to well established businesses which were building up large fleets of the new motorised transport which was steadily displacing the horse. By 1905 a number of large retail houses began to take an interest in deliveries by motor vehicle which allowed them to greatly extend their area of business, and to a large extent they were also attracted

8hp A1 (Dog Cart). The first Albion to emerge from the Finnieston Works in 1900 is pictured in the grounds of Heavyside Farm, Murray's family home near Biggar in Lanarkshire. It was powered by a water cooled petrol engine of Albion design which used two horizontally opposed cylinders in a 'fore and aft' alignment above the gearbox and rear axle. The rear axle design was based on sketches and components sent by Fulton while in the USA, where the bicycle type wheels on this first Albion were manufactured. The engine location greatly reduced the passenger accommodation area, although a rear facing platform provided limited space for items of luggage. This traditional 'dog cart' style body was soon available with the engine cover upholstered to form a rear facing bench seat. Versions were aimed

at potential clients well able to afford a price of around £280 plus options, a considerable sum in those days. The two seaters were favoured by landowners with their gun dogs; there was a four seat businessman's car, and a doctor's car available in both the two and four seat configurations. The open body, spoked wheels and tiller steering may appear rather basic to modern eyes, but the dog cart had many advanced features for the period. Although only one chassis was produced by the original 5 manual and 2 clerical employees in 1900, output the following year was 21 chassis from a workforce which had rapidly increased to 32. The 8hp model was available with optional wheel steering by 1902, and was produced until 1903 achieving a total output of 60 chassis with this engine.

by the advertising value of the larger bodies which these new chassis could carry. It will be noted in the photographs of early vehicles that although the motor industry was in its infancy, advertising had been around for much longer and many companies took every opportunity to publicise their product or services in many attractive and ingenious ways, using their vehicles as mobile billboards. The opportunity for publicity by Albion themselves was not missed, and large fleets belonging to well known names such as Harrods of Knightsbridge, London, often feature in early brochures. Harrods were one of many customers to remain faithful to Albion in those early years, and steady sales in the capital encouraged Albion to sign an agreement in December 1904 with the Long Acre Car Company of London, who subsequently became the sole concessionaire for all sales in England & Wales. Although cars continued to be sold as Albions, the arrangement allowed the sale of Albion commercial chassis as 'Lacres' with their own radiator design. This tie up was severed after an acrimonious

legal battle just five years later, but it had been extremely important to Albion at a time of rapid sales growth and allowed the company to gain a large share of this expanding market in the Capital and elsewhere.

The limited capacity of the works at Finnieston was soon under pressure and a much needed expansion was funded in 1902 following the conversion of the partnership into a private limited company, with John F. Henderson becoming a joint managing director with Murray and Fulton. Once established in a new purpose-built factory at Scotstoun as early as 1903, output, which at least in the early days always followed sales, continued to increase in a very satisfactory manner apart from a small dip in 1907. This early period must have been one of the most exhilarating times in the Albion story. The steady expansion and equipping of the new site was a full time affair, and pressure on the management must have been intense. Expansion continued on the site with single storey sheds, but in 1913 an elegant new sandstone faced office

8hp Engine. The engine of the dog cart had two cylinders of 4" bore and 5" stroke with a capacity of just over 2 litres, and typical of the period, produced a fairly modest 7-8 brake horse power. The engine developed by the Mo-Car Syndicate for their Arrol-Johnston dog cart used a rear mounted single cylinder engine with opposed pistons and a single crankshaft placed below the cylinders. This arrangement required rocking levers and long connecting rods between pistons and crankshaft, and would have been familiar to Murray and Fulton from their time with Mo-Car. However, the engine designed for their own Albion model used a simpler arrangement, with a central crankshaft and a horizontal cylinder on either side. The normal engine speed of 700 rpm could be varied by the driver from 300 to 1,000 rpm with an accelerator which adjusted a governor controlling the exhaust valve tappets. A lever at the driver's right hand controlled the power of the engine by varying the tension of the springs on the damped 'noiseless' automatic inlet valves and thereby altered the inlet charge to the cylinders. The cylinders and exhaust valve chambers were fully water jacketed, and water circulation was provided by a pump which was chain driven from the sprocket visible in this offside view of the engine. The crankcase and gear box were formed from a single aluminium casting, with the gears and shafts running in an oil bath. The first motion shaft of the gearbox was immediately below the crankshaft and provided splash lubrication of minor bearings, with the main bearings and crank pins positively lubricated. A Murray designed and patented low tension magneto was mounted on the nearside end of the crankshaft, and the governor was housed inside the crankcase.

Dog Cart Chassis. The generally robust construction of the chassis bears out the Albion claim that their car was not based on a 'voiturette' or lightweight bicycle-derived type, but was intended to be a sturdy workhorse capable of standing up to the variable road conditions of the day. However, the bicycle type spoked wheels and tyres fitted to the first chassis proved to be inadequate for the weight, and were soon discarded in favour of more dependable artillery pattern wooden spoked wheels with solid rubber tyres. The tiller steering arrangement is a feature of the earlier versions of this model, and the engine radiator can be seen mounted at an angle behind the front wheels, somewhat conveniently below the driver's and front passenger's feet. The magneto is mounted at the centre of the flywheel in this nearside view of a production chassis. The space taken up by the horizontally opposed engine was considerable, limiting rear accommodation and dictating the high set body style. Output from the engine passed through a leather faced cone clutch to a two speed constant mesh gearbox with reverse. An early synchronising mechanism using Albion patent combination clutches, allowed silent changes between low and high gear without the use of the clutch; useful when changing gear on hills, which could be negotiated at fully 5 mph in low gear. 13 mph was achievable at normal engine speed on moderate inclines in high gear, with an accelerator boosting the top speed to 19 mph. A single short chain

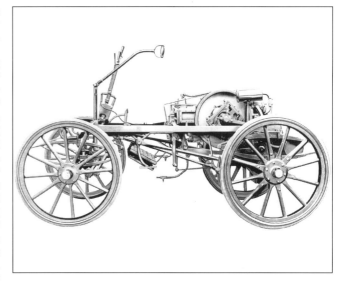

from the gearbox second motion shaft drove a compensating gearbox which transmitted drive to the live rear axle with spur gears. Setting the pattern for many future Albions, it had a foot operated transmission brake, and a hand lever acted on spoon brakes on the rear tyres.

A new office block was completed in 1913 to the west side of the existing factory at South Street, Scotstoun, and adjacent to the 1903 offices which can be seen to the right of the photograph. Designed by the architect Alexander Paterson in the style of 'symmetrical classicism', it housed the board room, the director's suite of offices and their dining room, and other general offices. This building remained a focal point of the factory until its demolition in the late 1970s.

block facing South Street was completed, fronting a new four storey reinforced concrete block of innovative design. Designed for extra machine shop space, a second identical block was erected the following year in 1914, completing a remarkable expansion in machining and assembly capacity in just over a dozen years since the assembly of the first dogcart in more modest surroundings. During this period of steady growth at Albion other names disappeared, the most famous being that of Argyll, who had overspent on an opulent factory at Alexandria, near Glasgow, with a capacity which was never fulfilled. Argyll's voluntary liquidation in 1913 sent shock waves through the industry, especially at Albion. This event must have convinced the directors at Scotstoun that the increasingly price sensitive car market could only be satisfied with well financed large factories producing high volumes of cars to keep unit costs as low as possible. It can be no coincidence that Albion ceased car manufacture in the same year, having come to the conclusion that the future of the business lay in the production of commercial vehicles and buses, not such a price sensitive market and much less of a gamble. Events were to prove this a shrewd decision as within a year, the First World War had

enveloped Europe and created an enormous demand for lorries, which continued to dominate factory output as each year of the war passed.

Evidently not anticipating the demands of the War, in the August of 1914 the directors proposed a 50% salary cut for themselves and that all staff on a one year agreement were to accept 2/3 of their salary. At a board meeting just 8 days later, this decision was held in abeyance after large orders from the Munitions Supply Department of the War Office were received. In 1915, the directors considered putting up a factory for manufacturing bodies but did not pursue this option, wartime capacity being fully taken up with rapidly expanding output of A10 chassis and shell cases. Patents were applied for covering a new type of rear axle, a new friction clutch, and an improved fluid pressure pump, and in August 1917 Murray was awarded a D.Sc. from Edinburgh University. Around this time, concerned that the oval inscribed badge on the radiator was 'hardly noticeable from a passing vehicle', the first production models appeared with the Albion 'scroll' design attached to the radiator tubing. Shortly afterwards, the Albion name was cast into the radiator top tank itself, and the scroll design became a prominent feature readily identifiable

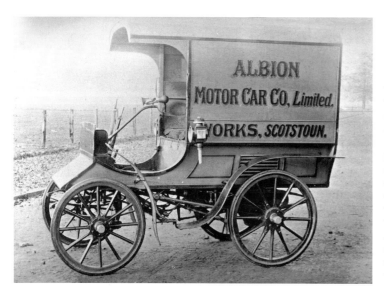

10 cwt Van. The first chassis to be assembled was retained by the company, and in 1902 the dog cart body was replaced with this 10 cwt van body, becoming both the first car and the first commercial vehicle in the company's history. The experience gained with this chassis was applied to the development of new models which would appear over the next few years, and this photograph of what was effectively a prototype for future Albion commercials is the only one known to have survived. This first chassis continued in use as a works van until 1905 clocking up over 40,000 miles during the period. Albion presented the vehicle to the Kelvingrove Museum in Glasgow in 1908 and it is now in the vehicle collection of the City Council's Transport Museum across the road in part of the Kelvin Hall, scene of many Scottish Motor Shows at which Albion products made their debut. Now devoid of a body, the bare chassis on display does however allow the many novel features to be seen in detail.

with the marque, reflecting a more confident outlook gained during the busy war years.

Chassis output peaked at 1,843 chassis in 1918, all 32hp A10s and over ten times the 1913 peacetime output of 155, making a grand total of 5,563 A10s supplied for the war effort. Only 3 days after the armistice on the 14th of November 1918, the Munitions Supply Department, perhaps not unexpectedly, abruptly cancelled the contract, but the momentum of wartime manufacture appeared to take some slowing down. With a considerable stock of parts in hand there was no option but to continue building these parts into vehicles for general sale. In fact, the War had denied many operators deliveries of new chassis from the factory, they had lost vehicles requisitioned by the Military and horses were also in short supply. Post-war production was merely satisfying what was to be a relatively short lived demand. The large number of newly demobbed army drivers fortunate to have survived this War, were no doubt full of praise for their trusty Albions, and would have been a considerable influence as they returned to civilian employment. All of these circumstances at least settled the future of the 3-4 ton A10 and the directors could now concentrate on the likely prospects for the remaining vehicles covering the 10 cwt to 2 ton range.

By May 1918, progress with the design of a new 25 cwt model, the A20, with a proposed 2 ton subtype, contributed to the decision not to resuscitate post war production of both the 2 ton A12 and the 10-20 cwt 15hp A14 of 1911. This meant that the range now consisted of only two models, the 20-30 cwt 20hp A16 which had just entered production before the onset of war in 1914, and the extremely successful 3-4 ton A10. Although typical of the cautious nature of the management, it was perhaps also another lesson from the Argyll demise, when in a failed attempt to gain market share they had increased the number of models. Negotiations in 1918 with the Munitions Supply Department resulted in a further post-war order for up to 778 A10s in December, but only a month later, an alternative offer was made to Albion of £30 per chassis in lieu of this order. In 1919, the Disposals Board of the War Office had started selling surplus chassis and the General Post Office established their Motor Transport Section with A10s purchased from this source. By the end of 1919, 484 of the reintroduced 20hp A16 model and 1,219 A10s had been produced, with the Scotstoun works now able to concentrate on the civilian production of only two models which were at least familiar to the workforce. ❏

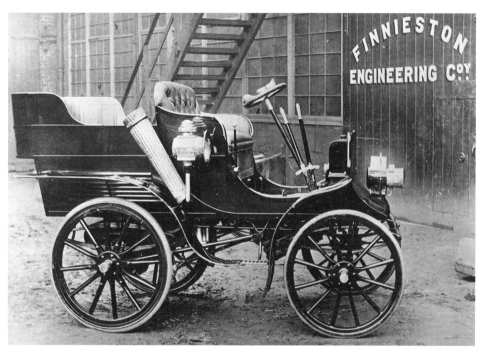

10hp A2 'Dog Cart'. For 1902, the 8hp dog cart was remodelled as a rear entrance tonneau with a 10hp engine, which was also offered as a £30 option on the 8hp dog cart. The tonneau-de-luxe had a wheelbase increased by 9" to improve the ride quality and provide more passenger space. The 10hp model was similar in overall appearance to the dog cart and saw the replacement of the tiller by the steering wheel which had initially been an option. Forward facing rear seats were now possible with the longer wheelbase and rear body overhang, and a wagonette with 6 seats was also available on this longer chassis. A fully upholstered seat was now positioned either side of a central rear entrance door, but the upright and top heavy body stance caused by the mid-engine layout was beginning to look out of place relative to the competition. However, it did follow the social trend towards placing forward facing passengers in the rear of the vehicle, rather than merely providing space for estate staff or luggage as dictated by the dog cart layout. The optional wicker storage container for the parasols of lady passengers signalled that the 'pleasure car' market was certainly being catered for by Albion with this 10hp tonneau-de-luxe, which was photographed outside the Finnieston works in Glasgow. The front seat would most probably be occupied by the proud owner, perhaps taking the wheel himself, or seated beside his chauffeur. This was a new position in the wealthy households of the day and would most likely have been a retrained estate worker familiar with more traditional horse power. John Lawson, the first chauffeur in Scotland, was employed by Murray's architect father John L. Murray at Heavyside Farm. Only 17 of the 10hp engined chassis were produced in less than two years with the 8hp dog cart continuing in parallel as a 4 seater trap, and both were replaced by the front engined 12hp A3 model in 1903.

12hp & 16hp A3. The 12hp A3 model of 1903 was the first new model from the recently occupied Scotstoun factory and had the first Albion engine with vertical cylinders. A larger 2.6 litre capacity was the result of increasing the bore of the two cylinders by ½" over the horizontally opposed engines. The use of a front engine allowed a much lower and completely new side-entrance tonneau body to be used, and early models can be identified by their sloping bonnet louvres, whereas later models and most Lacre versions had upright louvres. As with the 8 and 10hp models, the 12hp engine pre-dated the more sophisticated mechanical lubricator patented in 1905, but the main bearings and crankpins were positively lubricated, with sight feed lubricators for the cylinders and splash lubrication for the minor bearings only. For stiffness without weight penalty, the ladder frame chassis had tubular cross-members and was bolted together instead of being riveted, both features common to all future Albion chassis. A patented spring drive smoothed out the action of the leather faced cone clutch, and a long propshaft transmitted drive to a combined gearbox and differential, with dual chain drive to the rear axle. Braking was by a foot operated water-cooled transmission brake with locomotive-type cast iron shoes, and the handbrake acted on angled steel rims bolted to the rear wheels with a compensator arrangement. In September 1903, the model was entered in the 1,000 Miles Automobile Club Reliability Trials, gaining full marks for brakes, running gear, restarting on hills and condition after the trials. From 1904, performance was improved with a 16hp engine of 3.1 litres and the model proved to be the basis of a very successful range of cars, 10-40 cwt commercials and charabancs of up to 15 seats totalling 2,432 of the 12hp and 16hp chassis

including Lacre versions. In 1905, a 16hp car driven by salesman Ralph Wilson won the Gold Medal for 2 cylinder vehicles at the Scottish Reliability Trials, confirming the company's now well established reputation for reliability, often repeated in testimonials and reviews; in 1906 a motoring magazine stated that "the 16hp Albion is another way of saying reliability". The 16hp A3 was the first model to offer all of the recent Albion patents, with the adoption of the mechanical lubricator, the patent governor, automatic carburettor, and the spring buffers applied to silence the magneto ignition trip gear. The lever operated Albion-Murray patent governor had by now been developed into an integrated control which regulated engine speed, mixture and ignition timing (advance and retard). The driver was thus able to control the speed at which the governor closed the throttle on the patent automatic carburettor and once the required engine speed was set, it was maintained for all but the most severe inclines by this early form of cruise control. To ease starting, a half compression handle projected from the front of the engine and moved the exhaust camshaft along its axis to allow the engagement of a second series of cams. Originally underpriced at around £350 for the 12hp model, Albion lost money on the early chassis but soon recognised their error and adjusted the price accordingly. Sales started to fall by 1913, and discounts were authorised to boost sales with production finally ceasing in 1915. Although Lacre greatly assisted with sales of this model in their territory of England and Wales, competition in the London area with many 4 cylinder models available at a similar price to the 2 cylinder A3 put pressure on Albion to produce their own 4 cylinder engine, and a few days after meeting Lacre management, the board put in hand such a design.

Characterised by the brass radiator partly covered by the bonnet with its sloping louvres, this illustration of the A3 car shows how a much lower and up-to-date body layout was possible with the first of the front engined Albion models.

This 16hp A3 was delivered in 1912 and completed 16 years of service with Hawkes Brothers, Manufacturing Confectioners of Chelmsford. It travelled the equivalent of five times round the world without failing to complete a journey, and the company was so impressed that the Albion badge from the grille was mounted on an oak plaque in their office after the vehicle completed its working life.

A 12 seater charabanc was one of many body options available on the A3 chassis, and this Lacre bodied example operated between the Dublin resorts of Kingstown and Bray, where it is seen here in 1906. This vehicle operated through the previous year's summer season without a breakdown, with a daily run of 100 miles and a fuel consumption of 13½ mpg. Following the success of the model on this run, another A3 was ordered to extend the service to Enniskerry.

24/30hp A6. Aimed at the luxury end of the rapidly expanding 'pleasure' market and with an eye to increased Lacre sales in the London area, the entirely new side entrance A6 had Albion's first 4 cylinder petrol engine of 24/30hp, and was announced in September 1906. Available in 3 wheelbases to suit a variety of body types, it was undoubtedly the most handsome of the Albion cars. It featured a 4 speed gearbox, oil bath multiple disc metal clutch, dual braking system and the Albion-Murray patents already introduced on the A3. The governor was mounted on the side of the engine, and was gear driven from the inlet camshaft, with a mechanical lubricator mounted at the front of the engine. Mechanical layout was generally similar to that already established on the A3, with the exception that the longer engine resulted in a much shorter propshaft, and the clutch was moved rearwards to the front of the mid-mounted gearbox / differential unit. Engine output was 30 brake horse power, but it was rated at 24hp by the RAC and Treasury method of using the cylinder bore and number of cylinders to calculate a horsepower rating for taxation purposes, a system which remained common for many years. A range of around 240 miles was available from a 14 gallon fuel tank, which was pressurised by a small engine driven pump to force the fuel to the carburettor. Although just recently announced to the public, an example was entered in the 1906 Scottish Reliability Trials and was awarded a mechanical 'non stop' certificate, although experiencing a number of unexplained tyre failures. The A6 proved to be expensive to manufacture, reflected in a price range of £633 for a standard side entrance car, to £758 for the landaulette, about half as expensive again as comparable A3 versions. Production of the model ceased in 1911, with 57 built over 5 years of production. This new A6 owned by Thomas Whillens, is seen posed on a summer's day near Selkirk with his chauffeur proudly seated at the wheel.

This full page advertisement for the newly introduced 24/30hp A6 car was published in 1907. The vehicle featured, G 1025, belonged to joint managing director John F Henderson.

32hp A10. The 3 ton A10, powered by a new 4 cylinder engine with an RAC rating of 32.4hp, was introduced in 1910 and was one of the most important models to be developed by Albion in the early years. The commercial success of the A10 resulted in a production run of sixteen years with only two revisions, the Mark II of 1923 and the overtype Mark III of 1925, finally being replaced in 1926 by the shaft & worm drive Model 27. It had an open chain drive and can be identified by a 14 vertical louvre bonnet, the Mark II by 2 sets of 5 horizontal louvres and the Mark III with its overtype cab. The engine was unusual in having the four cylinders cast in a single block, with an integral cylinder head also incorporating the water pump. A high tension magneto was another first for Albion, and was introduced to eliminate the low tension tappet gear, the adjustment of which was considered to be impractical on commercial models of more than two cylinders. The engine was fitted with a mechanical lubricator and a governor controlling the carburettor, with the drive passing through a single disc clutch; all Albion patents. A 'Butler' type fabricated front axle used two 'I' beams riveted together, with an 'H' section rear axle of solid nickel steel. The straightforward and rugged construction of this model contributed to its phenomenal success and by 1912 it was available in 2, 3 and 3½ ton versions. A 4 tonner was introduced in 1913 using an uprated frame, springs and rear axle. The Albion philosophy of 'leaving nothing to chance' on this uprated model was demonstrated by the addition of two diagonal tie bars which strengthened the frame above the rear axle, a feature also used on other models from the A3 on. The frame was already amply braced with 2½" tubular cross-members which were by now an Albion hallmark. The van shown was originally purchased by Harrods, requisitioned by the War Department, refurbished after the war, and eventually repurchased for its original role with Harrods delivery service.

32hp A10 Charabanc. The 32hp A10 chassis also formed the basis of a variety of bus models and as the dropped frame specialised bus chassis was some years away, buses or coaches of this period were little more than lorry chassis with rows of bench seats. Typically with a door at each seat row and windowless sides, but variations included bodies with openings only at each seat row, and lorry charabancs without any side body or doors, their potential dangers mitigated somewhat by their limited top speed. Albion is credited as being the earliest user of the torpedo charabanc body which was first exhibited at the 1912 Scottish Motor Show, and shown in this illustration from the 1914 catalogue. This body type was named after their torpedo-like long smooth sides which were usually fully enclosed up to the window line. Seating capacities varied from 19 up to 29 seats on the A10 chassis, although smaller seating capacities were available on the well established 16hp A3 and on the 15hp A14, introduced in 1911.

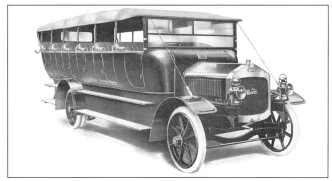

32hp A10 Double Decker. This 34 seat double decker was also listed in the 1914 brochure for the sum of £812, only £2 dearer than the 29 seat torpedo charabanc and the second most expensive model listed. Four of these buses were operated by Newcastle upon Tyne Corporation in 1919-20, but the existence of other similar examples with this body type is unknown.

15hp A14. The 4 cylinder A14 model for car and lightweight commercial use was introduced in 1911 to provide a direct drive (chainless) chassis for a 10-20 cwt van or lorry, a 8-10 seater wagonette (light bus), a taxicab, and also a range of cars of 2 to 6 seats. Originally intended to be fitted with a 2 cylinder engine by using 'half' of the 4 cylinder 32hp engine from the A10, it was found that the advantage of natural water circulation could not be retained without an unreasonably high radiator and bonnet. In addition, the width of this 2 cylinder engine could not be reduced to meet the requirements of the taxicab, and so the design of a 4 cylinder 15hp engine was brought forward. Governed for higher speeds of up to 32 mph, dependant on model, it had an optional accelerator pedal instead of the column mounted throttle lever. This was the first Albion engine to dispense with the Murray patent lubricator, which was replaced by an integral oil pump driven from the exhaust camshaft to recirculate lubricant round the engine. Ignition was provided by a Bosch high tension magneto, previously introduced on the A10. The shaft and worm drive was thought likely to make the taxicab model more popular and saleable, and it was produced in parallel with the popular light commercial chain driven 16hp A3, but never in the same quantity. In 1913, production of Albion cars finally ceased with this model and the Glasgow showroom closed at the end of the lease, despite a nation-wide trend of rapidly increasing car sales. H.E. Fulton, brother of co-founder N.O. Fulton, is at the wheel of this A14 in 1911.

25hp A12. The 25hp A12 of 1913 was originally designed to a War Office subsidy specification but subsequently modified for the civil production of this 2 ton, 16 mph chassis. In general, many features of the successful 32hp A10 were retained such as the chain driven rear axle, although with a new design of chain case. Chain drive was considered more economical and efficient for commercial use, and direct drive Albions at this weight range were still some years away. An innovation for Albion was that the four cylinders were cast in pairs, the inlet duct from the carburettor passing between the cylinder pairs from offside to nearside. A high tension magneto was used and with the Bosch Z4 model fitted, the timing was now controlled by a lever mounted below the throttle lever and connected directly to the magneto, by-passing the governor. Bolt-on steering arms were covered by a Rolls Royce patent and manufactured under licence, never a common

Albion practice. Intending to employ piston valves in the engine, they proved difficult to perfect and conventional poppet valves were fitted to production models. With an increased speed of 20mph, it was available in chassis lengths to suit buses and torpedo charabancs of up to 25 passengers. Ride quality was improved as a result of the standard fitment of relatively long 4' 6" springs which would have been a useful asset on this van for biscuit manufacturers, MacFarlane Lang & Company. Although output had rapidly built up in 1914, wartime emphasis on the A10 resulted in production rates diminishing until a final 3 were built in 1916, with a total production of about 180 chassis. Operating experience had shown up a number of minor problems which could not be dealt with due to the increasing pressures of wartime production. It was considered that work on all of the modifications necessary would have almost constituted a new model and it was therefore not reintroduced after the First World War.

20hp A16. Introduced in 1914 after 18 months of testing, the 30 cwt A16 was the first Albion model casualty of the First World War, with only 18 chassis built before production was redirected for large War Office contracts. The 3.3 litre 'monobloc' engine of 3½" bore and 5" stroke produced 20hp and was governed to a maximum of 1,250 rpm. There were no major innovations, other than extending chainless 'direct drive' into a slightly higher weight range and retaining a gear type oil pump as on the 15hp A14. Murray patent devices were still in use, including the governor, automatic carburettor, combined fan and pump and the Albion single disc clutch with a 3 speed gearbox. As with other high tension magneto models, the throttle lever only operated the throttle valve via the governor, the timing advance and retard being operated by a separate lever. Production of this model did not restart until 1918, and output then rapidly built up to 484 for 1919 and continued until December 1920, when the new 20hp A20 progressed through the fitting shop. Typical of the unstable times, prices of this model increased from around £475 at its introduction in 1916, to £860 for the home model by February 1920, with two further increases, each of 5%, in April and July of that year. Unfortunately, the A16 did not lie down quietly, as a problem surfaced in 1921 with wheels developing serious faults, incurring large warranty claims at a time of diminishing financial returns.

An early model A16 van with a brass radiator and 11 louvre bonnet, is pictured outside Albion's Manchester sales office, awaiting delivery to the Winnington, Northwich and District Co-operative Society Ltd., which operated in Cheshire to the south west of Manchester.

Later models of the A16 had a fabricated design of aluminium radiator which was bolted together using a top tank, sides and base to enclose the core. This 30 cwt van for Messrs W. Whiteley Ltd., of London, shows the early style of aluminium radiator with its rounded top tank and bold Albion scroll motif. The 9 bonnet louvres and the painted radiator help to identify post war versions of the A16. A similar radiator change took place on the model A10.

❧ THE OBJECTIVE OF THE BUSINESS MOTOR BEING PURELY COMMERCIAL, IT MUST STAND OR FALL SOLELY ON COMMERCIAL RESULTS.

❧ Initial cost is probably the least important item in buying a Commercial Vehicle. Successful business results are not obtained through a low purchase price. It is the maintenance and repair bill that affects the yearly balance sheet——the smaller the cost of upkeep, the larger the margin of profit.

❧ The design of an Albion 32-h.p. 3-ton Lorry enables it to be built fully 15 cwts. to 20 cwts. lighter in gross weight than most other makes. This effects a substantial saving in petrol consumption, repairs, and in the wear and tear of tyres——important items in upkeep costs.

❧ Under the worst conditions of Active Service, His Majesty's Government conclusively proved that Albion Commercial Vehicles cost less for maintenance than any other type of vehicle and spent less time in the repair shops.

❧ The big houses, leaders of commerce, unreservedly endorse the Government's opinion by adding Albion after Albion to their fleets.

❧ Load Capacity: 30, 50, 60 and 80 cwts.

COMMERCIAL MOTORS
ALBION MOTOR CAR CO. LTD., SCOTSTOUN, GLASGOW
London Office and Repair Depot: 21-22 Upper Rathbone Place, Oxford Street, W.1
Branches at Manchester, Sheffield and Birmingham
FOR TERMS OF BUSINESS AND GUARANTEE, SEE CATALOGUE

32hp A10 War Department Type. With the onset of the First World War, the military authorities began purchasing increasing numbers of a modified 3 ton A10 to their own specification. The 3 ton model was selected because military limits on gross vehicle weights for temporary bridge crossings gave the recently introduced 4 tonner no advantage. The War Office stipulated the fitting of a radiator guard with head lamp brackets, towing hooks front and rear, and the body had to have angle iron hoops with ridge poles, but no tarpaulin. Protection for the driver was limited to a canvas apron and canvas side doors in addition to a fixed roof. Further identifying features of this version were the vertical ribbing of the cast aluminium radiator, and larger diameter wheels, increased by 4" at the front and by 7" at the rear to improve ground clearance, particularly with regard to the rear chain drive. Almost four years of production of this model prior to the outbreak of the War allowed Albion to deal with any problems, nevertheless the factory did seek feedback during operations in France and incorporated the few minor improvements suggested. Company records indicate a War output of 5,563 A10 chassis alone, which contributed to a total output of almost 8,800 of this model, a perfect example of the right product at the right time. The post-war brochure proudly stated that 'official records show that they were unsurpassed for reliability and maintenance', and at the signing of the Armistice there were many still in War service. Chassis requisitioned by the Government from commercial operators saw military service in France and many were subsequently returned to civilian use after refurbishment, some with their original purchasers.

Three times every week convoys of A10s for the War Department were sent south on their delivery run. Albion offered to carry passengers on these 3 day convoys, and two passengers could be accommodated on each A10. For this the passengers paid a fee of 10 shillings which was handed over to organisations like the Red Cross. The year is 1916 and ten A10s are seen 36 miles from Carlisle on the south side of Shap Fell.

A10 advertisement circa 1919.

Two years later in October 1918, A10s of the War Department Type are seen transporting troops to the front somewhere in France.

This line drawing shows a plan view and section of the A10 chassis layout which was fairly typical of the early chain driven models. A relatively short propshaft was connected to a mid-mounted gearbox and final drive unit, with the chain case operating as a radius arm. The additional cross-bracing of the 4 ton frame to provide local stiffening was also adopted for the 3 ton War Department type and is clearly shown above the rear axle.

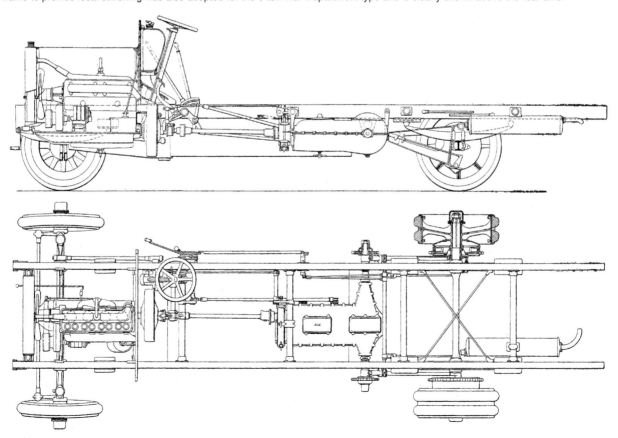

Chapter 2
Lows and Highs
1920 to 1929

The directors of Albion could surely reflect on a satisfying first twenty years, and in fairly confident mood they made plans to purchase 43 acres of ground at Blawarthill between Scotstoun and Yoker in the January of 1920. Unfortunately, the early 1920s were to mark the first period of the company's history when the previous steady rise in fortunes was dramatically reversed and along with the rest of Europe, Albion felt the sudden cold draught of recession. Adding to the problems of falling demand, the War Office placed around 20,000 surplus ex-military lorries onto the open market at low prices which further reduced any hope of demand for new chassis. In 1920 Albion purchased 959 ex War Office 3 ton A10s and initially

reconditioned these war damaged and nearly new chassis at Scotstoun, which were then sold with a six months warranty. As demand increased, a 21,600 sq.ft. sub-let was acquired at Clyde shipbuilders Barclay Curle's Jordanvale Works at nearby Whiteinch. This was a profitable exercise, but there was a price to pay as over the next few years the 3 to 4 ton market became saturated with thousands of ex-war surplus stock, and any headway in sales would not be in this weight range for some years. The purchase of a further 300 ex-WD vehicles was cancelled and the Jordanvale Works closed in August 1920. The remaining ex-WD chassis were refurbished at Scotstoun and took a full five years to dispose of. As the slump in demand

A general view of the Jordanvale Works in Whiteinch in which hundreds of war damaged A10s were refurbished. The chassis were completely stripped down, the components examined and replaced with new parts if worn or defective. The chassis were then re-assembled to the factory standard for new vehicles and given the same test procedure, with a small brass plate attached to the dashboard indicating the reduced guarantee of six months.

continued, a third reinforced concrete building was also cancelled, and the loss of income from spares and repairs was to be felt into the late 1920s.

Taking an opportunity for possible demand in the lighter weight range, the 20hp A16 began to be replaced with the 25 cwt 20hp A20 in December of 1920, after a 3 month delay due to market conditions. Output had by now fallen to a recent all time low and output for 1921, the year of a 3 month long miners' strike, was a total of 166 chassis or just over 3 chassis per week, a tenth of the previous year's output and a figure bettered as far back as 1906. Office staff levels fell from 433 in 1919 to 193 in 1921, but it was the hourly paid workers who bore the brunt of the pay-offs, with a drop from 1,697 in 1919 to 497 in 1921, only 29% of the 1919 figure (ref. Appendix E). By May 1921, new vehicle production had stopped, and although testing continued on experimental models, assembly of the A20 did not restart until October at the year's earlier rate of 3 per week. Further bad news came with reports of A16s developing serious wheel problems, and a plan to develop a 25/30 cwt electric vehicle for the London area and Railway Company local deliveries was eventually dropped in 1922.

The purchase of ground at Blawarthill was called off late in 1922, and efforts to keep the works fully employed resulted in an unsuccessful search for sub-contract work from car manufacturers. During this period the board had been anxious about competition, especially from the United States. They considered how they could contribute to a one-model-per-factory policy on an industry wide basis in the UK, similar to American practice, but it was soon realised that the market for any one model was not big enough to keep the factory busy. However, one lesson taken on board was that the American manufacturers were concentrating on accurate machining to eliminate subsequent work by assembly fitters and increase efficiency. By the end of 1922 annual output was up to 244, and although a modest increase over 1921, this was at least real growth. The upward trend was maintained with 606 chassis in 1923, exports accounting for 46% of the total.

Demonstrating more confidence in the future, new models were announced in 1923 with the A10 Mark II and the entirely new Model 24, also available as a bus with a low floor height, at that time a feature fairly novel in the bus market. The Government had recently introduced a subsidy scheme to create a pool of civil vehicles available to the military in the event of another conflict. A sample Model 24 chassis complying with the military specification was accepted in November 1923 and proved to be a successful development. For once, other manufacturers with similarly approved models could not compete on price, other than Thornycroft in late 1924. A chassis-testing rig was installed to reduce road testing and proved so successful, that another was ordered shortly afterwards. The first tooth-grinding machine to reduce problems with noisy gears and improve gearbox quality was also installed.

As the 1920s progressed, new models were introduced at the rate of roughly two per year, indicating that the design staff had been busy during the quiet period at the beginning of the decade and were also responding to changes in the road tax regime. By 1925, enough confidence had returned to the heavier weight ranges for a Mark III variant of the venerable A10 with a 'driver beside engine' or 'overtype' layout. Chain driven vehicles were becoming less popular however, and designs were soon in place for a replacement, although useful experience was gained from this first overtype. Later models greatly expanded the weight range on offer and others introduced many innovative features or layouts, such as the Model 35, an overtype with an easily removable cab and the unusual dual purpose '6 wheeler' version of the Model 24, which was an early form of articulated vehicle. In April 1925, an approach was made by Halleys at Yoker with a view to a merger, but the Albion directors were 'not disposed' to this idea, although acquiring the site must have had its attractions.

'Progress' was the fleetname used by W. Armitage & Son of Blackpool on this Pickering bodied PM28, which is seen here on the occasion of a visit to Blackpool by the Swansea Woman's Section of the British Legion in the summer of 1928.

A new lightweight 30 cwt goods model was proposed in 1925. As it was destined for a very competitive and price-sensitive market, much time was taken in development and testing, including the purchase of a 30 cwt Dennis chassis for comparison. Albion was having to fight more and more for sales as the smaller operators especially bought cheaper or 'lower first cost' vehicles, and in some potential export areas such as South America, a higher vehicle loss rate resulted in cheaper American models preferred to the higher quality and more expensive British marques. The directors were placed in a quandary as to whether to adhere to the traditional Albion practice of designing for overload conditions adding cost to the chassis, or abandoning their principles and designing for this rated load only as many of their competitors were doing. The option to develop this model into a 2 tonner was the deciding factor in designing for the higher capacity, thus building a cost handicap into the 30 cwt model and eliminating Albion from being a real player at this weight range. A separate site was considered for the sole assembly of this model, with the Halley factory an option as strenuous efforts were made to contain costs. When finally introduced in 1928 as the Models 40 & 41, it was made clear to sales staff that due to keen pricing of these models, alterations to suit customers would not be permissible.

As the motor industry showed signs of maturing even in these early years, it was essential for Albion to respond to market pressure and adapt. Design of a six cylinder petrol engine primarily for bus applications was started in 1926, appearing in 1928 as the 36/90hp EN53 option in the Model 26. In the same year, satisfactory results had been achieved from four wheel braking tests, just as the Metropolitan Police was demanding the abolition of the transmission brake on public service vehicles. Although operators were already pressing for power-operated brakes for 'the comfort of the driver', it was not until 1927 that experiments with Dewandre power-assisted units on a Model 28 chassis were carried out and subsequently introduced on the rigid 6 wheel Model 31 & 32.

20hp A20. With the oversupply of 3-4 ton chassis following the First World War, it made sense to concentrate on the lighter model range in what was to become an increasingly difficult period for sales. The A20 was introduced in 1920 and initially rated at 25 cwt or as an 11 passenger bus, but was soon uprated to 30 cwt or 15 passengers. Powered by a 20hp EN20 engine of 3½" bore, it had a governed maximum speed of 17½ mph on solid tyres and 20 mph with front pneumatics. The chassis was set lower than on the A16 it replaced and the introduction of inward facing flanges gave the frame a much tidier and more modern appearance, a feature continued on all future models. Provision was made for the optional 'Klersite' lighting set powered by a CAV 3-brush series wound dynamo, which was driven by a vee belt from the fan pulley and was sufficient for either one 6 volt 18 watt lamp, or two 12 watt lamps. Although the A16 had a gear driven oil pump, the trusty Murray lubricator was reintroduced on this model, perhaps a sign of problems with recirculating mesh-filtered oil. An Albion 'distance recorder' was fitted as standard, worm driven from the gearbox mainshaft and mounted on the offside chassis frame. This device was initially promoted for checking tyre mileage guarantees, rather than solely for measuring journeys and servicing intervals. A 2 tonner was introduced in 1922 following sales pressure, but it was underpowered, especially as a charabanc, and was eventually replaced by the Model 24. This A20 owned by Bentalls of Kingston on Thames, was a 25 cwt van with a detachable canvas top. It is shown with the typical combination for this model of front pneumatics and rear solid tyres, since the tyre manufacturer's recommended limit of 25-30 cwt for all round pneumatics could easily be exceeded by heavier loads. The neater radiator top tank design, and the flat side panels fitted with bosses to simplify the installation of the optional lighting set distinguish the A20 from the similar looking late model A16s.

Although buying in proprietary major components had been considered in 1927 and rejected, other expertise was brought in as required, in particular with instances of exhaust valve burning on Model 26 buses operating under 'arduous conditions'. The Model 26 EN50 engine and the new Model 40/41 EN52 engine designs were submitted to consultants Ricardo for criticism. They suggested design modifications to the cylinder head and opened up water passages, which were also adopted on the EN51 and later engines. However, this had happened over a crucial period as bus sales were beginning to grow in England after a fairly successful Scottish debut, and as competition with Leyland buses was particularly keen, any possibility of increased chassis prices was eliminated. The poor reputation gained during this period was later to be cited by the directors as a crucial factor in Albion's inability to capture a substantial part of the bus market, although there were other reasons which are dealt with in Chapter 5. As a result of these engine problems, the decision was then taken by the board to invite George Pate, a former employee, to rejoin Albion as Joint Managing Director, from his post as Chief Engineer and Director of engine manufacturers, D. Napier & Sons Ltd.

The amalgamation of bus companies during this period had a severe effect on Albion as fleets were standardised, and in an attempt to break into this buying power Dr Murray suggested buying a controlling stake in a public service bus company. This approach to ensuring a steady market for Albion buses was rejected by the board however, since it was felt that it might antagonise the railway companies, who were also large potential users of vehicles. Indeed shortly afterwards, LNER bought 50 Model 24 subsidy 2 tonners for local deliveries. A welcome diversion from these troubles and highlight of the year for the staff was a brief visit to the factory by the Prince of Wales, who had earlier opened the 1927 Scottish Motor Show in the newly rebuilt Kelvin Hall.

1928 was to see the first order from Merryweather for two chassis for fire engines, with the Albion radiator replaced by Merryweather's own design in a manner similar to that last seen during the Lacre agreement. 1928 continued a two year run of increasing output benefiting from bus and coach demand, although it was a disappointing year for goods sales. A reluctance to accept an increasing number of trade-ins resulted in further lost sales, and a successful 2 ton Thornycroft model was blamed

32hp A10 Mk II. In November 1923, Albion took advantage of rising sales with a Mark II version of the 32hp A10, readily distinguished from the original with 2 sets of 5 horizontal bonnet louvres. With thirteen years of production behind it, the model was given a new lease of life with a new engine top end using paired removable cylinder heads. Water circulation between the block and each head was provided for with three large countersunk holes, each fitted with a double conical rubber ring reinforced by a split brass centre. A repositioned exhaust manifold allowed improved access to the side valves. Retaining a 4½" bore, the RAC hp rating therefore remained at 32hp, but actual output was up by 10-15%. Altered gearing assisted in improving the road speed by 12% over its predecessor, and fuel consumption was some 20% better. Chain drive was retained as Albion still considered this best suited to heavy commercial vehicles as the lower

unsprung weight compared to a live axle, resulted in better rear tyre wear. The longer rear springs of late A10 models were carried over to this Mark II version, but otherwise chassis details were unchanged, enabling existing stocks of almost 40 A10s to be easily converted to Mark II standard. Another distinguishing feature of the Mark II related to the radiator top tank, on which the Albion scroll was smaller than previously used and was the last such design before the addition of the sun-ray motif on the Model 27 of 1926. Also clearly visible on this example are the A10s' characteristic straight frame members with their outward facing flanges, which extended well forward of the radiator for the front spring mounting. B7283 was a 3 tonner photographed in 1930 for owner Gailey & Roberts Limited, who were the Albion agents in Nairobi, the capital of what was then known as 'Kenya Colony'.

for a decline of sales in this sector. Production of the new 4 ton Models 34 & 35 was temporarily suspended, but undaunted by market conditions, Albion approached Harland & Wolff who had ground directly across South Street with a view to further expansion, but this was turned down. As the year progressed, coach sales also became uncertain as many operators traded on 'uneconomic terms', and the hoped for sales from railway companies were only partly fulfilled as they justified the purchase of cheaper machines because of the relatively low mileages being run.

By the end of 1928, Ricardo was encouraging Albion to investigate the use of diesels, and J.D. Parkes, London Sales Manager and a member of the board of directors had already been impressed by two diesel engines seen in service. However, they were not at that time considered by the directors to be sufficiently refined, especially for buses, and N.O. Fulton was minuted as remarking that the chance of diesels being of use was remote. Although a visit was made by Parkes to Germany in the January of 1929 where diesels were noted to be much more advanced,

it was not until early 1930 that a 4 cylinder Deutz diesel was purchased for experimental purposes for £340 plus duty, the cost of a complete 30 cwt chassis. Albion's delay in getting its own diesel off the ground was largely due to a lack of vision on the part of the directors, including, surprisingly, George Pate, who had been brought in following Albion's engine problems. Apparently hostile to this new technology, his main argument was that the price advantage held by diesel fuel would disappear as the oil engine became more popular and forced prices upwards, a possibility subsequently confirmed by the oil companies.

From early 1929, chassis output had shown a steady decline from a peak of 43 per week, to 5 per week by 1932. Production figures for 1929 were helped considerably by orders for a total of 223 rigid 6 wheelers from the India Office, one of the proposers of this type, and by the end of 1929, 6 wheeler output was 20 per week out of a total of 35. Although the rigid 6 wheeler had been designed primarily for military and export requirements, a 1929 regulation allowing increased permissible speeds on vehicles without

Model 24 (Goods). The 20-40 cwt Model 24 was another act of faith in view of the collapse of sales since 1920, and like the A20, was introduced into the sector of the market most likely to generate sales. It was the first model without a single 'A' prefix and the 25, 30 and 40 cwt versions had the new style designations prefixed with an 'L' for lorry, as the LA24, LB24 and LC24 respectively. Originally intended for passenger applications only, production started many months after details of the bus version was revealed to the press in January of 1923, and suggest a delay to allow the development of a goods version to counter the poor performance of the heavier versions of the A20. The Model 24 was a development of the A20 with a completely new engine, and production of both models overlapped from 1923 until 1925, when the A20 ceased to be built. Early goods chassis retained an A20 style radiator with its cast Albion scroll, and although using the same core, had different mountings and brackets. This was later replaced by the Model 24 bus radiator with its enamelled badge late in 1926, which was thus adopted on both goods and bus versions. The 24hp EN24 engine was matched to a new 4 speed GB50 gearbox introduced to suit a maximum

speed of 25 mph on pneumatic tyres, although front super cushion tyres and rear solids were also common in this transition period. Despite the reintroduction of the patent mechanical lubricator on the A20's EN20 engine, it was dropped on this faster model in favour of a gear type oil pump with gauze filtration. The oil pump was driven from a spur gear on the camshaft, but this engine subsequently proved to be weak with regard to cylinder wear. However, the reliability confirmed in extensive testing for the War Office subsidy scheme paid off with large numbers of this model exported and by early 1924, 210 chassis had been shipped to India alone for use on the North-West Frontier with Afghanistan. The ease with which the engine was controlled by the throttle lever and patent governor, the high ground clearance, and radiators proportioned for use in tropical climates undoubtedly helped the sale of large numbers to the Crown Colonies and other overseas markets. This van on a flour delivery run was operated by Messrs. Mansfield Gibson & Co., of Birmingham, and just visible below the maximum speed plate is a chassis mounted Albion distance recorder, a feature which became standard on all models from 1923 onwards.

trailers created a trend for longer wheelbases and multi-axle chassis for the heavier weight ranges. This market was important as it was recognised that heavy vehicle sales carried more of the factory oncosts. A sale in the heavy sector was reckoned by Albion to keep the competition out for 5-10 years, but to be tackled successfully, it was clear that it also had to have a competent family of engines.

1929 was also to mark the end of an important chapter in the Albion story with the resignation of Dr Blackwood

Murray in March after a long period of illness. Then shortly afterwards in June came the sad news that he had died, thus depriving the company of his enthusiasm and inventive talents. His ability to translate engineering challenges into working applications had been fundamental to the company he had co-founded and was so proud of. Although absent from board Meetings in recent years, he had kept in close touch with events, and his interest and advice had always been keenly noted. ❏

Model 24 (30 cwt Subsidy Type). A version of the Model 24 was introduced in 1923 to comply with a Government subsidy scheme to ensure a sufficient war time supply of requisitioned vehicles, and was known as the Subsidy Model 24 or SB24. Learning from the massive requisition of vehicles during the First World War, the War Office had decided that a number of specifications should be drawn up to allow vehicle manufacturers to produce models which would also comply with military requirements. Any owner who purchased such an approved model could claim a subsidy for a limited period. Although the British Army had a large number of 3 ton vehicles in use post-war, specification No. 11 for 30 cwt capacity subsidy vehicles was designed to provide a more manoeuvrable lighter model as a valuable transport auxiliary, available for impressment in a national emergency. A grant of £40 per annum was paid to the owner for a maximum of two (later three) years, which more than offset the £25 higher price. This was paid provided that the vehicle had a minimum of 24hp on the

RAC rating system, was capable of carrying 30 cwt, and that the type had been certified as fulfilling the required tests for the scheme. These included being fitted with pneumatic tyres of British manufacture, having a gravity fuel feed capable of supply on a maximum gradient of 1 in 4½ and being capable of 30mph for one mile on a good level surface. This 30 cwt Albion demonstrator operating from the London sales office was photographed in June of 1924, and made good use of the available body space to advertise the subsidy scheme. Apart from the requirement for pneumatic tyres, the subsidy model was externally indistinguishable from the standard Model 24.

Model 24 (Passenger). The higher maximum speed of the Model 24 was primarily intended for the bus and coach market and both applications were met with two main versions; a saloon type bus body of 20 seats and a coach, the latter fully described below. Although revealed to the press in January of 1923 for passenger applications only, both passenger and goods versions were formally announced at the 1923 Olympia Motor Show in November. The standard bus chassis used a neat new angular radiator which introduced the 'rising sun' on an enamel badge attached to the radiator top tank, and clearly visible in this view. It used a straight frame chassis common to the goods version and was one of the last to do so before the development of the specialised 'dropped frame' bus chassis on the Model 26 Viking in late 1925. Versions were designated in a similar pattern to the goods models, but with a 'P' (passenger) prefix and letter(s) denoting wheelbase and seating capacity variants. The PE24 standard bus chassis had a shorter wheelbase than the coach at 11' 9", with a typical overall body

length of 19' 0", width of 7' 9" and a 5' 10" centre line headroom. In addition, a 12 seater bus with a 10' 9" wheelbase was also available and designated PA24. Passenger comfort was attended to with extra long springs, with front super cushion tyres and rear twin solids as standard; the improved ride quality from pneumatic tyres all round was an extra charge option. This model was considered to have a reasonable turn of speed, geared to suit a governed 20 mph on solid tyres and 21½ mph on pneumatics, as well as returning the low petrol consumption expected by the operators. After the introduction of the larger engined 30/60hp Viking, the Model 24 passenger chassis continued to be listed for bus applications only, coach versions being dropped in favour of the Model 26. The two short wheelbase buses shown were supplied to the Education Authority of Glasgow for the transport of school children and were the forerunner of today's minibuses on similar duties. They are posed for the photographer in 1928 outside Victoria Drive Public School, just a short distance from the Scotstoun factory.

Model 24 (Viking). An 18 passenger coach based on the Model 24 introduced a model name into the Albion range for the first time, and the new 'Viking' name which graced this model was to appear on a variety of coaches and buses over the next 50 years. Introduced at the 1923 Olympia Show for the 1924 season, it was thought to be very desirable to have a coach based on touring car lines, and this high class model was intended to suit the more sophisticated patron who was becoming familiar with the de-luxe standard of travel from motor cars. To assist in its visual appeal, an elegant new radiator was introduced for this coach which was similar to that of the standard Model 24, but with the more rounded edges of a contemporary touring car. Minor detailing which featured ebonite inserts around the edge of the filler cap added to the smart and elegant appearance. Sharing the standard Model 24's straight-frame chassis, the PF24 had a longer 14' 0" wheelbase and required a two-piece propshaft with a support bearing. The floor height was low enough to require just one step, and with a passenger eye level of 6' from the ground, it would

appeal to "aged and lady passengers", according to a contemporary review. An 11' 3" wheelbase version of this model was also offered with a 14 seat body as the PC24, and with special springing was ideally suited for ambulance work. Provision for a spare wheel was not yet a standard feature of such chassis but could be accommodated by the coachbuilder, and a Kellogg make tyre pump driven from the gear box was fitted to ensure easy inflation of the pneumatic tyres. A new departure was a rear frame-mounted fuel tank with an 'Autovac' system using engine vacuum to draw fuel to an Albion-Zenith carburettor, and a 12 volt dynamo supplied the standard lighting system. This PF24 Viking was bodied by Simpson of Bridgeton, Glasgow and was the 1923 Olympia Show model. It was subsequently purchased by Sanderson Brothers of Glasgow, who later established Millburn Motors, the Albion concessionaire for Scotland. The 11 passengers about to depart from the Crianlarich Hotel in Argyll are comfortably spread out on this 18 seater, and appear to be well wrapped up against the elements for the journey home.

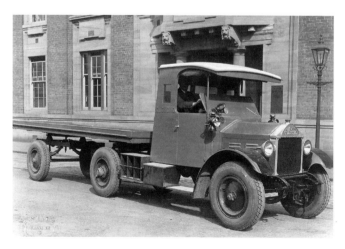

Model 24 (Tractor). Described as a 6 wheeled tractor-lorry, this variation of the Model 24 was intended for service in West Africa to be used both as a tractor pulling a two wheeled trailer, and as a conventional chassis. The tractor, or prime mover, was based on a 25 cwt Model 24 of 10' 9" wheelbase fitted with special springs to cope with varying loads, but with no modifications to the braking system, probably due to the strictly governed speed of 15 mph. Used as a conventional lorry it had an easily detachable 8' 0" platform body with a 3' 2" loading height running on 34"x7" 'giant' pneumatics with cast steel disc type wheels. With the platform body removed, a turntable was fitted above the rear axle to accept a 16' 0" trailer with a loaded platform height of 3' 8". Not having the modern fifth wheel's ability to rapidly uncouple and recouple, it was more of a body swap system. The trailer was interesting in that it was also fitted with a turntable above the trailer axle and a linkage ensured that it tracked the axle on the prime mover. This arrangement was said to be of particular advantage on rough deeply rutted roads which were common in many of Albion's export markets, and this model was supplied to the Crown Agents for service on the Gold Coast of West Africa where a 2 ton capacity limit was imposed.

Model 24 (2 ton Subsidy Type). Although the 30 cwt SB24 was the first Albion to be accepted for a subsidy grant, in May of 1925, the 2 ton Model 24 chassis with its 6" longer wheelbase, deeper frame and stiffer rear axle was also awarded a subsidy certificate in the same category. Designated as the SC24, Albion had reduced chassis weight by 1½ cwt to 35½ cwt, the maximum permitted by War Office specification No.11 for 30 cwt subsidy vehicles. 'Scientifically lightened to meet official requirements', according to early reviews, it was proposed that this would be achieved by making the front wings, dashboard and bonnet of sheet aluminium, and by substituting aluminium for the cast iron of the cylinder head pair. In practice however, it appears that aluminium cylinder heads may not have been introduced on production chassis and no details exist of any surviving

versions with this specification. 'Duralumin' was used for the dashboard support brackets and the handbrake rod adjustment nuts. From the 1st of May 1925, 'giant' pneumatic tyres had become a requirement of the Subsidy Scheme and the model was fitted with 34"x7" Dunlop Cord tyres all round. Other fitments included a positively driven mechanical tyre inflator, Tecalemit lubricator nipples, radiator protector bar, spring drawbar and towing hooks. Although subsidy models were consequently priced slightly higher than normal models, this was offset by the £40 per annum / £120 maximum grant income. This 2 ton SC24 prototype is seen with a trial body shortly after the vehicle had successfully come through trials at Aldershot, which would allow certification and enrolment under the War Department subsidy scheme.

32hp A10 Mk III. 1925 brought the Mark III, and final, version of the successful 32hp A10. This was Albion's first 'overtype', or 'forward control', chassis. A development of the A10 Mark II, it was not designed from scratch as an overtype; that honour would fall to the Model 35 of 1927 which would benefit from the lessons learned with regard to engine accessibility on this model. Featuring a relatively high driving position, the steering column descended to an auxiliary gearbox consisting of a bevel gear pair with a shaft leading backwards to the steering box proper, but despite the increased front axle loading from the overtype layout it was claimed that no additional drag was noticeable. Access to the engine was achieved with a removable sheet metal cover in the cab, and optional wings attached to the entry doors helped to provide similar access to that of the bonneted

models. More modern in concept, although with solid tyres lending an 'old fashioned' appearance, Albion had recognised the benefits to commercial operators of more efficient space packaging by producing the 3 and 4 ton models with wheelbases respectively 2' 0" and 1' 8" shorter than the Mark II equivalents. The retention of this chain driven model so late on however, had an adverse effect on 3 tonner sales for some years, even after direct drive models became available from late 1926 onwards. The example shown is in the livery of Chamberlain, King & Jones of Birmingham and is a platform lorry with a 'sling van body' or container. The strengthening brackets either side of the radiator were installed to stiffen the dash panel and prevent damage to the cab during the loading and unloading of the van body.

Model 26 (4 cylinder). Albion recognised that the rapidly growing bus market had different requirements, and in 1925 produced a specially designed chassis rather than an adapted lorry chassis as had been done with the Model 24, the first Viking. Building on the success of the Model 24, the Model 26 came with the new 4 cylinder 30/60hp EN50 petrol engine and had an overall weight of 3¾ tons, which allowed a maximum legal speed of 20mph on this chassis designed for pneumatic tyres only. Wheels ran on taper roller bearings but front braking had yet to appear, this model retaining a foot operated transmission brake with hand operated rear braking in line with Albion practice. This model was available as a 30 or 24-26 seater bus, and as a Viking coach of 18 or 14 seat capacity on slightly shorter wheelbases, all complying with the proposed Hackney Motor Vehicle regulations. Splayed rear chassis frame side members accommodated the spare tyre within the depth of the frame and avoided further reduction of the ground clearance on this dropped frame, low loading design. A 30 seater model carried out a non-stop run of over 800 miles to London and back in a weekend at the time of the model launch, returning 11 mpg and with no mechanical failure, despite constant running over the 2 days. Although not specially prepared for the run, it had by this time completed over 10,000 miles following extensive testing, and the bus

shortly afterwards returned to London as an exhibit in the Commercial Motor Show at Olympia. In 1927, the coach versions had increased seating capacities of 26 or 20 seats on wheelbases slightly longer than the buses. A 20 seat PNB26 'Monarch' luxury coach was also introduced on the longest wheelbase of 16' 3". Armchair seats fitted with armrests, pneumatic cushions and finished in hand-buffed leather, were in a 2 plus 3 arrangement facing forwards, except over the rear wheelarches where they faced inwards to a central oval table with folding leaves. The EN50 engine later developed problems with pistons and con-rods having to be changed under warranty, and a long running battle with burnt exhaust valves was only resolved with a Ricardo designed cylinder head. These troubles are not evident however in this photograph of a PNA26 Viking, which if nothing else had an impressively large set of tyres to enhance ride comfort. A typical example of the all-weather body popular in the 1920s, WO 2031 was registered in Monmouthshire and was a 26 seater coach supplied through Albion's London depot as a chassis to Messrs. Lewis and James of Newbridge, South Wales. The shorter radiator with starting handle projecting from below is the identifying feature of the 4 cylinder 30/60hp Viking engine and can be compared with the deeper radiator of the 36/90hp Viking Six on page number 39.

The dropped frame bus chassis was popular with operators due to its higher speed and low loading height, and was ideal for vans or pantechnicons which were often loaded and unloaded at street level. This example was based on a 30/60hp 29 passenger PK26 bus chassis of 16' 0" wheelbase, and was a type recommended and supplied by A.E. Keeling and Sons of Leeds to Prices (Tailors) Ltd., who were also based in Leeds. Keelings designed and built the body which had a capacity of 2,000 suits per load, and the first model was so reliable that a further two were ordered. This van was part of a small fleet of eight vehicles consisting of six Albions, which left the factory at 9 pm to arrive at their destinations by 8 am, delivering 10,000 suits per week. With all of the deliveries originally carried by rail, the decision was taken to transfer to road transport after the 1926 General Strike. The elegant and eye catching body with its sweeping curves allowed Prices to make full use of its advertising potential for their London shops.

DECISION ON EXPERIENCE

30/60 h.p. 32 Passenger Albion Overtype Rear Entrance 'Bus, one of a fleet supplied to London-derry Corporation.

30/60 h.p. 29 Passenger 'Bus, one of a number of Albion 'Buses purchased by the Metropolitan Railways.

30/60 h.p. 20 Passenger "Viking" All-weather Coach, with fixed back (Manchester type).

Model 28 (4 cylinder). The Model 28 bus was introduced in 1926, and was a development of the Model 26 bus chassis of the previous year. Incorporating suggestions made at the 1925 Motor Show, it had a low floor and overtype layout, and was ideally suited to maximum capacity bus operations. Easily recognised with its steering column projecting well in front of the radiator, the effect of a minor front end collision on the driver's ability to maintain control could only be guessed at. With the longest wheelbase of any of the bus models so far at 16' 3", it was designed for a maximum of 32 seats and took the seating capacity up to the limit of the licensing regulations. The engine and gearbox were inclined slightly downwards to give a straight drivetrain, using a split propshaft which drove the rear axle through a worm drive from David Brown & Sons. To keep floor height as low as possible, buses used an underslung worm arrangement which reduced clearance below the rear axle to just under 7", not a limiting factor in bus operations. Springs were also underslung in that they were attached to the underside of the axle and in line with Albion practice, were suitably long to give a comfortable ride, those at the rear being 5' 0" long. Other features appropriate to service bus operations included a self starter and the use of ball or taper roller bearings at all main points in the steering linkage to reduce driver effort as far as possible.

Photographed in December of 1927, this PM28 service bus was supplied to H.&W. King of Pollokshields in Glasgow and featured on the Cowieson stand at the 1927 Motor Show.

As with the bonneted Model 26, low floor pantechnicon bodies were a popular application on dropped frame bus chassis. GE 9872 was used for their removals business by Wylie & Lochhead of Glasgow, who also had interests in the motor trade, were funeral undertakers, and were highly respected designers and manufacturers of furniture.

Model 27. Delayed by the General Strike, the 2½-3 ton Model 27 of 1926 finally ended the 16 year run of the chain driven A10 and introduced a direct drive live axle into the heavier weight ranges. Concerned that advance news of this 3 tonner would harm sales of the A10, it was officially described as a 'Colonial 2 tonner' while under development. This subterfuge was at least partly true, since sales advice suggested that indirect drive chassis were unsuitable for unmade roads in overseas markets due to mud contamination of the chain. Powered by a 30/60hp 4 cylinder petrol EN50 engine with a 3 bearing crankshaft and Simms High Tension magneto, it was fitted with a dynamo as standard. Around 9 mpg could be expected from this engine, which was coupled to a new gearbox design with a separate selector box containing three selector shafts instead of two, allowing operation from varying distances to suit different bodies. Experience gained over the years ensured that Albion chassis were strong but light, and this model's modest chassis weight of 49 cwt was typical of a design philosophy which ensured reliability and safety in service. This commercial-only model retained solid tyres, but with optional pneumatics was governed to a maximum of 25 mph and intended for 'high speed' duties with double the maximum speed of the original A10 model. Front wheel braking of Albion design was introduced on the pneumatic tyred model only, operated by foot and in conjunction with the transmission brake via a compensator. In order to capitalise on the Albion motto that the vehicles were 'As Sure as the Sunrise', an eye-catching design featuring sun rays was cast into the radiator top tank, centred on a slightly smaller Albion scroll. Relatively higher speeds were attractive in many export markets due to the longer running distances, and this 3 ton LF27 supplied by agents Arthur D. Riley was operated by McEwen, Carter & Co. Ltd., in New Zealand.

The 30/60hp EN50 petrol engine from the Models 26, 27 and 28 had four cylinders cast in one block, with a pair of detachable and interchangeable cylinder heads. A Simms high tension magneto had an internal timing mechanism which was adjusted by a lever on the steering column. The governor operated a system of levers connected to a butterfly valve in a casing between the carburettor and the inlet passage, which was cast integral with the cylinder block. A chain driven dynamo was mounted in a cradle on the offside, and an optional strap mounted starter with detachable ring gear was also available.

Model 35. Albion continued to add to the range with this design in 1927 which was more innovative than it looked. Rated at 4 tons, it was the first Albion chassis to be designed from the outset as an overtype, whereas the A10 Mark III and Model 28 were successful adaptations of bonneted models. Powered by the largest engine thus far with the 35/55hp EN51B of 6.06 litres, engine accessibility, in comparison with the overtype A10 Mark III, was greatly improved by making the complete cab easy to remove. In only six or seven minutes, two men could unbolt and raise the cab with light lifting tackle; a cut out panel at the rear of the cab allowed the necessary clearance for the radiator and steering wheel to allow the chassis to be pushed back. While perhaps at first glance not the most elegant of Albion chassis with the unusual 'vee' shaped radiator and solid tyres, it was in fact completely up to date in concept and with a little development, might have been Albion's first tilt cab. Taper roller

bearings were fitted all round, and optional pneumatic tyres allowed the governed engine speed to increase from 1,250 to 1,600 rpm. A 5 tonner was introduced the following year in 1928 with improved braking, consisting of a Dewandre servo assisted foot brake acting on rear drums, and a hand operated transmission brake. In the desire to make the cab easy to remove, it had lacked rigidity and it suffered from engine heat and noise. A stiffened cab and a double engine cover was introduced in 1930, in an attempt to deal with these problems. At the same time, body length was sacrificed by extending the cab rearwards by about 3" to assist driver accessibility and to make the operation of the handbrake easier. A 6 tonner was introduced in 1931 with a more conventional flat fronted radiator, and some cabs used a three panel windscreen. Two panel windscreen versions had a very similar appearance to the 6 ton Model 37 of 1932.

RS 9214 is a typical example of a 4 ton LK35 of 1928 in the service of George Wilson of Aberdeen with solid tyres all round, and used with a drawbar trailer for the haulage of livestock.

The pneumatic tyres of the 5 ton LMA35 transformed its appearance and made it look as if it belonged to another era compared to its solid tyred counterpart. This Albion demonstrator is shown loaded with 5 tons of weights as used by the experimental department on test chassis.

Model 34. The bonneted 4 ton Model 34 was introduced along with the overtype Model 35 in 1927 and was always destined to be somewhat overshadowed by its more innovative partner. Production started a month later than the Model 35 and lasted a few months longer into May 1933. Although a 5 tonner was introduced in 1929, the uprating of the overtype version to 6 tons in 1931 was not repeated with this model. Powered by the 35/55hp EN51A engine, it had twin detachable heads, and ignition was by high tension magneto with an impulse starter. A Solex carburettor was fed by an Autovac, with the inlet manifold being heated by an exhaust gas jacket. As might be expected, it had a similar specification and running gear to the Model 35, but with a 3' 0" longer wheelbase of 14' 0". Optional 36"x8" pneumatic tyres increased the £800 chassis price by £120, but did allow a modest increase in the top speed to 23 mph from the 20mph of the solids. This LKA34 platform lorry complete with drawbar trailer, or 'dangler', is shown in front of Harrod's large furniture depository in London, which has now been converted into luxury apartments. Both units are loaded with 'sling type van' bodies which were in common use before the development of the international standard container of today.

(Overleaf) **Model 31.** Albion's first rigid six wheel chassis was the bonneted Model 31, designed around a subsidy scheme specification after interest in such a type was expressed from the War Office, the India Office, and the Crown Colonies Office. Albion had also become increasingly aware of the advance of other rigid 6 wheelers in the home market, although large home sales were not anticipated. Developed from a prototype 24hp 2-3 ton 6x4 chassis, it was first exhibited at the Olympia Show in November 1927, and was rated at 3 tons to suit the British Army's strict weight limits for operation over temporary bridges. 4 tonners were also sold to the Australian Defence Force and to Iraq, and that was also the rating used by civilian hauliers for the LK31, or subsidy specification SK31. A 30/45hp 4 cylinder petrol engine was initially installed, but the 30/60hp engine was also used with a larger radiator to suit tropical conditions. Unusually for a goods model, it used a dropped frame design similar to, but generally shorter than the bus models. The main innovations centred around the double rear axle arrangement, which was designed to a military specification to ensure a standard rear bogie regardless of the vehicle manufacturer. This enabled standard 'caterpillar' tracks to be attached to the rear wheels, which were stowed on platforms attached to the frame on either side. The specification also included Timken bearings on all wheels. Drive was by overhead worm, with the drive from the first rear axle passing direct to the worm of the second rear axle without a third differential. The rear arrangement was quite successful for the rough terrain work intended for these models, but for general haulage on surfaced roads could cause a torque 'wind-up' between the axle pair if tyre diameters differed substantially between the two axles due to differing sizes, or from tyre wear. Rear springs were twin inverted leaf semi-elliptic and were clamped to a central fulcrum bracket, with a system of torque rods linked to a tubular cross member absorbing the torque of the bogie axles. A production first for Albion was a foot brake assisted by a Dewandre servo, which operated on the second rear axle only. The handbrake operated on the first rear axle, with the front axle unbraked and with no transmission brake fitted. On WD models 36"x6" tyres were used with twins at the rear, with either 36"x8" rear singles or twins listed for the civilian version.

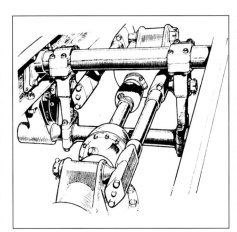

The layout for taking the torque of the axles of the military specification rear bogie on the Models 31 and 32 is shown in this detail. A frame cross tube was connected to a fulcrum bar with vertical members, and cushioning springs were employed in the ball pins of the horizontal torque rod ends.

This War Office type Model 31 from the Motor Transport
Department of the Royal Army Service Corps, Feltham, is
seen negotiating rough country on nearby Hounslow Heath,
with Corps members undergoing driving instruction.

In a civilian role but with the
36"x6" tyres and rear twins
of the WD and subsidy
specification, this 30/45hp
Model 31 was owned by
Australian carriers A.N.
White and supplied through
T.D. Chapman of Sydney in
1928. Fitted with a platform
body by A.H. Peters & Co.,
the crew appeared to enjoy
at least some home
comforts on the road with a
table and two chairs
strapped to the cab roof!

Model 32. The overtype Model 32 was the second of the rigid 6 wheelers to be developed for the War Office and for service in India, entering production in 1928 within 6 months of the bonneted Model 31. It had an identical rear bogie to the Model 31 and apart from the overtype layout, had a similar specification. Fitted with the 30/45hp EN57 engine and retaining the British military 3 ton rating, it proved to be an extremely successful export model, with a series of orders in 1929 alone for a total of 223 chassis for the Government of India. Destined for a hot climate, no cab was fitted and protection from the sun for the driver and crew was provided by a substantial canvas canopy reminiscent of wartime A10s. A special version with a six cylinder 36/90hp engine was also supplied, identified by a bonnet extension and the radiator in line with the leading edge of the front wheels.

A 30/45hp 3 ton Model 32 is pictured here on a short test track constructed within the factory grounds at Scotstoun and shows how the rear axles could cope with obstacles on rough terrain. This was one of the 223 chassis supplied to India.

This 4 tonner for the Gas Light & Coke Co., of London was photographed in September 1931 and was bodied by their own coachbuilders. This body type was used for the delivery of domestic appliances, but a platform version was also used to deliver coke to new building estates with unmade roads.

Model 40. The replacement for the 30 cwt Model 24 was introduced in 1928 with two versions, one of which was the 'home' Model 40, powered by the 4 cylinder EN52C of 20/36hp. Like the Model 41, a new combined engine and gearbox unit was used, with an open clutch 'pit' for easy access, and three-point mounting of the complete unit. A centrally mounted gear lever was introduced in 1930. Identified by 5 bonnet louvres, its similar looking Model 24 predecessor had 6 louvres, and was more likely to have solid tyres all round. The Model 40 employed an underslung worm drive which allowed a lower floor height without the intrusion of the worm gear, and became popular for 14-17 seat local service buses. The Models 40 & 41 were

only announced after considerable development and an intense effort to control costs for launch into a very competitive market sector. Chassis price was £365, rising to £440 with a box van body. A body weight of under 9 cwt met the 2 ton unladen weight limit for a £25 road tax. Apart from the fan which was belt driven, all of the auxiliary components were positively driven and included a dynamo for a 12 volt lighting set. Transmission braking had now been abandoned on this lighter model at least, in favour of more conventional methods with both hand and foot brakes operating shoes in 17" drums at the rear. An unusual feature on this pneumatics only model was the inclusion of a spare wheel with a solid tyre to ensure a usable spare at all times. Baillie Brothers Ltd. of Hawick Street, Yoker operated this 16 seater bus on local services between Glasgow and the Dumbarton area. The lower floor height possible with the underslung worm gear is evident when compared with the Model 41 below.

Model 41. The companion to the Model 40 was the 'export' Model 41, also rated at 30 cwts and with a technical specification generally similar to the Model 40. The principal difference was in the use of an overhead worm drive to increase ground clearance under the rear axle from 8" to 10" and intended for the unmade roads more likely in export markets at that time. In practice, this model was also sold in the U.K., and with its higher floor line was more common as a van or light lorry where floor height is of less importance. The Model 41 was also used as a school children's ambulance for the transport of children with special needs, or as a shooting brake for the estate owners who may have possibly been Albion's first customers. An LB41 from the Motor Transport Section of the

General Post Office is shown with a special body designed for use as a telephone utilities van, with sufficient light stores for 3 days work. This versatile body was capable of carrying 6 men plus the driver and was also equipped with a small bench attached to the rear of the bulkhead which could take a vice or be used as a foreman's writing desk. The GPO had a fleet of these high speed vans for light wiring duties in rural areas which could support a number of squads. A trap door visible at the front of the van body allowed telegraph poles to project over the cab, and ladders would be attached to the side brackets. The GPO was an extremely important customer for Albion in the inter-war years, purchasing around 1,600 vehicles in the light to medium weight sector.

Model 26/28 (Viking Six). The bonneted Model 26 and overtype Model 28 were revised in 1928 with a new petrol engine of 36/90hp, and the first Albion six cylinder, designated EN53. For 26 and 31 passengers respectively, these 'Viking Six' models were at last given an engine which provided the valuable increase in power and refinement essential to this market sector. Retaining many of the features of previous engines, the EN53 did also inherit some of the exhaust valve burning problem of the 4 cylinder EN50 until the final Ricardo cylinder head designs were introduced. Continuing with an exhaust jacketed induction manifold and fuel feed by an Autovac, there were also new features such as a special 'snap' pick-up arrangement on the carburettor to ensure rapid acceleration, and an 'Auto Klean' oil filtration system. To comply with London Metropolitan Police recommendations and to cope with the higher weight and speed, front wheel brakes were fitted as standard. The rear brakes were of an interesting twin shoe design, having a wide pair of shoes for the Dewandre servo assisted foot brake and alongside, a narrower shoe pair for the handbrake. The 36/90 radiator was much deeper than before and extended below the starting handle, with a cowled fan providing the necessary forced cooling. The longer bonnet of the six cylinder engine and the raked windscreen of the Model 26 added particularly to the elegance and impression of speed.

The 26 seat bonneted Model 26 Albion demonstrator shows clearly the deeper radiator of the 36/90hp six cylinder engine and the ebonite fillers on the radiator cap first seen on the Model 24 Viking. This Albion demonstrator coach was fitted with a type of 'all weather' roof which could be slid back for good weather, and had a fixed rear portion to accommodate the additional luggage rack.

The Strachans bodied 26 passenger long distance coach belonged to Tourist Motor Coaches (Southampton) Ltd., and ran between Southampton and London daily. The appearance of the overtype Model 28 Viking Six was perhaps less successful with the extended bonnet protruding forward of the front dash of the half cab producing a semi-overtype effect. The ladder allowing access to the overhead luggage rack is clearly visible underneath.

Chapter 3
Expansion and Competition
1930 to 1936

Throughout the early 1930s, developments regarding oil engines had been continuing and Albion was now doing its best to keep up with events. Negotiations took place with Beardmores to design an engine exclusively for Albion in order that chassis alterations would be kept to a minimum on installation, but although Beardmore engines were offered, it is not recorded whether these engines were the result of such an arrangement. Bus sales continued to be uncertain for some time and work on a new light bus was suspended in view of the developments with diesels. A 6 cylinder Beardmore diesel, on loan for a month, was installed in an experimental double decker bus, and two experimental double deckers were also undergoing road tests, the 6 wheel Model 85 and the 4 wheel Model 80, the latter with Glasgow Corporation Transport (GCT).

A potentially rewarding opportunity came in October of 1930 from Babcock & Wilcox, which was associated with a Spanish company wishing to manufacture commercial vehicles under licence in Spain for a minimum of 15 years. Unfortunately Albion was unsuccessful as in December it was announced that Saurer of Switzerland had secured the

contract. Albion wisely avoided being tempted into business with Russia, and decided not to quote in 1931 for up to 300 goods vehicles of 3½ to 5 tons with a two year credit period. Trading links were attempted with the Continent however, and although Belgium had seemed the most likely opening as Albions had operated there since the First World War, no connections were eventually established.

Although the company had not manufactured a car since 1913, it was still known as the Albion Motor Car Company Ltd. Noting the fashion for shorter names, Joint Managing Director H.E. Fulton suggested that the name be shortened to Albion Motors Ltd., which was approved at the 1931 Annual General meeting. A difficult trading year closed with substantial orders from the Indian Government for 116 modified 30 cwt chassis and an additional 23 rigid six wheelers for the India Office. This was followed two months later with an order for 27 Model 43 buses from the Nizam of Hyderabad's State Railway in India, which over the following years would prove to be a loyal customer.

A somewhat surprising development came later in 1933 from the Durban Municipal Authority, who had indicated a requirement for trolleybuses. At that time GCT had applied for powers to operate trolleybuses, and Albion assumed that if a suitable bus was developed for South Africa, then it could also be of interest to Glasgow and other municipal authorities. Perhaps aware of the intense competition from Leyland Motors with more conventional models, the Albion directors appeared to be keen to develop another potential market and a prototype was later produced for inspection by GCT representatives. By September 1934, the experimental trolleybus chassis was on the road for tests, but the project was not developed further for two reasons. Firstly, there were difficulties in sourcing proprietary components, which in any case produced a chassis of limited component value to Albion; and, secondly, there would be difficulty breaking into a market already dominated by an established group of trolleybus manufacturers.

An experimental EN75 oil engine newly installed in a bus chassis was however not running successfully and the production of excessive smoke resulted in Ricardo again being called upon to redesign the Albion cylinder head, which was installed 6 months later in May 1934. Later reports from trials of the Ricardo head diesel with W. Alexander & Sons subsequently proved to be satisfactory,

Bus and Coach Chassis – The Victor.

Model 48/49. The second model to follow the 'V' naming style was the Model 48 'Victor' introduced in 1929, but only two examples were built before being replaced by the Model 49 in 1930. The Victor light bus was perceived as a 'big bus scaled down' and was powered by the 4 cylinder 20/42hp engine. As a 20 seater bonneted bus for town and village services, it had an overall length of just under 22' and a narrow body of only 6' 0", ideal for narrow country roads. The chassis was factory fitted with full width channel type body bearers, which were bolted to the frame at the front and the rear of the chassis, also acting as a guide to body width for coachbuilders. As used before in bus chassis, the engine and gearbox unit was slightly canted down to give a straight drive line to the underslung worm of the rear axle via a split propshaft with fabric flexible joints and a centre support roller bearing. Servo assisted braking with the manually adjustable Dewandre unit was similar to that used on recently

introduced models, and in common with other bus layouts the fuel tank was mounted on the frame, instead of the gravity fed dash mounted tanks of the goods models. In 1933 the engine was replaced by the 23/60hp EN68 and three versions were available on two frame lengths, a 4-abreast 20 seat PH49 on the shorter frame and on the 1' 8" longer frame, a 3-abreast 20 seat PHA49 and a 4-abreast 24 seat PHC49. GS4145, a 1934 PHA49 was owned by Christisons of Blairgowrie, Perthshire, and is parked outside Messrs Alexander McAra, Albion concessionaires, East Dock Street, Dundee.

Model 114/115. The overtype Model 115 'Victor' was a revised version of the 1930 Model 49 'Victor' announced in early 1934, with a bonneted Model 114 in production three months later. The capacity of the original 20-24 seat 'light bus' was now available either as a 24/26 seat, 14'-6" wheelbase PH115 or a 30/32 seat, 16'-4" wheelbase PK115. To compensate for the increase in seating capacity, a slightly more powerful 23/65hp EN211 engine was installed with a 3/8 inch larger stroke and 5 bhp more than the previous year's 23/60hp EN68 revision. Contemporary reviews noted that although the power output was still below average for a bus of 32 seat capacity, performance was acceptable despite a rear axle ratio selected for economy. The EN211 featured a transversely mounted high tension magneto driven by a skew gear, with a water pump on the nearside driven in tandem with the dynamo and a much more accessible distributor and contact breaker, with no auxiliaries on the offside. The Victor was now the only chassis in the range not available with an oil engine option. Braking was upgraded from the single servo of the Model 49 to the triple set up previously introduced on the much larger Model 80 'Venturer' double decker bus, using a frame mounted main servo unit with an auxiliary servo on each stub axle. One of 3 owned by Hicks Brothers of Braintree, Essex, this PK115 had a Waveney 32 seat coach body with roof mounted luggage compartment, and was new in December 1936.

but it was almost a year before Albion was satisfied with its durability and pressed on with a 6 cylinder version. It made good commercial sense in the short term to satisfy the growing demand by offering oil engines from other manufacturers, allowing the company time to develop an oil engine range of its own. However, when Glasgow Corporation Transport purchased 110 double deckers late in 1934, Albion was disappointed to receive an order for only 50. Unfortunately, GCT experienced engine problems with the first batch of 20 Beardmore-engined Venturers and withheld some of the payment – hardly a good omen for future sales.

In June of 1934, George Pate, by now sole Managing Director, announced to the board that in his opinion Albion 'had lost the boat in the passenger market' and suggested concentrating on goods chassis. Albion was losing out in two main areas: competition in the bus market and mass-produced chassis in the lighter weight ranges. Both factors produced downward pressure on prices, especially as other manufacturers, particularly Leyland, aggressively reduced theirs. John F. Henderson thought that the passenger and goods markets would move apart, just as cars and commercials had done in the early history of the industry, and circumstances were certainly indicating where the future lay for Albion.

1935 was to mark another break with the past, when Dr. Murray's original partner and co-founder, Norman O. Fulton, died after a short illness. Although, like Murray,

an experienced and capable engineer, Fulton's talents and interest had been as organiser of the business, and he had ensured from the very early days of the company that an efficiently run organisation would greatly contribute to its prosperity. He was much respected by all and sadly missed. Fulton's death, coupled with the departure of other long serving board members from Albion's early days, meant that the management of the company was now in the control of George Pate, elected Chairman shortly after Fulton's death. Despite Pate's early doubts, progress with the design of 4 and 6 cylinder diesels was well under way, but there was still a need to buy in diesel engines from other manufacturers, with Gardner, Beardmore, Dorman and Perkins oil engines offered as alternatives to the Albion petrol designs if required.

Halley Motors had finally gone into liquidation in the October of 1935, and the Yoker factory, without machinery, was purchased by Albion for £13,500, so there was at last an opportunity to relieve the pressure on space at Scotstoun. As development and testing of new engines and entirely new model ranges proceeded into 1936 for launch later that year, the Albion directors must have felt that they had been on a roller-coaster ride over the previous fifteen or so years, but many hard lessons had been learned. Successful attempts had been made to rationalise models and production, and they were acutely aware of the importance of manufacturing costs, especially relevant to the lighter weight ranges. ❏

The Valkyrie.

Model 65. To satisfy the demands of the economy urban bus market, the Model 65 was announced in 1930 with a similar layout to the Model 28 of 1926 and retaining a steering box projecting well ahead of the radiator. Also designed for 32 passengers, it introduced the third of the six 'V' bus names, 'Valkyrie'. It was fitted as standard with the 4 cylinder 5 litre EN60 engine of 30/60hp, with the 4⁵⁄₁₆" bore of the similarly rated EN50, but with a ½" longer stroke. Identified by a simplified but still elegant new radiator based on the earlier curved top tank first seen on the 'Viking', it was available in 'driver beside engine' or half-cab layout,

an arrangement which was to be commonplace for many years to come. In what was now becoming standard practice, front wheel brakes were assisted by a Dewandre servo, and in keeping with the arduous duty of this type of chassis, a centralised group of chassis-mounted oil nipples helped to reduce servicing times. There were three sub types, the PX65, PT65, and PW65, the second letter in the prefix indicating progressively longer wheelbases. This PW65 was owned by Strachans of Ballater and had a 32 seat bus body by Northern Counties. It was registered AV5191.

Model 67/69. In 1933 the Model 67 'Valkyrie' was introduced as a 32/36 seat bus or coach with the 4 cylinder petrol EN200A of 35/80hp as standard, but offering a variety of Albion petrol or oil engines, or proprietary oil engines as alternatives. Revised gearbox and axles were specified, but otherwise the model followed closely the layout and specification of the PW65 which it replaced. It was available only in the longest wheelbase for maximum length bodies of 27' 6", which meant that only the 'PW' variant was built. The illustration shows a 32 seat front entrance Brush bodied Model PW67 in service in Halifax delivered to Hebble Motor Services Ltd. in March 1934. A year later the Model 67 was redesignated as the Model 69 with the EN200B engine as standard.

Model 141. The Model 141 'Valkyrie' was introduced in December 1935 as a 40 seat bus or 35 seat coach, replacing the Model 69 'Valkyrie'. There were two sub-types, the PV141 and the PW141, having a variety of Albion petrol, Gardner oil, or the 6 cylinder Albion-Ricardo oil engine. The PV141 had power units generally above 7.5 litres, the latter below this figure, while the 'P' prefix denoted 'passenger' model. The shorter bonnets of the PW141 allowed for extra passenger accommodation or an extra row of seats. A four speed gearbox, underslung worm axle, and vacuum servo assisted brakes completed the specification on both types. The model had a short life span ending production in December 1937, having been replaced by the new Valkyries, the CX9, 11 and 13. A 32 seat Duple rear entrance coach body was fitted to AV9216, a 1937 PW141 for Sutherland of Peterhead. It had a Gardner 5LW engine.

Model 145. In August 1936, production began of a 6 wheeled single deck bus chassis aimed at busy urban services and the luxury coach market. Like the Model 85 'Valorous', it took advantage of the 30 feet maximum legal length for 3 axle chassis and used an identical frame cross-section to the 9 ton N553 but with the usual bus type dropped frame profile between front and rear axles, along with additional stiffening. Designated the Model 145 'Valkyrie', it usually had a trailing rear axle bogie, but double drive was available to order. Long springs of thinner section than the N553 were fitted for a more comfortable ride and an underslung worm drive came with a variety of ratios to suit operational or engine requirements. Braking was applied to all six wheels, using the triple servo arrangement now virtually standard on all recent models. There were two sub-types, the PR145 and the PW145, the differences relating to engine size and seating capacity as per the 2 axle PV141 and PW141. Seating capacities were 40-44 for the bus, or 34-40 for the coach. However, the PW145 with its longer engine required the bulkhead to be moved back, and this reduced the capacity to 39 or 40 seats maximum. Single wheels of 9.75"x20" were fitted all round.

The Model 145 shown above is on a road test for a motor magazine in early 1936. Mr Richard Twelvetrees, a well known motoring journalist of the period is conducting the road test with passengers on temporary seats on top of test weights. It must be wondered how an accurate assessment of the finished vehicle's riding qualities could ever have been obtained under these conditions, to say nothing of the safety implications!

A finished PR145 with 39 seat Cowieson coach body with stepped waistrail and smart whitewall tyres. The coach is seen in Glasgow Road, Paisley, passing Barshaw Park on a Young's service to West Kilbride when new in 1937. It was fitted with an Albion-Ricardo six cylinder oil engine of 7.32 litres. Only 28 chassis were built, of which none survives today.

The Valiant.

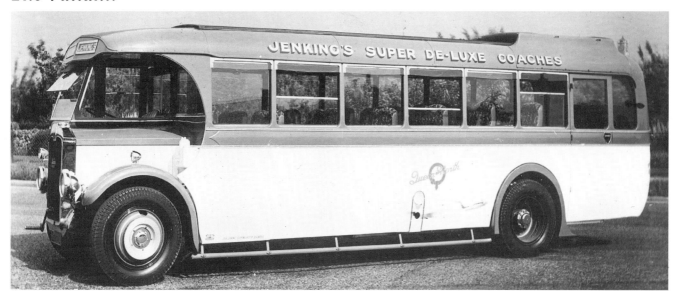

Model 70. The new 'Valiant' Model 70 of 1931 was not an improved 'Valkyrie' Model 69 as the model number might have suggested, but was a completely new design altogether. It had a front axle set back to give a better proportioned appearance to the front end of the vehicle, and had a six cylinder engine as standard. But most importantly, it had a maximum width frame similar to the type later used on the M80 'Venturer' double decker. It could achieve 50 mph on level roads with its 6 cylinder EN70 engine and was priced at £1,630. The Valiant was, therefore, a top flight touring coach chassis suitable for long distance work. A notable innovation for Albion was that the engine was an overhead valve design, with the valves set at an angle, and almost horizontal sparking plugs positioned opposite the valves, with a triangular section combustion chamber. The design of the valve gear had in fact been patented in 1919 by Murray, and used exhaust valve seat inserts along with a duplex chain driven camshaft and automatic tensioner. In line with the easy maintenance philosophy of earlier bus models, three banks of Tecalemit chassis lubricators were fitted to the chassis to ensure that no nipples were missed in difficult-to-reach locations, especially from night-time servicing routines. Jenkings Super De-Luxe Coaches, a Blackpool operator, purchased this 1933 'Valiant' PV70 with Burlingham 32 seat coachwork. Registered FV 3655, it subsequently received a new coach body in 1950 and went on to give a few more years service with a new operator.

Model 71. In December 1934 the PV70 was replaced by the PV71 'Valiant', which had different engine options and revised front and rear axles. The revisions appeared to follow similar improvements which had been introduced on the Model 81 'Venturer' at approximately the same time. The Venturer and the Valiant had much in common, but the Valiant was built to maximum legal length of 27' 6", this being 1' 6" longer than that allowed for the Venturer double decker. BOE 397 was a PV71 demonstration vehicle with fully fronted coachwork, and was used by the Ellison Electric Switchgear Company of Birmingham.

The Venturer.

M80. Announced just prior to the Scottish Motor Show of 1932 in Glasgow's Kelvin Hall, Albion's first purpose-built double decker was the Model 80 'Venturer' for 51 passengers, allowing 24 seated on the lower deck and 27 above. Generally similar to the single decker 'Valiant' PV70 with its six cylinder engine, it was fitted with the more powerful 43/100hp EN80A power unit, this engine retaining the overhead camshaft and horizontal sparking plug arrangement first seen on the EN70 of the 'Valiant'. Other engine options were the EN85 7.82 litre unit, or the choice of Beardmore or Gardner oil engines. The complete chassis was as usual designed to be strong yet as light as possible and to this end frame members were reinforced with nickel steel flitch plates. The foot brake operated on all four wheels with assistance from a Dewandre triple servo arrangement, with a main servo unit on the frame for the rear brakes and a smaller auxiliary unit mounted on each stub axle. Maintenance considerations included the Tecalemit centralised lubrication system using three banks of nipples and the use of a traditional Albion layout of exposed clutch and separate 3-point mounted gearbox. Standard tyres offered were high pressure 35"x8" all round, or alternatively, a low pressure set with 40"x10½" on the front axle and twin 38"x9" rears. Seen at the Kelvin Hall before the opening of the Scottish Motor Show in November 1932 is the first complete M80 built. Although exhibited in Glasgow Corporation Transport livery, it was an Albion demonstrator which was later sold to Young's of Paisley in 1934 after trials with GCT. A Cowieson 51 seat body was fitted.

(Below) **Model 81.** The Model 81 'Venturer' introduced in 1935 was of a very similar specification to the Model 80 which it replaced except that a new rear axle was fitted and the options of petrol engines were no longer available. The oil engines offered were the Beardmore HOE 8.36 litre or the Gardner 6LW 8.4 litre units, but the Beardmore proved to be less reliable than the Gardner engined examples, and many of these engines were changed for better known types during the course of their working lives. XS 4132 was a Gardner engined ex-Young's M81 acquired by Western when that company was taken over in 1951. It is seen at Renfrew Ferry, about a mile from the Yoker Works, on the south bank of the River Clyde.

The Valorous.

Model 85. In 1933 Albion designed the Model 85 double decker to tackle the high capacity end of the bus market and this 6x4 chassis was given the grand title of 'Valorous', the sixth and final 'V' name and the shortest lived. Built to take advantage of the maximum legal length of 30 feet for 3 axle chassis, it may have been inspired by the AEC Renown, of which large numbers were purchased by the London General Omnibus Company in the early 1930s. Officially classed as an experimental vehicle, only one example was built, and after the development and testing period it was bought by Young's of Paisley, a faithful Albion operator for many years. This efficient and well run organisation had a fleet of over 80 Albion buses covering an aggregate of 5 million miles per year, and was ideal for extended trials of new models. Conveniently close to the factory at Scotstoun on the other side of the Clyde, Young's were based in the Renfrewshire town of Paisley, at that time a busy mill town of cotton spinning, thread and ribbon manufacturing. Pickering built the 60 seat bodywork, and it was sold out of service in 1944 to a showman with no record of it existing after 1945.

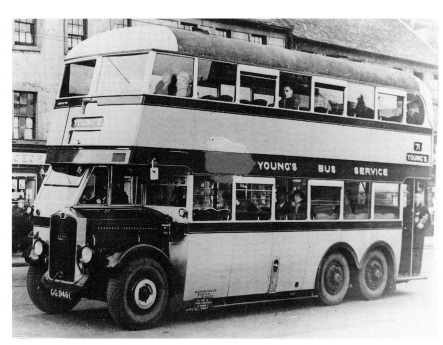

Light and Medium Goods.

Model 43. 1930 saw the introduction of the bonneted 2 ton Model 43 based on the 30 cwt Model 40 but with a deeper 7" frame, larger tyres, 12' 6" wheelbase and overall length of 19' 7". Fitted with the 3.2 litre EN58, this engine was rated at 20/42hp, similar to the Model 40s' 20/36hp EN52C, but with a ⅜" longer stroke and notable for its large bearings to extend overhaul intervals. Using a single cylinder head and dry liners, the engine also had a Zenith carburettor and some Ricardo influence from a split induction system and shrouded inlet valves. This 'shrouded' valve design was used in many Albion engines and improved gas flow at the point of initial valve opening, giving the effect of a high lift cam without the disadvantages. Four wheel braking was employed and the handbrake used a separate set of rear shoes of the same width as the front shoes, a general arrangement first seen on the Models 26 and 28 of 1928. Although 32"x6" tyres were fitted as standard, a feature reflecting the overseas market was the option of a narrower front axle fitted with wider 8" tyres, thus making the front and rear tracks 'standard' and rendering the machine suitable for deeply rutted roads. A Model 43 three-way hand operated tipper delivers a load of bricks to a building site in the Glasgow area in the early 1930s.

Model 44. The Model 44 was an overtype chassis introduced in 1931 for the lighter weight range of 2-2¼ tons, an alternative to the bonneted Model 43 of the same capacity introduced the year before. As with all overtypes, the Model 44 had the advantage over the bonneted '43' of a smaller turning circle and a wheelbase 1' 3" shorter, sufficient to allow a one piece propshaft. The engine was the 20/42hp EN58 petrol 4 cylinder with all auxiliaries grouped on the nearside in the usual fashion, and particularly suited to overtype installations with their limited access from the cab interior. The only offside mounted auxiliary was the magneto which was driven by a skew gear cross shaft and protruded through the cab floor between the steering column and the pedals. Since the overtype cab layout had no space for the dash mounted gravity feed fuel tank of the bonneted models, the frame mounted tank necessitated the fitting of an 'Autovac' mounted under the nearside seat alongside the battery. Considerable effort was made to reduce heat and noise by the use of a double skinned sheet steel engine cover containing a suitable ventilated air space and with a layer of asbestos attached to the inner sheet to minimise radiated heat. On the left in this view is a Model 44 owned by Woods Bottle Works of Portobello and on the right is a rare Model 41 overtype.

Model 46/47 & Model 463/473. The 2½ ton bonneted Model 46 and overtype Model 47 introduced in 1931 were uprated versions of the 2-2¼ ton Models 43 & 44 respectively, with the same 20/42hp EN58 engine of 3½" bore and 5" stroke. Front wheel brakes were not included to keep the price down but were available as an option. Chassis weights were too high to achieve the 2.5 ton unladen weight limit, which would have saved £5 in tax and allowed the maximum speed to be increased from 20mph to 30mph. In the early 1930s new vehicle taxation rules had a considerable influence on the success of certain models and Albion, like other manufacturers, had to respond quickly to the changing demands of the market. To take advantage of tax changes for unladen weights not exceeding 3 tons, two further sub-types designated 463 and 473 uprated to 3 tons capacity were introduced in 1932. These uprated models, with front brakes now standard, also had a small power increase with the fitting of the EN68 of 23/60hp. In common with the lighter weight ranges, the gearbox was mounted to the engine as a single unit, but with the clutch easily accessible from an open clutch pit. The overtype is represented here with this Model LHA473, which was supplied to Bertram's Foundry, Edinburgh. The bonneted truck is a Model LHB463, one of three supplied to Thomas Allen Ltd., who continued to use Albion lorries in all weight ranges on contract to Guinness well into the 1960s.

Model 50/51. Two of the new 1931 models were the 3½-4 ton bonneted Model 50 and its stablemate, the Model 51 overtype, both retaining a steering box projecting well ahead of the radiator as on the Models 28 and 65. Powered by a side-valve 4 cylinder 30/60hp EN60 engine, this chassis followed what was now standard practice, with pneumatic tyres, chassis mounted fuel tank and full lighting set, and certainly looked a thoroughly up to date vehicle. A new radiator design still following traditional lines now had a honeycomb grille which was said to improve the appearance of the vehicle, less important on this commercial model, although still a factor in the overall image. Perhaps surprisingly in view of the four wheel braking

now common on the bus models, this 30mph commercial had no front brakes, at least as standard fitments, and had a foot operated servo assisted rear brake with the hand or parking brake connected to a transmission brake. The 4½" wide rear brake shoes could be replaced without disturbing the hub bearings and the centralised lubrication system first seen on the passenger models was used, with rigid pipes feeding oil to the spring shackles and other vital points. Scott of Gorebridge used this three year old LKA51 seen here on the left in this view in 1935. The prefix L meant lorry, while K was related to weight range and A to the wheelbase. On the right is an LHB473 3½ tonner with typical Kirkness and Innes cab built in Leith.

Model 52/53 & Model 520/530. Introduced at the 1933 London Olympia Show, and among seven other new and revised models on display, were the 4 ton capacity bonneted Model 52 and overtype Model 53, available in two and three wheelbases respectively. Despite the surprise announcement of Albion's first compression-ignition engine, the EN75, the standard engine offered was the 4 cylinder petrol EN205 of 30/65hp, but EN75, Beardmore, Dorman and Gardner oil engines were offered in response to customer demand. Albion referred to the diesel as an 'oil' engine and following their belated commitment to this more reliable power source, Albion went on to become one of the most enthusiastic users of oil engines in the lower weight ranges. Braking on this 4 ton model followed a well tried Albion arrangement, using foot operated servo assisted rear brakes and a hand lever operated transmission brake of 12" diameter by 5" wide. An increase in payload to 5 tons in June 1935 resulted in models being revised as the M520 and M530. This well used K52 articulated timber lorry did not offer much protection from a shifting load in the event of an accident. A Gardner 4LW was fitted and the unit hauled a Dyson pole trailer.

Model 126/127. At the forefront of a successful series of low chassis weight / high payload models, Albion announced the bonneted Model 126 and the overtype 127 in September 1935, with payloads from 3½ to 4½ tons. Despite a ½ ton greater payload than the 4 ton 463/473 models they replaced, an unladen weight just below the 50 cwt threshold meant that they could operate at a 30mph maximum speed and with a £30 annual road tax. Three overtype 'J' (later 'K') prefix versions were offered with identical wheelbases to the only recently uprated but now superseded Model 473. Only one bonneted chassis was available on the longest wheelbase and designated HL126 with a rated capacity of 3½-4 tons, but the larger figure was only permissible with a forward positioned load. A modified design of radiator was fitted, slightly taller with narrower sides and more rounded lower corners, cooling a slightly more powerful EN211 or EN212 engine. Producing 23/65hp, it had a 3/8" longer stroke than the Model 473s' 23/60hp EN68 and an Amal fuel pump feeding a Zenith carburettor. A new feature for the driver was an electric indicator on the dash to warn of oil pressure failure. Great attention was paid to vibration damping and the front engine joint allowed rotational and sideways movement, with only vertical motion allowed at the rear. The gearbox was no longer operated by a right hand lever but had a central ball type lever which had to be turned through 180°, facing forwards or rearwards for use in the overtype and bonneted models respectively. Both overtype & bonneted models later received a 'K' prefix, and by mid 1936 this model had been uprated to 5 and then 5½ tons, still achieving an unladen weight below 50 cwt. Towards the end of the 1930s a number of warranty claims were received relating to rear axle failures. Although overloading was suspected as a contributory factor, claims were honoured and a larger diameter worm drive assembly was introduced.

EMC 533 was a KS126 operated by the Ham River Grit Co. Ltd. of London from 1936. It had Wood single ram tipping gear, weighed under 2.5 tons and carried a payload of 3.5 to 4 tons, which could not have been more than two or three bucket loads from the one cubic yard bucket on the Ruston Bucyrus mechanical excavator in the background. Headlamps, nearside mirror and wiper were deemed to be unnecessary accessories, and direction indicators were still some years away, but at least the driver had adequate ventilation.

Six KS127 tippers ('S' for short wheelbase) were delivered to Fife quarrymasters, Bell Brothers, in 1939. The two in the foreground were equipped with Edbro three way tipping gear, while the other four had Woods Hoist end tipping equipment. Five tons of gravel could be carried, and the vehicles weighed in at under three tons. Albion 4 cylinder petrol engines of 3.89 litres capacity were fitted, and the price of each chassis was listed at £435.

Model 118/119. Introduced in 1935 to replace the Models 40/41 in the 30/40 cwt payload sector, the Model 118 bonnet type and 119 overtype were the lightest chassis in the range, but followed closely the design of the 126 and 127 models. Four engines were listed during its five year production run, two Albion petrol units and two oil engines. The standard unit was however the EN216 four cylinder petrol engine of 3.39 litres capacity driving through a 4 speed gearbox to an overhead worm rear axle. Vacuum brakes were provided which acted upon the rear axle only, and the list price of the chassis was £322. Castlebank Laundry operated this fleet of B119 models and Holland Coachcraft of Gateshead built the streamlined bodies.

Model 122/123/125. In 1935 the bonneted Models 122 and overtype Model 123 replaced Models 43/44 in the 2 to 2½ tons weight range. They shared the identical specification of engine, gearbox and axle equipment as the lighter M118 and 119 types with only tyre equipment and perhaps springing differentiating the two ranges. As with the lighter range two wheelbases were available of 10' 9" and 12'. For 3 tons the near identical Model 125 was available, but with four wheel braking. A 1936 CL122 two and a half tonner is pictured beside a new 1953 FT21 three tonner, which was then the lightest in the range. It was likely that the FT21 was the CL122's replacement, which was probably the reason for the photograph. The C prefix indicated a weight range of 2 to 2½ tons, and the L denoted the longer wheelbase.

Model 129. The KN129 six ton 6x2 model of 1936 introduced a series of lightweight six wheelers which in later years was to become the mainstay of the company's production. It was based on the Model 127 using the same engine, gearbox, and driving axle, which was complemented by the provision of an extra trailing axle. Light axle loadings allowed it to operate in places where other 6 tonners could not, which was of particular interest to some overseas operators. Holmes, Mullen and Dunn operated this 1500 gallon petrol KN129 tanker in Belfast in 1937.

Heavy Duty Goods.

Model 36/37. In 1932 within only a year of the introduction of the 6 ton version of the overtype Model 35, a replacement arrived with the Model 37 rated at 5 to 6 tons and accompanied by a bonneted Model 36, the first normal control 6 tonner. A main feature of these models was that the position of the front axle was moved rearwards by several inches, giving a very distinctive and easily recognisable 'long nose' appearance on the bonneted model. This was an arrangement adopted by a number of manufacturers which conformed with popular demand of the period, and which was said to gain

optimum axle loadings. Along with the low chassis weight, this arrangement allowed a gross load of 7.5 tons for this '6 tonner' while remaining within legal axle and gross weight limits. Both models were available in two wheelbases depending on the capacity, but the bonneted models were somewhat unusual for that period in that the front axle was in the same position as on the overtype, an arrangement which became commonplace thereafter. Benefiting from a more powerful 35/70hp 4 cylinder side valve EN65A engine compared to the 35/55hp unit previously fitted in the Model 35, the overtype models continued with the air cooled double skinned engine cover to reduce cab heat. Provision was made in this chassis for the fitment of a diesel engine with the minimum of alteration and although an Albion oil engine was still a year away, engines from Gardner, Beardmore and Dorman were available as options by early 1933. The long nose is apparent in this view of a Model 36 petrol tanker for Redline Glico Ltd. registered in London in September 1933.

Model 56/57. The first of the 1933 models to go into production, the overtype Model 57 and a companion bonneted Model 56 which followed in October, were heavy duty maximum legal weight versions of the 5-6 ton Models 37 & 36 introduced the previous year and retained the same set-back front axle arrangement. For non-trailer work the power came from the 38/85hp EN70 introduced with the 'Valiant' bus, but for trailer hauled duties, the 43/100hp EN80 from the 'Venturer' was offered. Gardner and Beardmore 5 and 6 cylinder diesel engines were also available for solo and trailer work respectively. At that time, the model number was often given a prefix letter and the wheelbase indicated with a second prefix letter (e.g. 'L' Long, 'S' Short), whereas post second

world war models used a suffix letter. Three overtype versions had wheelbases of 12'-0", 14'-6" and 16'-6" and were listed as the 'PS57', 'P57' and 'PL57' with both versions featuring low loading heights from underslung rear springs. The two bonneted versions, with 14'-6" and 16'-6" wheelbases, were the 'PS56' and 'P56' respectively. This common 'engine forward' arrangement was intended to maximise load space and, indeed in bare chassis form, both overtype and bonneted versions only differed visually in the position of the steering wheel and scuttle/dash panel. A Gardner 6LW was fitted to this PS56 with Crane trailer operated by Edward Jacobs (Pty) Ltd. of Johannesburg. Timber for use in mines was carried.

Opposite: **Model 58/59.** Described as a 10 ton chassis but designed for a 12 ton gross load, the overtype Model 59 commenced production in April of 1933, with a bonneted Model 58 not available until early 1934. They were Albion's first heavy duty chassis and officially designated with a 12-13 ton 'R' prefix as the R59 and the RL59 with 14' and 17' wheelbases respectively. The shorter version fitted with a platform body could easily achieve an unladen weight of 6 tons and thus be subject to the lower annual tax of £90. This model was fitted with a trailing (non-driven) second rear axle, the rear bogie configuration having no resemblance to the earlier 6x4 War Office subsidy Models 31 and 32. Whereas these earlier models had been designed for unmade roads, this chassis was based on the recently introduced 6 ton 4x2 and was intended for general haulage work only, although heavy triangular stiffening plates between the rear axles and additional cross bracing might have suggested otherwise. Powered from an uprated version of the 6 cylinder petrol EN80, the 7.8 litre EN85

had a ¼" larger bore and produced an additional 10 bhp. This engine followed recent practice with an overhead valve or 'raised camshaft' design, and the timing gear utilised a Renolds triplex chain, with automatic tensioner, driving the camshaft via an intermediate gear and also driving the fan, magneto and the dynamo and water pump shaft. The Gardner 5 or 6LW oil engine was also available as an option.

(Above) A Gardner engine was fitted to this sturdy looking bonneted R58 mobile water distilling plant with equipment by Weirs of Cathcart, Glasgow, and destined for use in Italy. It is seen conducting hill start tests in Gardner Street, Partick, about 2 miles from the Scotstoun factory, and a favourite location for these sort of tests over a long period.

(Below) A 5LW was fitted to this R59, a 1935 2000 gallon petrol tanker owned by C.T. Bowring of Birmingham. Unfortunately, none of the range of two and three axle heavy duty Albions with set-back front axles is believed to survive today.

Model 54/55. Exhibited at the November Motor Show of 1933, the bonneted Model 54 and overtype Model 55 had actually both been in production since May. They were maximum load two axle chassis limited to an 8¾ ton gross load (including body) within a 12 ton gross vehicle weight. In keeping with the traditional Albion approach of eliminating all but essential features, the chassis was straightforward, light but strong and capable of carrying a legal payload almost twice its unladen weight of just under 4 tons. Not requiring the output of the six cylinder overhead valve unit, both overtype and bonneted models used the new 4 cylinder petrol 35/80hp EN200, with the same 4"x5½" bore and stroke of the

1927 35/55hp EN51. Despite retaining a side valve layout, the EN200 produced a considerable increase in power output over the EN51 for the same 6 litre capacity, a clear indication of the pace of engine development over six years. Chassis price was £710. This Model 54 was bodied by Harvey Brothers of Strathaven in 1933 and is seen on a delivery run in Paisley for Charles Moore, bottlers, Glasgow. The driver had worked with Moores since before the First World War on horse drawn vehicles, which were not phased out by them until March 1948. Incidentally, the driver was the second last man off the beaches at Gallipoli and returned from the War to work with Moores until his retirement.

Model 540/550. The bonneted Model 540 and its equivalent overtype the Model 550 were developments of the Models 54 and 55 introduced in 1935, but with an increased payload of 6 tons. Of similar if not identical external appearance to the older models, they shared the same EN200 6 litre engine with a choice of diesel proprietary engines, but had new and presumably heavier duty axles front and rear. CRK 374, a 1937 MS550 with Duramin cab and body and Bromiloe and Edwards end tipping gear was operated by Surrey based Gilchrist Road Services Ltd. The M prefix referred to the weight range and was not in this case an abbreviation for 'Model', while 'S' indicated short wheelbase.

Model 547/557. The bonneted Model 547 and overtype Model 557 were improved maximum load 2 axle 6 to 7½ tonners, which started production in May and September 1935 respectively. Now incorporating triple-servo brakes, a new type of rear axle and a higher and narrower radiator which was said to give the vehicle a better appearance, it was capable of hauling a trailer giving it a gross train weight of 15 tons.

The Shell Company of South Africa took delivery of this P557 fuel tanker in 1936, which was one of nine Albions in the fleet. The prefix 'P' in this case denoted the weight range, and was not related to the similar prefix used on passenger vehicles. The decompression lever on the left hand side of the radiator indicates that the power unit is most likely a Gardner 5 or 6LW. This lever was provided to aid the starting of the engine when an electric starter was not fitted. To start the engine on the handle the driver would turn the decompression lever to the vertical position, which would prevent the exhaust valves from closing. This would enable the engine to turn much more easily, as no pressure was created on the compression stroke. When enough momentum was gained with the aid of the large flywheel, the decompression lever was turned to the closed position, whereupon the engine would usually start.

A Gardner engine was also fitted to this bonneted PS547, which was the type preferred by the Shell Company of Australia. It hauled a 2000 gallon tanker.

Model 549/559. The Models 549 and 559 of 1935 were six wheelers which replaced the 12 ton R/RL58 and 59 introduced two years previously. Now suitable for loads of 13 tons, they returned the front axle to a conventional forward position in the chassis, and the rear bogie was available with either a trailing third axle or as double drive. Four vacuum cylinder servo units provided what was then considered to be a high degree of braking efficiency, and an unusual feature was that the handbrake as well as the foot brake was servo assisted from a fifth servo unit. Unless handicapped with heavy bodywork, the unladen weight was less than 6 tons, putting it into the £90 taxation class at 1933 rates. The standard engine was the petrol EN80D 6.97 litre engine, but also offered was the 7.81 litre EN85 petrol unit. Diesel options were the Gardner 5 and 6LW motors, and in practice these were the more popular choices in this weight range.

A Gardner 6LW was fitted to this R559 supplied to the Bromsgrove Sand Company Ltd. of Worcestershire on 14th February 1936.

The second vehicle shown is an R549 10 ton three way hydraulic tipping wagon with large section tyres as supplied to Lanark County Council Highways Department in December 1936. Again a Gardner 6LW engine was fitted, and the offside exhaust manifold of this engine required that additional clearance was required for the steering column, which resulted in the protrusion on the side of the bonnet on all Gardner-engined examples.

Model 553. Designed to fill the gap between the maximum load 7½ ton 4 wheeled models and the 12-13 ton heavy duty 6 wheelers, the N553 catered for the payloads of 8-9 tons denoted by its 'N' prefix. The first of two 3 axle models which started production in the summer of 1936, only one wheelbase was available, but with a variety of engines. Offered either in 6x2 configuration with a trailing second rear axle or as a 6x4 with a double drive bogie, both drive set-ups were available with single or twin rear tyres. An open clutch was fitted, with the 4 speed gearbox mounted separately and driven by a duplex fabric joint at the gearbox end, both features being regular Albion practice on all but the lighter models. Powered by the 43/100hp EN80 or 49/110hp EN85 6 cylinder petrol engines, oil engines offered were the 6 cylinder 55/90hp EN76 or the Gardner 5LW, the latter conveniently fitting the engine bay without major modification. With a rear bogie design similar

to that first seen on the 1933 Model 59, local stiffening of the frame was achieved using deep bolted-on brackets and two cross tubes, the upper tube carried the spring trunnion brackets and the lower located the two torque arms, one for each axle. Braking was by vacuum assisted servo but the usual triple servo arrangement was uprated with an additional auxiliary servo mounted on the inner frame, which doubled the effect of the main servo unit to the rear. In standard trim with EN80, the chassis price was £995, with the 5LW Gardner costing an additional £200 and adding almost 2 cwts. The Gardner option was fitted to this fine example about to be delivered to George Picket, Haulage Contactor, Stourbridge in 1937.

Model 561. Models introduced during the early 1930s had ensured that any weight range gaps were well covered, and the 15 ton overtype Model 561 of 1936 now extended the payload capacity upwards as an 8x4 chassis based on the 12-13 ton R/RL559. The standard engine fitted was the 6 cylinder 49/110hp EN85D petrol, but the Gardner 6LW appears to have been a much more popular choice. With a 'T' prefix indicating its 15 ton capacity, the T561 had in common with other Albion chassis a generous body allowance without exceeding the unladen weight limit of 7 tons for this class of model. The bare chassis weighed 5 tons 6½ cwts, with the diesel option adding another 5 cwts. This provided an allowance of around 1½ tons for what would of necessity be a fairly substantial body. A four speed gearbox was standard with an optional fitment of an overdrive, having an indirect ratio 50% higher than fourth. Unlike the Model 559 with its optional trailing axle, only the fully driven rear bogie was available on this model which used overhead worm gearing. Braking followed the pattern introduced on the R/RL559 with four vacuum operated Dewandre servo cylinders for the main braking, with a fifth unit assisting the handbrake operation. On this four axle model, the foot brake operated on the four driving wheels and on the two wheels of the leading axle, with the handbrake operating on the driving wheels only. Young's Express Deliveries used this 15 ton dropside wagon on long distance haulage between Scotland and England. Production ceased in February 1938 with the arrival of the CX7 and none of the type have survived.

Model 563. Having developed the 8 wheeler, all the componentry was in place to construct a twin steer six wheeler or 'Chinese six', as they were known. The N563 could carry a similar 9 ton payload as the conventional six wheeler, but without the additional cost of two extra wheels and tyres and their maintenance, and without the penalty of tyre scrub associated with orthodox 6x4s. The chassis shown is believed to be the only one of its type built and is seen at Scotstoun in December 1937. It was superseded by the CX27 which started production in 1938.

Military and off road vehicles.

Model 131/133. The WD131 was a 6x4 chassis for the War Department which appeared in November 1933 and had a production run of 3½ years. It had a fully articulated rear bogie and was fitted with an EN206 four cylinder engine of 5.02 litres capacity. The forward positioned front axle afforded protection to the radiator, but the design allowed for the fitment of an optional Gardner 5LW engine, for which a short bonnet extension was provided ahead of the dash panel. This gave the Gardner engined examples a more conventional appearance with the radiator in line with the front of the axle. In 1936 the slightly heavier Model 133 was supplied to the India Office with Gardner 6LW engine and chassis mounted winch. The WD133 had a longer bonnet and heavier tyres, 13.50x20 singles all round. Pictured in South Street is a WD131, supplied to the War Department in September 1936.

Model 136/137. The bonneted Model 136 and overtype Model 137 were 6x4 cross country vehicles chassis supplied to South African Railways between 1935 and 1938. One of a fleet of 26 in service in 1938, some had bus bodies, and others like this one had combined passenger and goods bodies. There were four compartments, the foremost for the driver and guard, followed by five first and eight second class passenger compartments, and the rearmost was for goods and luggage, five tons of which could be carried. Another 5 tons could be carried on a trailer. The EN85 six cylinder petrol engine was not fitted with a governor, thereby allowing extra revs in emergencies, but the driver was provided with a tachometer so that engine revolutions could be monitored. To cope with the dusty conditions, a particularly large oil filled air cleaner was used. The bodies were built in the company's own workshops and the complete vehicles measured 8 feet wide by 30 feet long. By 1946 these machines had clocked up around 220,000 miles, an impressive figure bearing in mind that most of this mileage was completed on unmade roads and tracks. Only four of the fleet had been withdrawn by that time, either having been destroyed by fire, or having sustained accident damage which was not economically repairable.

Model 463 (AM 463). Following trials of a number of manufacturers' chassis in November 1934, a contract was awarded by the Air Ministry for a substantial number of two axle chassis to fulfil a number of roles. Albion used a special version of the Model 463, which was given the prefix AM (Air Ministry) and deliveries to the RAF commenced from 1935 onwards. The radiator protector bar, generous ground clearance provided by large 9.00x20 tyres, and front mounted Grüss air springs to soften the ride while off road, all contributed to the very rugged appearance of the finished vehicle. Some were fitted with even larger 10.50x20 tyres for duties in particularly difficult terrain. Two engines were listed, the 4.42 litre EN213 or the 3.89 litre EN217, and these and all other running units differed from the standard Model 463. A variety of bodies was used, but the most common type was as an ambulance like the one illustrated here. Some were used as the basis as an articulated platform lorries and one is shown below. A large number were demobbed immediately after the war, and many were converted or rebodied for a variety of civilian uses by specialist contractors.

Albions featured in an advertisement for Gourock Ropeworks in 1936.

Chapter 4

The War Intervenes – New Truck Models
1938 to 1950

A new model range was introduced at the Commercial Motor Show at Earls Court in November 1937, using a new system of model designation, where the prefix type letters were based on the first and last letters of the alphabet, e.g. AZ, BY, CX, etc. For the heavy CX range, an entirely new design of overhead valve 4 and 6 cylinder direct injection oil engines was introduced, which were numbered EN233 and EN242 respectively. Designed from the outset as diesel engines, they were also used as the basis for two new petrol engines (EN236 and EN245) replacing petrol engines of similar size. Other features of the engines were an aluminium crankcase (later replaced with cast-iron), and twin cylinder heads on both the four and six cylinder units, one head for each bank of two or three cylinders. The oil and petrol engines were completely interchangeable, and for the first time in the Albion heavy range, the engines were unit mounted with the gearbox. The diesel's tendency to rough idling was dealt with by a complicated three point flexible mounting system, incorporating a rubber block mounted on a tubular cross member at the front, and two special bell-crank levers with coil springs at the rear. Compared with the system of bolting the engine direct to the chassis frame, the arrangement gave a very satisfactory vibration-free ride.

At the other end of the range was the light AZ series, which had been built in small numbers since 1936, but the onset of the Second World War upset the introduction of the latest production model, the AZ5 in 1940. However, the FT3, also introduced in 1940, and intended as a replacement for the popular 127 range, was produced in limited numbers for the civilian market during the war. These and a small number of bus chassis delivered up to 1942 were the only civilian vehicles manufactured, as for the next five years the capacity at the factory was taken up with military output. Indeed the Yoker Works were taken over for the production of .38 Service revolvers, and the new 'D' factory, east of Balmoral Street, became engaged in the manufacture of torpedo engines for the Admiralty. Chassis production was taken up mainly for the Ministry of Supply and a significant range of military vehicles was produced. viz. BY1, BY3, BY5, CX6, CX22, CX23, CX24, CX33, EV1, FT11 and FT15. The least successful of these was the 30 ton tank transporter WD.CX24, which the company complained was being used for purposes for which it had not been designed or tested. It was one of only three types supplied as tank transporters during the

---

South African Orders

As you were informed last year, I paid a visit to South Africa early in 1937 to study the operating conditions at first hand. I paid another visit at the end of the year, partly in connexion with our business arrangements there and partly to show those interested what we had designed and were putting into production to meet the special South African requirements. In June of last year we received a very substantial order from the South African Railways and Harbours; and apparently at the beginning of the previous month someone in the Cape Parliament had asked a question there about the satisfactoriness of vehicles supplied to the South African Railways and Harbours. As the answer was public, there can be no breach of confidence in giving the gist of the answer made by the Minister of Railways, as reported in the *Johannesburg Star*:—

One concessionaire had supplied 44 German chassis, of which 37 had developed major defects. Another firm had supplied 5 German chassis, of which 4 developed major defects. From one firm 45 British chassis were obtained, and of these 5 developed major defects and 11 minor defects. From another firm 46 British chassis were obtained, in none of which were there any major defects found, but 24 had minor defects. From still another firm two British chassis were obtained and both developed major defects. Of the 29 chassis obtained from Reunert and Lenz Ltd., none had major defects and two had minor defects.

Reunert and Lenz Ltd., are our concessionaires for the Union of South Africa, and the 29 chassis referred to are "Albion" chassis. I think you will agree we could have nothing finer as a testimonial. We hope to merit an equally good report with the chassis we are now exporting.

Extract from George Pate's Chairman's Report, April 1938, on the subject of the reliability of Albions.

war, the others being the American-made Diamond T, and the Scammell Pioneer. Unlike the Albion, both of these had proprietary engines.

The need to offer proprietary diesel engines in the 1930s had resulted in engine manufacturing capacity becoming significantly under-utilised, so it made sense to remove the options of proprietary engines now that in-house designs were available and fully developed. When civilian production started again after 1945, therefore, Albion engines became standard across the entire model range and no proprietary engines were offered in any model. In 1939

the stroke of the 4 cylinder EN233 had been increased to 6 inches to become the 6.6 litre EN234, and in 1947 the same procedure was adopted for the 6 cylinder EN242, which became the 9.9 litre EN243. This again put Albion at the top of the league as the producer of the largest oil engine in Britain. These big oil engines had gained a reputation for smoothness and reliable running, which was perhaps the basis for an enquiry from Guy Motors of Wolverhampton in October of 1946. Guy enquired if Albion was interested in supplying up to five hundred EN242/243 engines from 1947 for installation in Guy trucks and buses. The board

War Department Second World War Trucks.

BY1. The BY1 light 6 wheeler was a 6x4 3 tonner, the first of which was tested at Farnborough in November 1936. Although a further 20 had been built by April 1937, quantity production does not appear to have started until February 1938. The BY1 had a 4 cylinder EN215 engine of 3.89 litres capacity, basically the same engine which was used in the Model 127, which, although said to have good torque characteristics, was underpowered in this application. Power from the petrol engine was taken through a four speed gearbox and two speed auxiliary box to a fully articulated double drive bogie. Vacuum servo assisted brakes acted upon all six wheels, which were shod with 9.00x20 tyres. Seen at Scotstoun when new is one of a batch of BY1N petrol tankers for the Air Ministry. It was a BY1 which played a leading role in the 1940's Ealing Studios film 'The Foreman Went to France.'

BY3/BY5. In June 1940 the BY1 was replaced by the very similar BY3, which now had a 6 cylinder engine, the 4.25 litre EN278, and gearbox modifications. The EN278 engine was basically the same engine introduced in the FT3 in 1940, except that the aluminium head was replaced with one made from cast iron. After 2 years of production the BY3 was superseded by the BY5, another very similar machine but powered by a slightly larger 4.6 litre six cylinder EN280 petrol engine. Externally the BY5 could usually be identified by a new radiator incorporating a pressed copper top tank in place of the more distinctive cast aluminium unit, this being easier to repair in the field, but the changeover may not have co-incided exactly with the change of model. The vehicle shown is a model BY3N, which was 25 years old when photographed in 1966 in the service of the Kenyan Ministry of Health, Division of Insect-Borne Diseases, having started life in 1941 with the British Army as a Bacteriological Laboratory. Production of the BY models finished in May 1945 and only one example is known to survive.

opined that while this would need to be considered as a matter of policy, an objection to such a transaction would be unlikely. Albion's ultimate response to Guy is not known, but severe shortages of iron castings were already affecting Albion's own production at Scotstoun, while the engine shop would have required expansion to meet such requirements, when there might be no guarantee of continued business. Guy subsequently bought locally made Meadows engines to supplement the standard Gardner supplies.

Model names were introduced on lorries at the beginning of 1948, when two new models were announced, the FT35 'Clansman' and the FT37 'Chieftain'. These new trucks, particularly the latter, were to become perhaps the most important in the company's history, spawning a whole range of lightweight buses and commercials, which were to become the basis of the company's success in the 1950s and 1960s. At the heart of the success of the FT37 was the four cylinder EN286 engine, an entirely new direct-injection, overhead valve oil engine, which had been under intensive development since 1938. A specially patented feature which was unusual in oil engines was the method of providing vacuum for the brakes. An automatic bypass valve fitted alongside the throttle valve was designed to shut with the operation of the throttle, but to open automatically when the engine dropped to idling speed. This allowed vacuum to build up in the reserve tank on the overrun. This device, which was similar to one used by Crossley, obviated the need for an exhauster and helped keep the unladen weight of the complete vehicle below 3 tons thus allowing 30 mph operation. Four point flexibly mounted with the engine was a new five speed gearbox which was specially designed to make the best use of the new engine's torque characteristics. This combination of engine and gearbox resulted in a truck which set new levels of fuel economy, reliability and longevity, and helped the company compete with the cheaper petrol engined offerings from Bedford, Ford and Commer.

A full range of petrol engines continued to be offered during this period, although demand in the heavier weight ranges was increasingly restricted to export models. In 1947 a decision was made to discontinue the AZ models without replacement because of competition from mass producers, and because of concern that the range of models was too extensive. The lack of an export market and the non-availability of an oil engine for this model may also have been factors. It took two or three years for AZs to run out, but the range which was left was still one of the most extensive offered by a British manufacturer, and all with a very high percentage of in-house content.

In contrast to the situation which developed after the 1914-1918 war, large numbers of ex-service vehicles were not available to a home market desperate to replace worn out vehicles, and at the same time the Government was placing great emphasis on exports. Taking the Government's exhortations on board, the directors chose to concentrate on the export market as this was also a method of ensuring better supplies of raw materials. Overseas managers recalled from Australia, New Zealand, India and South Africa reported on the performance of Albion products in these territories and what was needed to satisfy future requirements. The British Construction and Use Regulations had produced a product for the home market where minimum engine size and lightweight construction was the order of the day, but this produced a chassis which was not suited to the rugged conditions overseas. On the basis of the continuing feedback from overseas, a suitable range was developed for these markets, and by the end of March 1950 the sales figures for the first three months of the year indicated that export sales now accounted for more than 50% of production. Although increased export sales meant increased allocations of steel and iron supplies, all of which were in very short supply, the downside of this was less profits as export chassis were sold at lower prices. ❏

WD.EV1. The WD.EV1N model was a 3 ton overtype 4 wheel drive model, the first 4x4 produced at Scotstoun, which despite its low payload utilised engine and transmission parts from the heavy duty CX range. The 6 litre EN236 four cylinder petrol engine from the CX1 was fitted, which drove through a four speed constant mesh gearbox to an auxiliary gearbox, and thence to the front and rear driving axles. The vehicle shown was built in 1938 with a Strachans of Acton general service body, and is believed to have been the only one made. It carries a Middlesex registration number, which was part of a block reserved for use of government departments. Development and testing continued until the end of 1939, but the model was then superseded by a new design, the FT11.

WD.FT11. A development of the WD.EV1N, the WD.FT11N was a 3 ton 4x4 truck for the British Army which started production in May 1942 with either a machinery or general service type body, and with a coachbuilt cab, the top half of which was removable. Overhead worm axles were fitted front and rear with hydraulic shock absorbers on each wheel, and a pressed copper radiator similar to the BY5 was specified. The 6 cylinder EN280 petrol engine of 4.57 litres was installed, driving through a four speed gearbox and two speed relay gearbox, high ratio being intended for road work and low for cross country. To stop wind up between the front and rear axles a third differential was provided which could be locked when the going got tough. Several hundred were supplied before production ceased in August 1944.

WD.CX6. Based on the CX5 overtype civilian model, the bonneted WD.CX6 was a 10 ton 6x4 general service truck, of which less than 200 were supplied to the British Army between June 1940 and June 1941. It differed primarily from the CX5 in that servo assisted hydraulic brakes were fitted rather than vacuum brakes, although the rest of the specification was very similar to the standard CX range. The CX6 was basically a civilian design with conventionally sprung rear bogie, but the model was never offered on the home or export markets.

WD.CX24. The 20 ton tank transporter, the WD.CX24S, commenced production in March 1942, and was designed to haul a tandem axle semi-trailer. The complete vehicle weighed 15½ tons, measured just under 44 feet long by 9 feet 5 inches wide at its maximum, and carried a Scammell 8 ton vertical winch with a cable length of 430 feet. The trailer with Albion 4 wheeled bogie was constructed at Albion's Yoker Works, and was connected to the tractor unit by a ball and socket coupling, where 8 bolts secured the two halfs of the ball pin. The trailer was thus uncoupled by removing these bolts, having first disconnected the wiring, air pipes and winch. The CX24 was powered by Albion's biggest engine yet, an EN248 engine of 10.5 litres capacity, being petrol driven like the tanks which it was designed to carry. It drove through a unit mounted four speed constant mesh gearbox to a 2 speed reduction type auxiliary gearbox mounted amidships, and thence to fully articulated twin overhead worm axles. Twin 50 gallon fuel tanks, one on each side of the chassis, were fitted. The CX24 was, however, the least successful of the wartime military range, as engine and other problems

quickly developed. Overspeeding of the engine caused failures, perhaps aided and abetted by inadequate brakes. These were air pressure servo assisted, the Clayton Dewandre air compressor being chain driven from the main gearbox, and the front axle was unbraked. The company wrote twice to the authorities complaining of the use that the vehicle was being put to. Firstly, Albion complained that engines were being run at speeds for which they had not been tested, and that Army alterations to scraper rings could have grave consequences. Secondly, it was pointed out to the Chief of the Imperial General Staff that other modifications did not make the vehicles suitable for cross country work. Mark II and mk. III versions later appeared with several modifications, including fitting rev counters with the maximum permitted revolutions clearly marked with a red line, but really the problems were never entirely resolved and the truck was eventually downgraded to carry cargo such as plant and earthmoving equipment for the tank regiments. Later models could be identified by the offset position of the radiator cap, earlier models having these centrally mounted.

WD.CX22. Based on the civilian model CX22 which went into production 5 years earlier, the WD.CX22S commenced production in 1943, although at least one prototype was sent to Farnborough for testing in March 1941. It is often confused with the similar CX24, but was designed as a heavy gun tractor and was never used as an articulated unit. Being longer than the CX24 and also wider, it had a particularly massive frontal appearance, and certainly gave the appearance of a formidable machine. It hauled a gun weighing 14 tons, the total moving weight of the laden outfit being 29 tons 4 cwt. Originally to have a petrol engine, the order was changed to an oil engine in June 1943, the engine being the EN244 unit of 9.1 litres and by this time manufactured with a cast-iron crankcase in place of one made from aluminium. Other differences from the CX24

were the provision of heavier tyre equipment with single rears. This model also had a Scammell 8 ton power winch operated by a shaft from the PTO on the gearbox mounted behind the cab. As on the CX24, a Clayton Dewandre air compressor, chain driven from the main gearbox, provided air pressure for the brakes on the two rear axles, the front axle being unbraked. The prototype had a cast aluminium radiator, but production examples had the more usual military copper top tank type, but much shorter than that used on the CX24. Production finished in May 1945, and they lasted much longer than their tank transporter cousins. Most appear to have acquired 'G' registrations in 'civvy street', suggesting a demob date of around 1968/69, although some were retained longer.

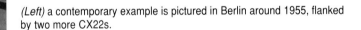

(Above) Followed by a Bedford QL and a Dennis Max, a preserved WD.CX22S heads a parade through St Helier celebrating the 50th anniversary of the liberation of Jersey in May 1995. The truck had done less than 10,000 miles when acquired by Albion Club member Colin Bent in 1970, and is now on permanent display at the Imperial War Museum, Duxford.

(Left) a contemporary example is pictured in Berlin around 1955, flanked by two more CX22s.

WD.CX23. The WD.CX23 was a 6x4 general service truck, basically the overtype version of the CX24 tank transporter model, and was designed for payloads of 10 tons. Introduced in 1941, a year before the CX24, it had vacuum assisted hydraulic brakes rather than full air brakes, and an EN244 oil engine rather than the larger petrol unit, this being preferred for an artillery vehicle. The EN244 was basically the same as the EN242 bus engine except that it had no belt driven auxiliaries. The model was later developed for South African Railways, and a fuller technical description is given on page 77. Several hundred were made during the war years.

WD.CX33. The twin engined WD.CX33 was the most powerful vehicle built by Albion Motors, and two prototypes were manufactured, one in 1943, the other the following year. They were designed for use as tank transporters, towing a 3 axle low loading trailer, and had the capability of recovering disabled tanks from the field. The first prototype had all 8 wheels driven as originally built, but appears to have been converted to an 8x6 at some later stage. On this machine the first two axles were steerable, while on the second prototype axles numbers 1 and 4 were steerable. Both prototypes had two EN248 six cylinder 10.5 litre petrol engines mounted side by side, and situated behind the driver's cab. There were two starting handles provided which are visible on the front panel. Both engines had their own clutch and gearbox, one power train driving axles one and four and the other driving the intermediate axles. The

driver's cab differed in external appearance on each prototype, but both machines had a three piece windscreen and the driver sat in a central position behind the middle section. There was also a rear cab which was provided for control of a power winch. At the end of the war one found its way into the service of the Bristol Aeroplane Co. Ltd., where in 1947 it was used to tow the Bristol Brabazon from the flight shed to assembly shed for final finishing work. In May 1952 the second prototype was in use towing a trailer loaded with concrete blocks with a combined load of up to 115 tons on a bridge testing exercise for the Ministry of Transport. At that time it was reported that the vehicle retained 8 wheel drive and that the first and last axles were steerable. At 20.92 litres of combined engine capacity, the Albion CX33 must surely have been the largest engined road truck ever built in Britain.

WD.FT15. The WD.FT15N was a 6x6 development of both the FT11N and BY5 intended for use as a low silhouette gun tractor. It had a semi-forward control layout to reduce height to a maximum of 7 feet 6 inches, which was said to facilitate shipment overseas. Assembly began in April 1945 with the 4.57 litre petrol engine, by then designated EN281. As with the earlier model, a similar two speed relay gearbox was fitted with

lockable third differential, but this time with the provision of a power take-off for a Turner 8 ton winch. The brakes were vacuum assisted hydraulic, and Luvax shock absorbers were fitted on the front axle only, the articulated suspension of the double drive bogie making such provision at the rear unnecessary. To provide waterproofing to a level of 5 feet 6 inches, the induction pipes, crankcase breather, and all ventilation pipes were taken to a point above this level. Approximately 150 had been supplied before the contract for 500 was cancelled in January 1946.

The AZ range.

AZ1/AZ3/AZ7. The AZ series started production in 1937 (the first prototype appearing a year earlier) as an intended replacement for models 118 and 125, the lightest of the Albion range, but were not listed before the war. The first model was the four cylinder AZ1 for loads of 30 cwt and then the 6 cylinder AZ3 for up to three tons, but only a few were built before hostilities forced the withdrawal of the model. Production resumed in 1945 with the 4 cylinder AZ5 and 6 cylinder AZ7, with similar payloads to the prewar models, but again not many of the latter were made before the model was replaced by the 4 cylinder AZ9 later in 1946. The AZ models differed from the rest of the Albion range in that they had an Albion spiral bevel rear axle, the only model in the Albion range to be so fitted, and being the lightest in the range had only 6 stud wheel fixings front and rear. New in 1946 to Galbraith's stores was this 6 cylinder AZ7N bread van, with a body designed to carry 140

dozen loaves on 70 bread boards. Galbraith's ran a large fleet of Albions in all weight ranges delivering foodstuff to their numerous stores throughout Central Scotland from their base in Paisley. The small headlamps are typical of the type fitted to many new deliveries during the later war years and for some time afterwards.

AZ5/AZ9. By the end of 1946 the range had been rationalised to only two models, the AZ5 and AZ9, two virtually identical models for loads of 45 cwt and 58 cwt respectively. It appears that only tyre equipment and perhaps springs differentiated the two models. Being somewhat similar to the prewar models which they replaced, the AZ5 and AZ9 still retained design features like a centre accelerator right up until production ceased in 1949. Early models had the 2.84 litre Albion EN271 petrol engine, whereas later models like this one had the larger 3.04 litre EN272 unit, and braking was by means of Lockheed hydraulic brakes, which were not servo assisted. The postwar AZ series could normally be identified by the front bumper which joined the two front wings. A typical delivery to Kilsyth Co-op was BWG 361, an AZ9N supplied in the summer of 1948. Albion had an almost complete monopoly of the Co-op mobile shop van market in Scotland from the mid-1930s to the mid-1950s, its only rival being Karrier. Many of these Co-op vans had long lives and survived into the 1970s.

AZ2/AZ8. There were two bonneted AZ models, the AZ2 and the AZ8, and only one of each was made. Seen here at Scotstoun in June 1937 is the AZ2 chassis, a right hand drive model possibly intended as the basis for a light fire engine. The AZ2 was the bonneted version of the AZ1, both of which were fitted with the earlier EN270 four cylinder petrol engine. In April 1947 a decision was taken to discontinue the AZ range in an attempt to rationalise the company's output. Production took a year or so to run out, before Albion left this payload sector, returning only briefly with the Cairn of 1955.

The FT range.

FT3. Introduced in 1939 to replace the popular model 127 range, the FT3 was a 5 to 6½ tonner fitted with a 6 cylinder side valve petrol engine, 4 speed gearbox, overhead worm rear axle and vacuum servo assisted hydraulic brakes. It continued to be available in small numbers to essential civilian users during the war, and remained in production until 1953/54, making it Albion's longest lived model. In the late 1940s the standard frontal appearance of all FT series lorries and buses, petrol or oil, looked the same, but the FT3 could be readily identified by the absence of a sump immediately behind the number plate. All FT3 lorries had a 6 cylinder 4.26 litre petrol engine designated EN277 with a sump positioned to the rear of the front axle.

(Above) FUS 916 was a postwar FT3L with a demountable livestock container, one of three delivered to British Railways, Scottish Region, in 1948. The container was built by Penman of Dumfries and had a capacity of 150 sheep, 55 pigs or 12 cattle. Before nationalisation, Albions were popular with the various railway companies, but after the formation of British Railways very few indeed were ordered.

(Below) Always popular as brewer's delivery lorries, two FT3s are seen waiting to leave Blair and Co.'s Alloa Brewery.

FT3A. Around 1948 a number of improvements to the FT3 model resulted in the introduction of the FT3A range, which included engine modifications, and the adoption of axles from the newly introduced Chieftain range. G. & C. Moore of Bridgeton, Glasgow, undertook to modernise the look of their new FT3AL by fitting a thoroughly up-to-date cab which concealed the Albion front dash and radiator. The bodybuilder of HGD 948 is unknown, but they produced a pleasing and functional layout with curved windscreen, twin wipers, nearside mirror, access step in rear of wing, and stirrups at both ends of the platform. The tailboard carried a large advertisement for Guinness, which was bottled locally by Moores. It was new in 1950.

FT3A6W. An additional model for the FT3 range was the FT3A6W lightweight six wheeler, effectively a successor of the Model 129 of 1936, and primarily intended for overseas markets where axle loadings were critical. Some examples did enter service in Britain, and John Biesty, a Manchester contractor and coal merchant, took delivery of this tipper in 1950. Powered by the Albion EN277 4.25 litre 6 cylinder petrol engine through a 4 speed gearbox, both rear axles were driven, and the handbrake was also applied on both rear axles.

FT5/FT21. The FT21 was a 3 tonner, one of two new models announced in 1949. Originally introduced in 1947 as the FT5 to bridge the gap between the AZ9 and the FT3, the adoption of front and rear axles from the new Chieftain range resulted in the change of model number to FT21 two years later. The FT5 / FT21 models were based on the FT3, but with a four cylinder 2.8 litre EN271 petrol engine, being exactly two thirds of the six cylinder unit in the FT3. Lighter tyre equipment was also specified, and a short wheelbase model was also available. Being the only models in the three ton category, they were kept in production after the Leyland takeover. They did not get the facelifted front with recessed headlamps and flared dash which the oil engined variants in the FT range acquired in 1949/50, and the general appearance remained very similar to the Model 127 of the mid 1930s. By June 1953 difficulty was being experienced finding customers for petrol engined FTs, which resulted in a price reduction of £200 per chassis. In a fleet run by Milanda Bread, this particular FT21, dating from 1952, was one of a batch re-engined with Ford 4D diesel engines in 1957. The conversion was carried out by Millburn Motors of Glasgow. This photograph was taken when the van was new and the type of sump fitted identifies the original Albion 4 cylinder petrol engine.

FT7/FT23. The other new model was the FT23 four tonner, similar to the FT21 except for heavier springing and tyre equipment. Sheffield Corporation Lighting Department specified the FT23 chassis for this new tower wagon which was new in July 1951. The FT23 was introduced in 1949 to replace the FT7, the adoption of Chieftain axles in the FT23 being the main difference between the old and new models.

(Bottom) **FT35.** Model names for commercial chassis were introduced for the first time in 1948 for the new Clansman and Chieftain and this is a pre-delivery shot of a 'Clansman' FT35L biscuit van new in 1949 for the United Co-operative Baking Society, Glasgow. The Clansman was a lighter version of the Chieftain and could carry a payload of 5 tons, compared with the 6¼ tons of the Chieftain. The same 4.88 litre EN286 oil engine was fitted, which could be identified by the front mounted sump with row of studs along the bottom, but the fitment of a starting handle was unusual on this engine, and was generally discontinued after 1949. Slightly smaller tyre equipment (34x7in as against the Chieftain's 35x7.5in) was the only way of identifying the chassis externally.

To carry the new model names a design for a radiator badge incorporating a Saltire and thistle was submitted by Mr J.B. Creighton, at that time a fitter, for which he was paid £25.

FT37. The 'Chieftain' FT37 6¼ tonner was the model which established Albion's market position in the light to medium sector and enabled the company to compete with cheaper petrol engined offerings from Bedford, Ford, and Commer. It was designed to weigh in at under 3 tons unladen, which allowed 30 mph operation, and was one of the few chassis to be offered in this sector with an in-house diesel engine. The success of the model was due, firstly, to the economy and durability of the new 4.88 litre EN286 oil engine, which, including derivatives, was to remain in production for nearly twenty years, and, secondly, the new 5 speed gearbox designed to make best use of the new engine's torque characteristics. First gear was a crawler gear for steep gradients, and fifth was direct top, which enabled a high ratio rear axle to be fitted. Early models had an upright dash and exposed headlamps as on this example delivered to D. & J. Sibbald in 1949.

It's not an easy job selecting a suitable name for a new model lorry or bus, but the work thus entailed is well worth the trouble because a good name is definitely a publicity asset. In the case of the two new Albions launched this week, the company posted notices in the works asking for suggestions. The response was overwhelming, over 600 names were submitted from about 300 employees. The names supplied by the largest number of entrants were: *"Chieftain"* (28), and *"Clansman"* (25) and these have been chosen for the two new models. The management have also decided on *"Claymore"*, *"Clydesdale"*, and *"Challenge"* for future models, and the S.M.M.T. has been asked to register all 5 as Albion model names.

Another early Chieftain was this FT37L supplied to preserve manufacturer Powells Products Ltd. of Low Fell, Gateshead, on 23rd June 1950 by local Albion agent F.W. Cawthorn. Excellent fuel consumptions of more than 20 mpg were said to be achieved, but the weight of the van body brought the unladen weight of the complete vehicle up to 3 tons 4 cwt, which meant that it was restricted to a top speed of 20 mph, although it was capable of almost twice that speed. Vacuum assistance for the brakes was provided by the patented Albion vacuum generation valve fitted on the EN286 engine. This worked well enough on the open road, but on this van it failed to generate enough vacuum while manoeuvring in confined spaces on tickover. This resulted in heavy pedal effort being required which was more inconvenient than dangerous. OBB 767 was sold for £75 in October 1964 to H.J. Martin, a Newcastle Haulage Contractor, who fitted a platform in place of the van body and used it for another three years. At least 95 FT37s are believed to survive today, testifying to the popularity and durability of the model.

Newspaper article January 1948. At that time only buses had model names, all beginning with 'V' – Victor, Viking, Valiant, Valkyrie, Venturer, and Valorous, and obviously the company must have stipulated that model names for commercials had to begin with 'C'. With the exception of 'Challenge', all the names mentioned here were eventually used, and the 'C' rule was not broken until 1956 when the Reiver name was introduced for 6 wheelers. Later two more 'Cs' appeared for 8 wheelers, Caledonian and Cameronian. No petrol engined FT lorries ever received model names, and no CX or HD series commercials received names either.

FT38. The bonneted Chieftain was the FT38, which was listed only as an export model. Almost all of Albion's competitors in the lower weight ranges, Bedford, Ford, Commer, Austin and Morris either offered or standardised on bonneted types, and Leyland's Comet also came in normal control form. It was strange, therefore, that Albion dropped the bonneted models for the home market after the war. Despite this policy some did appear on the home market to special order. Pickfords operated a furniture van, a contractor ran a tipper, and a West Lothian haulier had a platform lorry, all of these being bonneted FTs. Berger Paints operated this FT38 in New Zealand, and the 'oil engine' plate on the bottom of the radiator dates it as 1950 or earlier.

In this line-up of FT models five FT35 'Clansman' oil engined pantechnicons with new curved dash and recessed headlamps are seen nearest to the camera outside Slumberland's Birmingham factory in 1951. Further away from the camera are a number of petrol engined Albions, most likely FT3Xs or AXs, which were the nearest petrol engined equivalent of the FT35. The vans with the small headlamps are older model FT3s dating from the mid-1940s. In 1951 a new version of the Chieftain for pantechnicon work was introduced, the FT39ALF. This was basically a special long wheelbase version of the FT37 but with some of the refinements of the 'Victor' FT39 bus chassis. A wheelbase of 17 feet gave a body length of 22 feet which was ideal for loads of a light but bulky nature. Slumberland took some examples of the FT39ALF which were similar in appearance to the Clansmans shown.

FT101. The FT range was expanded for heavier payloads in 1949 when the appropriately named Clydesdale was introduced as a tractor unit only. It had heavy duty axles from the CX range which could be identified by the 10 stud wheel fixings, and the first model to be introduced was designated FT101S. However, the rest of the specification was similar to that of the Chieftain and Clansman with the use of the EN286 engine and 5 speed gearbox. This is a very early Australian example, one of the few which were built with the pre-1950 vertical dash and exposed headlamps. It was capable of hauling a respectable load of 13.5 tons.

FT102. The bonneted Clydesdale was the FT102 and this is an FT102S tractor unit with 1500 gallon trailer operated by Caltex Oil (Africa) Ltd. seen here in 1954. As with the overtype Clydesdale, the 4 cylinder EN286 oil engine drove through a five speed gearbox to heavy duty axles front and rear. Although a bonneted Clydesdale was shown at the Earls Court show in 1956, the model was not listed after September 1952, and the tractor unit shown may have been among the last production models built.

FT103. Above: Introduced in 1949 about a year after the equivalent petrol engine model, the FT3A6W, was the 'Clansman' FT103N 7½ tonner with the same EN286 engine and 5 speed gearbox as the Chieftain FT37. Designed primarily for overseas conditions where axle loadings were critical, it had a short production run of only two years. This example with livestock body was supplied to an Australian operator in 1950. In many ways the 'Clansman' FT103 lightweight six wheeler was the forerunner of the hugely successful Reiver, which was still in production some thirty years later.

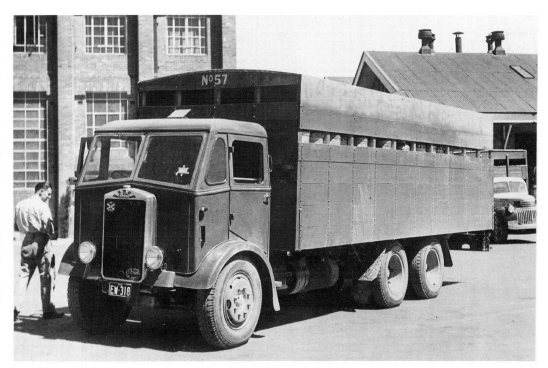

On 16th June 1979 this REME 'Clansman' FT103N, still in the ownership of the British Army despite its 29 years, made an appearance at the Albion Motors 80th Anniversary celebrations. Larger tyres with single rears were the main differences between the civilian and military model. It was one of 60 supplied to the armed forces around 1950 for use as mobile workshops in the Motor Transport Section. Ian Maclean, Registrar of the Albion Club and the Albion Vehicle Preservation Trust, is in the driving seat taking chassis number and other details from the 'Caution' plate to be included in the Register of Preserved and other Surviving Albions.

This photograph illustrates the changes in the appearance of the FT oil engined range between 1950 and 1951. The Manger's 'Chieftain' FT37 on the left has the upright dash and exposed headlamps of earlier models, while the 'Clydesdale' FT101 on the right has the new curved dash and recessed headlamps which were introduced in 1949 on the Victor bus and a year later on commercials. The Chieftain has lost its 'Albion Chieftain' badge – usually known as the 'Saltire' badge – from the offside top of the radiator grill, but retains the 'Albion Oil Engine' plate on the lower nearside. The Clydesdale, however, still has its 'Saltire' badge, but the lack of an 'Oil Engine' plate is probably correct as these appear to have been dropped by the end of 1950. Both vehicles were registered in London in 1950/51.

The CX range.

CX1. Although introduced at the Commercial Motor Show in November 1937, the 7½ ton CX1 had already been in production for several months. There was a choice of three engines, the EN233 oil and EN236 petrol engines of identical 6.0 litre capacity, and the Gardner 4LW oil engine. Unit mounted with the engine was a four speed constant mesh gearbox which transmitted the power to the usual overhead worm axle. For Albion's first unit mounted gearbox in a heavy duty chassis, special attention was paid to clutch ventilation, which was effected by a positively induced air circulation system. Anniesland Motor Transport of Anniesland, Glasgow, specified the 4LW for this CX1L platform lorry which was delivered in 1941, although it may have left the Scotstoun Works two miles away a year or so earlier. The obligatory wartime masked headlamp and white painted wings are evident in this view taken at the junction of Bearsden Road and Temple Road. The location is not much changed today except that Bearsden Road, which runs under the railway bridge, is now a busy main road and certainly not a location where you would now park a lorry to take a photograph.

CX2. The bonneted version of the CX1 was the CX2, which started production in 1938 for similar payloads of 7½ tons. After the war proprietary engines were not offered in the CX range (or any other range for that matter), and the 6.0 litre oil engine had been increased to 6.6 litres to become the EN234, being exactly 2/3 of the EN243 which was installed in the CX3 after 1948. Schweppes (Transvaal) Ltd. of Johannesburg took delivery of this CX2N in 1948 with EN234 four cylinder oil engine. It returned a fuel consumption of 13 to 14 miles per gallon despite a great many stops in a day's work. After the war the CX2 model, like other bonneted trucks in the CX and FT ranges, were listed as available only for overseas markets. The CX1 and CX2 models were discontinued in 1950 having been effectively replaced by the FT101.

CX3. The CX3, introduced in 1937 for payloads of 7¼ tons, shared the same frame as the CX1, but had reduced maximum load space behind the driver's cab because of the longer six cylinder engine. Ironically the smaller engined CX1 could carry an extra ¼ ton payload due to the lighter engine in an otherwise identical chassis, although the CX3 could tow a trailer.

(Right) Seen here when new in 1949 is a fine CX3L 6¾ ton dropside lorry fitted with the later EN243 9.9 litre engine, and supplied to British Road Services. Albion employed its own worm and segment steering on all CX models, the design of which utilised a steering drop arm situated well forward on the chassis. The drop arm is visible here and a cut out was provided in the panel below the offside headlamp to allow for forward movement of the arm when right hand lock was applied.

(Below) Albion's large oil and petrol engines were powerful and unstressed, and capable of completing high mileages on long distance trunking operations. In this view, the arrival in Pretoria, South Africa, after a five day journey from Lusaka, Northern Rhodesia, appears to cause something of a stir as the driver of this late 1940's CX3TR 9.9 litre engined articulated pantechnicon gets directions for a removal drop. The journey via Bulawayo and Mumbwa foreshadowed a regular service by Van den Berg's Transport Ltd. over this long route, for which more Albion outfits with sleeper cabs and Fruehauf trailers were purchased.

CX4. The Shell Company of Australia operated this CX4 3000 gallon articulated tanker for transporting fuel oil from Adelaide to Perth, a journey of 1,720 miles. The cab was a locally sourced 'Adelaide' pressed steel product, but looked as though it was borrowed from another lighter truck. The full designation of this particular truck was CX4ST, and in keeping with the post 1937 chassis designations, even numbers meant bonneted and the equivalent overtype chassis was generally the odd number which preceded it – so this was a bonneted 4 wheeler Short wheelbase, Tipper from the CX range. A full range of Albion tractor units was still a few years away, and shortened tipper models were popular adaptations. The model number generally varied according to weight range, and was not always related to the number of wheels.

CX5. The 12 ton six wheel overtype in the CX range was the CX5, available as a 6x2 or a 6x4, like this example delivered to Mechans Ironworks. Mechans were situated almost directly across the road from the Albion works in South Street, Scotstoun, and supplied all the straight frames to Albion at the time this photograph was taken. Mechans would thus be purchasing some of their own steel when they took delivery of this CX5N platform lorry in 1949. The photograph was taken outside Haldane and Menteith Villas, Anniesland Road, Scotstoun, which was only about half a mile from the Albion factory. Albion's photographers used this location over a long period, and fifty years later the villas are largely unchanged, although new houses have been built where the trees once stood. Mechans ceased trading in 1969.

A 1947 CX5N with 345,000 miles 'on the clock' picks up a load from the SS *Robert Coryndon* at Butiaba, Lake Albert, Uganda, in 1953. The *Robert Coryndon* was built on the Clyde and shipped out to Africa in pieces not exceeding 10 tons, and delivered by road on Albions to Lake Albert where it was finally assembled. The CX5 was one of three similar machines with Brockhouse trailers operated by Kenya and Uganda Railways and Harbours, and operated a service between Masindi Port, Lake Kioga, and Butiaba, a distance of 75 miles on unmade roads. The cabs and dropside bodywork on the lorry and trailer were built in the company's own workshops.

CX7. Edinburgh Contractors Arnott McLeod ran a number of CX7s with dropside or tipper bodies. This sturdy 13 tonner CX7T was taken into the fleet in 1949 when it is seen delivering a load of bricks to a new housing site. Nearing the end of its production run at that time, this 8 wheeler was fitted with the latest EN243 oil engine of 9.9 litres capacity, which was by then the only power unit listed for home use. However, ten years previously when Arnott McLeod took delivery of one of the first CX7s with the then new EN242 of 9.1 litres, two other power units were available, the EN245 six cylinder petrol of similar capacity, or the Gardner 6LW oiler. Vacuum assisted brakes were employed on all axles except the leading axle, which was unbraked. Postwar models had vacuum assisted hydraulic brakes.

CX21/CX23. The CX21 8 tonner of 1938 and CX23 10 tonner introduced a year later were heavy duty six wheelers with fully articulated double drive bogies designed for overseas markets where much of the running would be over unmade roads. One of a fleet of SAR.CX23s owned by South African Railways completes the 800 mile journey from Cape Town with a load of machinery for a bottling plant at a new Pepsi Cola factory in Johannesburg in 1948. The 29 ton load was made up of 9 tons on the lorry and 20 tons on the trailer. The vehicle had just completed 40,000 miles when the photograph was taken, and was believed to be less than 2 years old. Like its bonneted equivalent, the WD.CX24 tank transporter, It was equipped with the 10.5 litre petrol engine, EN246 in this application, this being the largest commercial vehicle engine offered by a British manufacturer at the time. It had a separately mounted step down gearbox, fully articulated twin rear axles with low pressure tyres all round, 12.00x20in. at the front, and 14.00x20in. singles at the rear, all of which enabled it to negotiate rough and muddy conditions well beyond the capabilities of the normal 4 or 6 wheeler. An exceptionally large 'Visco' oil bath air cleaner was fitted to deal with dust thrown up on unmade roads and the extra large 'tropical' radiator was cooled by a six bladed fan closely cowled. To maximise ground clearance, the rear frame was splayed out at the rear to accommodate a 14in spare tyre. The bodywork was built by Wevell Bros. who were located next door to Albion's Johannesburg Depot.

CX27. For loads of 10 tons came the CX27 in 1938, the company's second twin steer model, with the two steering axles set well back to ensure that they carried a good proportion of the payload, and to enable the rear axle to stay within its 8 ton limit. It was said that the advantages of a twin steering six wheeler were excellent road holding, and the elimination of tyre scrub associated with conventional 6 wheelers. Vacuum assisted brakes were employed on all wheels, and the handbrake operated on axles numbers two and three. This is a 1939 example with Gardner 5LW engine, which carried 15 tons of newsprint for a Leeds newspaper, 10 tons on the lorry and 5 tons on the trailer.

CX29. The CX29 was a 6x4 model also introduced in 1938, very similar to the CX5, but with a shorter wheelbase, lighter springs and lighter tyres and designed for loads of 10 tons. It replaced the Model 553, and did not reappear after the war. The Royal Navy took delivery of this CX29 dropside truck in 1939.

The DW range.

DW1. The DW series of models appeared briefly in 1939/40 for payloads of between 2 and 5 tons. Although said to be an export only model, this early DW1S patrol van entered service for Glasgow Corporation Police Department in 1939. It was designed to accommodate 20 policemen, and a cell for one prisoner was provided at the front offside, just behind the driver. It had a 4 cylinder EN212 3.9 litre petrol engine, the same as fitted to the model 127, but with a transmission which gave it a top speed of 50 mph, a significant speed for its time.

DW3. Three model DW3L 15 cubic yard moving floor refuse wagons supplied to Port Elizabeth Municipality in South Africa in 1939. The DW3 was effectively a four cylinder FT3 series model for overseas markets, where there was less stress on lightweight construction and low speed limits. Production of the DW range ceased at the beginning of the war and was never restarted, being effectively replaced by the FT range.

Demobbed

Many WD.CX24s were demobbed soon after the war and quickly found work as prime movers or recovery trucks. Said to be the largest recovery vehicle on the road in South Africa in 1951, this CX24 was put on the road at Albion's Johannesburg Depot, with a 9.1 litre EN242 oil engine replacing the original petrol unit. Recovery tackle included a Morris 6 ton travelling lifting block and a power winch, and a large steel cage for ballast weights was provided at the front. Sufficient fuel was carried for a range of up to 300 miles, which, coincidentally, was the distance of the longest recovery in its first year of service. Most CX24s had the usual military copper top-tanked radiator, but some had the cast aluminium radiator like the one shown. There was another similar truck at Cape Town, and both of these were modelled on an original machine based at Albion's Yoker service works at Glasgow, which was sold in 1972, and still survives today. The truck shown was still very active at the Johannesburg Depot in the late 1960s, but its ultimate fate is unknown. The Johannesburg Depot became a Ford dealership.

1938 advertisement for CX7 8-wheeler.

Chapter 5

Missing the Bus – The Decline of the Passenger Vehicle Market, 1938 to 1950

Albion had been an important bus manufacturer throughout most of the 1930s, and when bus production resumed after the war, the company soon had a model in all sectors of the market. Indeed, the full range which was offered by 1947/48 (Victor, Valkyrie, Viking, Valiant and Venturer) was not exceeded by any other British manufacturer. All were specified with a very high content of Albion parts which included a choice of Albion petrol or diesel engines. This was despite 1947 bus production accounting for only 16.5% of the company's output, 9.9% for the home market and 6.6% for overseas. It was clear that supporting such a diverse range without a wider customer base could not continue to be viable.

In 1946 Chairman George Pate had left the company in acrimonious circumstances, which resulted in the appointment of Jackson Millar as Chairman, and Hugh W. Fulton, son of the co-founder, as Managing Director. At a board meeting in April 1947 a few months after Fulton's appointment, he addressed the problem of the company's extensive model range. Referring to the company's entire output, he declared that the range would have to be cut down, and that there should be no more sanctions of the dropped frame type of chassis. This, he said, would mean that the company would drop out of the passenger vehicle market in Britain with immediate effect.

However, this did not come to pass immediately as important orders for double deckers for Sydney, Cape Town, and Glasgow were coming through, and two new dropped frame models (the CX37 and the CX39) were just coming on stream. Despite these new models sales continued to decline, although how much of this was due to the effect of Fulton's cutting down strategy, or just market forces, is not known. In 1948, around 350 CX buses entered service, more than half with overseas customers, but in 1949 this had dropped to approximately 150, with less than half being exported. In March 1948 Glasgow Corporation Transport asked the company to tender for the supply of 145 double deckers for delivery in 1949/50, but the invitation was turned down in a decision which was said to disappoint GCT's General Manager, E.R.L. Fitzpayne. Fulton was a lorry man, and it was clear that the end was in sight for the dropped frame range.

Basically there were two reasons for the company dropping out of this market, and it is necessary to go back some years to understand the reasons for Albion's decline as a mainstream bus manufacturer. Firstly, Albion was late in entering the double deck market, with the first purpose built design appearing only in 1933. Other manufacturers like Leyland and AEC had a head start by introducing dropped frame double deck designs in the mid 1920s. Secondly, and more importantly, Albion concluded around the same time that the petrol engine would remain dominant, and were therefore slow to develop their own compression ignition engine. This was a most serious mistake, because by 1935 most of the larger Scottish operators had decided to standardise on diesel engines and Leyland was the main beneficiary. Their 8.6 litre engine, available from 1933 and developed from an earlier oil engine design, became very popular among the larger Scottish operators. By 1938 when Albion had its own suitable designs ready, Leyland had assumed a dominant position on Albion's home ground, which the Scotstoun company was never able to challenge again.

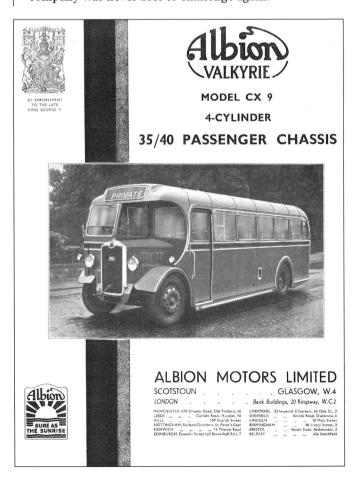

Albion's increasing vulnerability had been demonstrated by an item in George Pate's first Chairman's address at the 34th AGM of the company on April 28th, 1935. He noted the increasing demand for diesel buses, but pointed to the distinct unfairness, in his opinion, of the Chancellor's failure to reduce tax on petrol, thereby continuing an indirect subsidy on imported fuel oil. This was immediately challenged in a letter to the *Glasgow Herald* by W.J. Thomson, Chairman of SMT and associated bus companies, who denied that any such subsidy existed. He claimed that the fuel oil his companies used was not imported, but was entirely home produced from shale mined in the Lothians. The SMT group were enthusiastic users of diesel buses, and Pate's pleas fell upon deaf ears, as the market share of oil engined buses in Britain expanded by 36% in the next two years alone to the continuing detriment of petrol driven buses. On top of this SMT became Leyland concessionaires for Scotland after 1st July 1938, and it was not surprising that SMT

and its associated companies, which included W. Alexander & Sons, Western SMT and Central SMT, did not place any substantial orders from the independent Albion Motors again.

Design and testing work continued on an engine suitable for the double deck market and around May 1936 an experimental EN240 engine was fitted into US 1214, a 1933 Venturer M80, which was formerly an Albion demonstrator sold to W. Alexander the same year. The EN240 was almost certainly of the indirect injection type, and was said to have given satisfactory results despite having broken a crankshaft 6 months into the trial. As a result of these and earlier tests Albion decided that engines of the direct injection type were more suitable for passenger vehicle applications. In March 1938 the experimental engine was changed for a direct injection EN242, while a similar installation was fitted in a Venturer, probably an M80, of Young's Bus Service of Paisley. These early oil engines appeared to have run satisfactorily, but

The Valkyrie.

CX9. Introduced in 1937 was the CX9 with four cylinder petrol (EN236) or four cylinder oil (EN233) engine, both of identical swept volume of 6.05 litres, with the Gardner 4LW as an alternative. The CX9 was the smallest engined chassis in the Valkyrie range, but had potentially the largest seating capacity. As it shared the similar frame and wheelbase of the two other popular Valkyrie models with longer engines, the 5 cylinder CX11 and the 6 cylinder CX13, it consequently had up to an extra foot of passenger space behind the engine. This was enough to provide an extra row of 4 seats, making it potentially a 40 seater. Sometimes referred to as the CX35 in early technical reports, it was more often bodied as a bus than a coach, and the majority of chassis went abroad, mostly to India. A larger 4 cylinder oil engine was introduced in 1939, the EN234 of 6.6 litres capacity replacing the EN233. Spanning a longer production period than any other Albion passenger model, assembly ceased in 1950, by which time the stock of this model was proving very hard to dispose of at home. The last Valkyrie built for a British customer was KSM 566, a 1950 CX9 with Scottish Aviation fully fronted 35 seat coachwork, which was still being used by its original owner when pictured here in the Scottish border town of Moffat in October 1963.

did not return the same level of fuel economy as the Gardner engine. As full production of the CX range got under way, no more was heard of the experimental transplants and it is assumed that the two converted buses retained their more modern power units until the end of their days.

The war then intervened and apart from a handful of chassis delivered up to 1942, Albion was not allowed to build buses during the war years. Only Guy, Daimler, Bristol and Bedford were permitted to build new bus chassis during this period, with AEC and Leyland assembling unfrozen chassis from stock parts. This resulted in the loss of important customers like Young's, Scotland's largest independent operator, who in 1939 had a fleet of 114 vehicles, 85 of which were of Albion make. Gardner engined Guys and Daimlers were added to the fleet during and immediately after the war and no more Albion buses were ordered.

By the time the full CX bus range reappeared in 1947, it was too late to make an impact in the larger domestic fleets. The Venturer, for example, was probably a better product than some of its competitors which sold more strongly, but the double deck market in particular depended on selling a large number of chassis to a relatively small number of customers. With proprietary engines no longer available in Albions, conservative bus engineers did not want to introduce a new type of engine into their fleets. And to make matters worse, Albion's biggest customer for double deckers, Glasgow Corporation, was standardising on fluid transmissions, which Albion did not offer, while Red & White, its second biggest customer in the UK, was nationalised in 1950 and ceased to buy Albions.

The revamping of the CX bus range with even bigger engines and imposing looking frontal designs in 1948 had failed to stem the decline, and, apart from the mainly export straight frame Viking, no direct replacements were planned when the new HD range was introduced in 1950. In May 1951, shortly before the Leyland takeover, the newly introduced Viking HD61 was the only heavyweight bus chassis listed, alongside the lighter FT3AB and FT39 Victor bus chassis. No CX bus chassis were listed, and the last CX buses built were the 25 CX37SW eight feet wide double deckers for Glasgow Corporation, the chassis of which were delivered to the Corporation's Knightswood Garage later that year.

It had taken four years for Hugh Fulton's 1947 edict to be implemented, and the dropped frame models had been allowed to run out along with the rest of the CX range, rather than face immediate close down as had been originally proposed. From then on it was intended that the bus range would consist only of straight frame versions of commercial chassis.

Contrary to popular belief, therefore, it was not new owners Leyland who axed the heavy bus range, but with commercial vehicle sales buoyant and bus sales declining, the company took the decision to withdraw the range themselves some time before Leyland became involved. The independent Albion management, led by new men at the top, took the view that the range had to be cut down, and the slow selling, more complicated dropped frame models were the obvious choice. The directors appeared to have accepted that the market for the front engined half cab single decker was in terminal decline, and that the market for double deckers was effectively lost to competitors. ❏

CX9 (pantechnicon). Some bus chassis received van bodies because their gearing or low frame made them especially suitable for these duties. This CX9 Valkyrie 5½ ton Brockhouse-bodied pantechnicon van was supplied to the Royal Navy's Service Depot at Coventry in 1939, and was used for the transport of complete aeroplane wings during the war.

CX11. The CX11 had the distinction of being the only chassis in the CX range which was not offered with an Albion engine, the specified engine being the Gardner 5LW. At £1090, this made it £190 more expensive than the larger Albion engined CX13, and £265 dearer than the CX9. Since only Albion engines were offered after the war, the CX11 was not made after 1939. A design for a 6 wheeled version, the CX15, was well advanced in 1938, this being one of two new models to replace the model 145, but the outbreak of war ensured it never got to production. ASA 303 was a 1939 CX11 with a 32 seat Duple coach body for Strachan's Deeside Omnibus Service of Ballater. The CX11 is an extinct model, as there are no known survivors.

CX13. The CX13 was the flagship of the range with a choice of three six cylinder engines, the EN245 petrol or EN242 oil engines of similar 9.1 litres capacity, or the Gardner 6LW. Production of Valkyries ceased during the war, and after the war only Albion engines were offered. A six wheeled version, the CX17, was designed but never reached the production stage. Like the CX9 and CX11, the CX13 could have an optional overdrive gearbox, which would increase the top speed by 50%.

The first CX Valkyrie built was this CX13 with Gardner 6LW engine and Duple 32 seat coachwork. It is seen here in the condition in which it appeared at the 1937 Earls Court motor show before entering service with Red & White of Chepstow. The Red & White group of companies included Watts (Factors) Ltd. who were Albion concessionaires, and ensured the group's allegiance to Albion products until Red & White's purchase by the British Transport Commission in 1950.

Pictured at Lochranza on the Isle of Arran almost thirty years later is CHH 740, another Duple-bodied CX13, but with an Albion oil engine. The date was 12th June 1966, and the coach was in the ownership of Lennox of Whiting Bay, having been new to Blair and Palmer of Carlisle in 1948. It was sold to a contractor at the end of the summer season.

CX14/CX20. In the post 1937 model numbering system even numbers were bonnet types and the equivalent overtype chassis was generally the odd number which preceded it. Thus it is reasonable to assume that this CX14 fire engine delivered to Glasgow Corporation Fire Brigade in 1939 was a bonneted version of the 'Valkyrie' CX13 coach, and would have possessed a dropped frame and underslung worm rear axle. London Fire Brigade also took a similar machine, but that was a CX20, a bonneted version of the wide frame CX19 double deck chassis. An EN245 petrol engine of 9.1 litres capacity was fitted featuring dual ignition with twin sparking plugs, a governor and a tachometer. Special chrome radiators like this were often supplied on emergency and other special vehicles.

CX25. The CX25 was an additional model in the Valkyrie range, which was supplied to only two customers in 1939, seven for Glasgow Corporation, and the remainder for South African Railways, the latter examples being 8 feet wide. The EN242 oil engine was fitted to the Glasgow deliveries, while the SAR batch had EN246 petrol engines. Externally it looked the same as the other Valkyrie models, the CX9, 11, and 13, which shared identical frames, but the CX25 had a one inch shorter wheelbase, a wide frame and offset differential and drive line. The CX25 was, therefore, basically a longer double deck chassis, somewhat similar but not identical to the contemporary CX19 decker. CUS 855 was one of the Glasgow deliveries, which was well into its twenties when photographed at Greenfoot Garage, Glenboig, in the mid 1960s, when in the ownership of John Carmichael (Highland Bus Service) of Glenboig. Carmichael operated a number of Albion CX double and single deckers on stage service and private hire work and expected to get 220,000 miles between engine overhauls on these and the larger EN243 units. It was claimed that in the history of the company no Albion-engined Albion was ever towed home from a tour or private hire, and that gearbox and worm drive axle problems were unknown. On being sold CUS 855 lasted a few more years in private hands before being broken up.

The Viking.

CX41 (petrol). The Viking name was resurrected in 1948 when this CX41, the first of this model type, was delivered to South African Railways, having previously been exhibited at the first postwar Commercial Motor Show at Earls Court in October of that year. The CX41 was a straight frame chassis with 12 inch ground clearance for overseas markets, and there was a degree of collaboration with SAR in the design of the vehicle. This show vehicle was 36 feet long by 8 feet wide and was billed as the largest 2 axle single decker built by a British manufacturer at that time. It had an MCCW luxury coach body with seating for only 33 passengers in aircraft style luxury seats. Both doors were pneumatically operated, and the coach was fitted with air conditioning, individual sun blinds, a public address system and a radio. It was powered by a special version of the EN256 petrol engine of 10.5 litres capacity developing 175 bhp with the aid of twin carburettors. The large, hotter running petrol engine required extra cooling which was provided by a newly introduced larger capacity radiator. This could be identified by the positioning of the lower mounting points, which were built into the centre of the radiator sides rather than fitted externally as on standard CX oil engined models.

CX41 (diesel). The oil engined Viking was fitted with the standard bus radiator, and this example was delivered to Bombay State Transport in 1949. The engine was the EN243B 6 cylinder 9.9 litre unit. The CX41 was effectively a passenger version of the CX3 lorry, and Albion saw this model as a way of staying in the heavyweight bus market when dropped frame models were eventually withdrawn. The model was provided with a front dash intended for fully fronted bodywork, but the Indian bodybuilder apparently decided in this case that a half cab was more functional. The operating conditions obviously dictated the need for a heavy front bumper. Only 30 CX41s were built, all of which were exported, before being superseded by the similar 'Viking' HD61 in 1950.

The Valiant.

CX39 (diesel). By offering a number of the new Valiant passenger chassis for very short delivery, Albion managed to secure a proportion of the private coach market in 1949/50. Wiltshire operator Thomas's Luxury Tours took delivery of this CX39N with Burlingham 33 seat coachwork in March 1950. Like the Valiant models of the 1930s, the CX39 'Valiant' was a wide frame single deck chassis which had more in common with the Venturer double decker than contemporary Valkyrie models. It was one of two models introduced in 1948 which provided a stay of execution for the heavyweight bus range. It differed from the model it replaced, the CX13 'Valkyrie', in that it had an improved frontal design, new EN243 9.9 litre engine, wider frame and offset drive line and differential similar to the CX37 double decker. It was usually supplied with a separate overdrive gearbox controlled by a second gear lever situated behind the driver on the left hand side, which brought the speed up to 60 mph depending on axle ratio. This combination of performance and top speed was not matched by any other coach on the road at that time. However, the success it deserved was not forthcoming. Production ended in 1950, as operators changed over to more modern underfloor engined designs, although the last Valiant did not enter service until July 1951, marking the end of the dropped frame coach chassis by Albion Motors.

CX39 (petrol). Fifty CX39LW 'Valiant' chassis commenced delivery to South African Railways in 1948 and were delivered at the rate of 3 per week from the Port Elizabeth factory of Bus Bodies (South Africa). Running units were the same as those used on the CX41, but unlike the Viking, the Valiant was a genuine dropped frame single deck bus chassis. These buses had the large 10.5 litre petrol engine, and the semi-circular grill on the side of the bonnet is a Visco air filter specially fitted to deal with the dusty operating environment. Like the Viking, the Valiant was one of these rare vehicles in the motor industry which was given a model name, but which did not display that name anywhere on the chassis or finished vehicle.

CX39 (pantechnicon.) Bus chassis were always popular for pantechnicons, because their dropped frame meant a low floor for easier access and greater load space for a given vehicle height. As with all dropped frame models the standard worm axle was underslung, so that the drive was taken in the bottom of the unit rather than the top as on straight frame models. Medwood's furniture removers of Durban operated this oil engined 'Valiant' CX39LW with locally built body by Flambo. It was new in the late 1940s, and was still in service with its original operator some 25 years later, but its ultimate fate is unknown. The suffix LW indicated a chassis which was longer than normal, and was 8 feet wide.

The Venturer.

CX19 (home). The CX19 was introduced in 1938, a year after its single deck equivalent, the CX13, but differed mainly from the single deck model in that it had a wider frame and an offset worm drive and differential. This meant that the engine, gearbox and driveline were all inclined at a slight angle to the frame to provide a straight driveline from engine to rear axle. When it reappeared after the war, the model was substantially unchanged, but towards the end of 1948 the radiator design was altered. The small rectangular badge which had been used on bus models for almost 30 years gave way to this new design, which had the word 'Albion' cast into the top tank with rays spreading from it, in a variation of the design used on commercials for many years. At the same time the screw on filler cap was replaced by a quick release sprung hinged cap of attractive and practical design, while the 'Albion Venturer' badge (or 'Valkyrie' for single deckers) continued to be affixed to the grill on some,

but not all deliveries. However, only a small number of chassis received this radiator, before the rays were dropped, and the name 'Albion' appeared in larger lettering on an otherwise identical top tank. Around the same time the 'Albion Oil Engine' badge emerged on the lower nearside radiator, having first appeared on commercials in 1947. Some, if not all, of this batch of 'Venturer' CX19s built in 1948 with MCCW bodywork for Glasgow Corporation received this intermediate 'sunrays' radiator. After overhaul or accident damage any radiator was liable to be fitted, and for this reason the 'sunrays' radiators found their way on to other Albions in the fleet, from prewar examples to the last batch eventually delivered in 1953. However, B30 (EGA 36), still retained the correct style of radiator when seen passing through George Square on driver training duties in 1960. It was withdrawn and scrapped the following year.

CX19 (overseas). The biggest purchaser of CX19s was New South Wales Department of Road Transport and Tramways which purchased 160 between 1939 and 1949. Seen here taking a corner with a full load of passengers in the North Hyde district of Sydney in the late 1960s is one of a 1947 batch of CX19W eight feet wide Venturers with local bodywork by Commonwealth Engineering. The 9.1 litre EN242 engine, the largest oil engine available in a British built double decker when introduced, would have been put to good use on Sydney's hilly routes, but none of the even larger engined CX37s was ever purchased. Albion was pulling out of the double deck market by the late 1940s and it is quite possible that they did not tender for this market after this date.

CX37 (overseas). The CX37 replaced the CX19 in 1948 and kept Albion in the double deck bus market for another three years. Three of the fifty 'Venturer' CX37LW double deckers which were delivered to the Reef Section, South African Railways Road Motor Services in 1950 are pictured in Cape Town in the 1950s. Powered by a 10.5 litre EN256 petrol engine, they were the last and largest petrol engined double deckers built by a British manufacturer and at 30 feet long by 8 feet wide they were also the longest 2 axle British built double deckers at that time. The Coventry Radiator Company supplied all the cast aluminium radiators used by Albion at that time, and this batch was fitted with the wider type for the larger and hotter running petrol engine, being the fourth type of radiator used on the Venturer in as many years. The 66 seat bodies were by Bus Bodies (SA), an associate company of Metro-Cammell Weymann, which may explain their typical British styling.

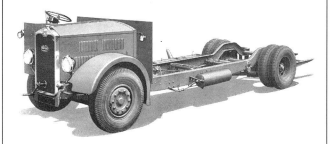

THE ALBION "VENTURER"
48/56 PASSENGER DOUBLE DECK MODEL

THERE are probably few classes of operation which make such heavy demands on the chassis as that of the double deck bus in urban areas where high peak loads and frequent stopping and starting are encountered. In this sphere the Albion " Venturer " has fully maintained the reputation for economy and durability which it acquired amongst users on its introduction some years ago.

The standard power unit is a 6 cylinder oil engine of the direct-injection type having a particularly good torque characteristic at the lower speeds, thus ensuring a quick " get-away " from rest. The gearbox is bolted to the engine casing, the complete engine-gearbox unit being carried in the frame by a special flexible mounting which

minimises to a marked degree the engine vibration imparted to the frame.

The transmission line is offset in the chassis, the worm driven axle pot being to the nearside, thus allowing the fullest advantage to be taken of the dropped frame so as to secure a low floor level.

The driver's comfort has been given careful consideration and the controls are conveniently placed, the handbrake being on the right hand, and the speed change lever on the left of the driver.

The chassis weight is such that 56-seater buses can be built without exceeding the fully-laden weight limit of 11 tons set by the Ministry of Transport Regulations.

From pre-war publicity leaflet.

Two Venturers, a CX19 and a CX37 are seen at Glasgow's Parkhead Garage in 1960, showing the earlier and later types of radiator fitted. Differences between the CX19 and the CX37 were slight, but, in addition to other minor improvements, the CX37 had the larger 9.9 litre engine, a 3½ inch shorter wheelbase, different tyre specification, and a revised frontal appearance. The CX37 also required a cut-out in the front panel to allow forward movement of the steering drop arm, a feature not found on the CX19. Otherwise the frontal treatment of the CX37 was neat and attractive, but this was slightly marred on the Glasgow examples by a modification which was carried out by the Corporation to the first batch of 65 early in their lives. Problems with radiator mountings called for a special bracket to be fitted behind the lower mounting points which required the radiator to be moved forward two inches with consequent lengthening of the bonnet and side panel. At the same time, the rubber block which formed the front engine mounting was changed for a steel spring arrangement similar to that used on the WD.CX22. The access holes on the engine side panel were provided for checking and filling the engine oil, a feature which was standard on the CX37, but was a later modification on the CX19. Glasgow did not operate a long life policy for its bus fleet, and being the only manual gearbox buses in the fleet by the early 1960s, the days of the Venturers were clearly numbered. The CX19 had a Roberts body and was sold in 1960, and the CX37 had a Brockhouse body and was withdrawn in 1963. One Glasgow Corporation Venturer, a CX37, survives today.

CX37 (home). Conservative bus engineers did not want to introduce non standard engines into their fleet and this was exemplified by the conversion carried out on the batch of sixteen CX37 'Venturers' delivered to Western SMT in 1949. Between 1952 and 1954 the Albion 9.9 litre engines were removed and replaced with Gardner 6LW engines in a programme which eventually saw the elimination of Albion engines from the fleet. As with the Glasgow examples, bonnet extensions were also required, but this time to accommodate the longer Gardner engines. In their new specification they continued to clock up very high mileages on some of the longest double deck stage services in Britain. But by 1961 there were only 20 CX Albions left in the fleet, and their early demise came soon afterwards. Some found new owners like this Alexander bodied example which was with its third operator when photographed in the service of Dunoon Motor Services in the summer of 1962.

The Victor.

FT3AB. The 'Victor' FT3AB was introduced in October 1947 as a lightweight bus chassis with a straight frame for overseas use. It used the same small 4.25 litre 6 cylinder EN277 and 4 speed gearbox as the FT3 goods models, but unlike the goods models, the sump was located at the front of the engine, this engine type being designated EN277E. Other refinements included wider springs and hydraulic dampers. The FT3AB soon found customers on the domestic market, but when used as a coach with heavy bodywork and carrying a full load of 31 passengers and luggage, it was found to be underpowered. To address this problem, the six cylinder 4.6 litre engine from the BY5 became standard from 1949. In this form the engine was called the EN282, and production of the model continued until 1951. Bus versions could carry more passengers and this is a Duple 32 seat bus body on an FT3AB belonging to D. Morrison of Lochwinnoch.

FT39. The FT39 'Victor' appeared a year later, and was, effectively, the passenger version of the FT37 lorry, differing only in electrical equipment, road springs, wheelbase, and the provision of hydraulic shock absorbers front and rear. In 1949 the frontal appearance was modernised with the curved dash and recessed headlamps, and some examples, particularly for coach applications, acquired fully fronted bodywork which totally enclosed the Albion radiator. Despite having an engine of less than half the size of the top of the range CX39 'Valiant', the combination of the new EN286 engine and flexible 5 speed gearbox enabled it to make good progress on the open road, while having the capability of climbing any reasonable gradient that it might be expected to meet. First gear was a crawler gear, and fifth was direct top, and the operator could, of course, specify an axle ratio suitable for the type of operating conditions in his area. BKS 288 was a 'Victor' FT39N with Scottish Aviation 31 seat coach body owned by Kyle Brothers of Kelso.

Chapter 6
The KP Experiments

Towards the end of 1947, an enquiry was received from W.G. Ramsay, Manager of Road Motor Services, South African Railways (SAR), which prompted one of the most expensive development programmes in the company's history. He enquired about the possibility of Albion supplying an engine considerably larger and more powerful than the existing EN256 10.5 litre petrol engine, which was already the largest commercial vehicle engine offered by a British manufacturer. SAR was Albion's biggest single customer, and they were looking for trucks with top speeds of up to 50 mph powered by engines of 250 - 270hp. for their increasingly heavy haulage duties. The Albion management considered that if they could not supply this market, someone else would, which would open the door for a competitor to capture all of the SAR business. So over the next few months the company considered designs for a straight six engine of 17.9 litres capacity or a flat twelve cylinder horizontally opposed engine of 14.6 litres. The latter used components of the four cylinder EN286 oil engine, successfully introduced in 1948 in the FT37 lorry and FT39 bus.

The EN286 had been ten years in testing and development, and it was felt that the latter option could provide the basis of a series of new multi-cylindered engines, which might eventually replace all the engines manufactured by the company. This would produce a high degree of standardisation by creating a whole range of power units with common components from the 286 engine.

This is the EN1200/2 twelve cylinder oil engine before it was fitted in the KD23. It had just undergone 745 hours of bench testing, during which one of the main crankshaft bearings failed. The crankshaft was then rebuilt using the latest RHP roller bearings. The engine had 2 fuel pumps, 2 air cleaners, and 4 cylinder heads. There was also a 12 cylinder petrol engine designated EN1200/1, but this was never used in a vehicle.

Horizontally opposed engines were compact in terms of length, but width limitations dictated that they would not fit in a conventional front mounted position, but would have to be carried in an underfloor configuration.

The company had already been looking at underfloor designs in 1947. At that time design work on the FT31 and FT33, underfloor-engined versions of the FT3 lorry and bus chassis had reached an advanced stage but had not been put into production. Underfloor engines were being introduced by competitors, with AEC and Leyland planning new bus models for introduction in 1949 and 1950 respectively, and Sentinel and Dennis had been developing underfloor-engined commercials. As engines were getting bigger and noisier, it made sense to place them amidships under the chassis, which would result in quieter, uncluttered cabs with more crew space. With these factors in mind, Managing Director Hugh Fulton flew out to South Africa on 4th September 1948 for a meeting with SAR managers and came back with the promise of substantial orders if the company could develop a high powered truck which met their requirements.

Thus in October 1948, under the control of Chief Designer, J.A. Kemp, who came to Albion from Maudslay in 1934, work started on a number of prototype engines with 4, 6, 8 and 12 cylinders. Arranged as pairs of 2, 3, 4

and 6 horizontally opposed cylinders with a central crankshaft, the engines shared a common bore and stroke and were designed to use pistons and other components from the EN286. A feature of these engines was the use of roller bearings of large diameter for the main bearing journals, developed by Albion in collaboration with bearing manufacturers Ransomes, Hoffman and Pollard. As the bearings were unsplit, this necessitated a crankshaft which was built-up of machined sections, rather than the conventional single machined forging.

During the summer of 1949 Kemp travelled to Arbon in Switzerland to visit Saurer, which was the only European manufacturer of automotive engines using built-up crankshafts with roller bearings. The Swiss company discussed freely the technical complexities of using multi-cylindered built-up crankshaft engines, and Kemp returned to Scotland with useful information having extended an invitation to Saurer's technical people to visit Scotstoun at any time in the future. The built-up method of assembly suited Albion's long held philosophy that all components should be maintained with basic tools, as this crankshaft was bolted together instead of using other solutions such as the press-fit method. This allowed a damaged section to be replaced without the need to replace the whole crankshaft, and the sections could be standardised for all engines regardless of size.

The KD23 with the 12 cylinder 14.64 litre oil engine was said to have performance which was far ahead of any other heavy vehicle on the road in Britain when used on long distance haulage between Scotland and England in 1951. The engine was mounted under the chassis, which meant that a straight frame could be used. The drawback of this was that in order to give the engine sufficient ground clearance for overseas conditions, the frame was much higher than usual as is evident in this view taken in Glasgow in 1951. Also evident is the massive tyre equipment, 13.00x20 at the front and 14.00x20 singles at the rear.

The range was known as the 'KP' series of engines and there was a total of six prototypes developed as follows :
- A 4 cylinder of 4.88 litres capacity, given type designation EN400, was run on one of the Experimental Department's engine test beds, but was never used in a vehicle.
- A 6 cylinder of 7.32 litres capacity, type designation EN600, went into a CX chassis and was used in the Albion transport fleet.
- Two 8 cylinders were made, both of 9.76 litres capacity and designated type EN800. These were installed in the specially designed KP71 bus chassis.
- Two 12 cylinder engines of 14.64 litres were built, one petrol (EN1200/1) and one oil (EN1200/2). However, the petrol unit was found to be too thirsty and never left the Experimental Department. The oil engine went into a special 6x4 chassis designated KD23, and was eventually sent to South Africa for extensive testing.

The two KP71 buses were the longest lived of all of these experimental vehicles, and were put to work in completely different operating environments. The first KP71 was delivered to Glasgow Corporation with a 35 seat Scottish Aviation bus body in 1952 and entered service on local stage services. Meanwhile the second was put to use on Western SMT's Glasgow to London service, and fitted with 30 coach seats in a Scottish Aviation body of completely different styling. They remained in use until 1959 and 1955 respectively before being returned to Albion.

The 12 cylinder KD23 was a one-off built mainly from the components of a former WD.CX24 tank transporter chassis, but with a new frame based on that of the overtype WD.CX23. Other differences from the CX range were Marles cam and double roller steering and a five speed constant mesh gearbox sourced from the new HD range. A conventional front mounted radiator was fitted and the final appearance of the vehicle closely resembled the CX23 model, which had been supplied in large numbers to South African Railways.

Upon completion, the chassis was tested by the Experimental Department for 700 miles, and thereafter it went into service on long distance haulage between Scotstoun and the Midlands of England, carrying loads of about 10 tons, making a maximum gross weight of about 20 tons. From May to September of 1951 a total of 10,500 miles was clocked up on these duties, and an Albion report noted that ". . . the performance of the vehicle, with its 240 bhp engine, was far ahead of any other heavy vehicle on the road." Certainly, in terms of its swept volume of 14.64 litres, it was probably the largest engined rigid vehicle on British roads at that time.

The truck was then delivered to Birkenhead docks and shipped out to South Africa where it commenced extensive testing in November 1951 in the territory for which it was intended. It was put to work for South African Railways where it apparently created a very good impression with the SAR personnel through its ability to shift heavy loads over long distances, in about half the time taken by most other types of vehicle. Apart from loss of coolant in its early days of testing due to local boiling in the cylinder block, the vehicle was said to have operated successfully in South Africa. The overheating was cured by the fitting

When initial testing work in Britain was completed, the KD23 was sent to South Africa late in 1951 for testing on the sort of duties for which it was designed. In somewhat less severe conditions than those which wrecked the engine in February 1953, the KD is shown negotiating a typical wet road during its trials in South Africa. On being shipped back to Glasgow, the engine and other major components were stripped down for examination, but Leyland had other plans for their new subsidiary and the remains of this amazing vehicle were eventually broken up.

of a larger capacity radiator, but a number of minor problems, such as numerous oil leaks, do not appear to have been fully resolved on this prototype. The brakes, being based on those of a CX24 tank transporter, were also found to be inadequate.

Much of the mileage was accumulated on unsurfaced roads where dust was a severe problem. When it did rain, it was usually in the form of a deluge, which then formed into floods, and this proved to be the KD23's undoing. While negotiating a badly flooded road in February 1953, water was ingested into the engine via one of the two air cleaners causing serious damage to the pistons, valves, etc. The vehicle was shipped back to Glasgow later that year for a thorough strip down and examination, but it was never repaired. By that time Leyland were in charge and had other priorities. They preferred the big six cylinder type and had already asked Albion to finalise the design of their own 15.2 litre 0.900 engine. As for the rest of the KP range of engines, they would not be needed either, as Leyland would supply all engines larger than the EN286. Albion's role as Leyland's subsidiary was now to produce trucks and buses at the lighter end of the market, and the KP Experiments were

effectively dead. Apart, that is, from one last trial. . . .

Leyland was very keen for Albion to re-enter the 30cwt market, which Albion had left with the withdrawal of the AZ models. The Claymore was already under development using a four cylinder engine based on components of the six cylinder Leyland 0.350, which would cater for 3 ton loads, but there was a need for something smaller.

A final horizontally opposed engine was developed using EN286 parts but this time the unit was a two cylinder air cooled engine. Albion had previously acquired a German air cooled Deutz engine for experimental purposes, but more importantly, had recruited George Lee from the Bristol Aeroplane Company, whose expertise in air cooled aero engines could now be put to good use. The engine was coupled to a Self Changing Gears automatic gearbox of Daimler design and installed in a lightweight chassis which was given the code LD1 (LD for Local Delivery). However, the experiment was not a success. The engine was too rough and noisy to warrant further development, and finally the new 30cwt model known as the Cairn was introduced in 1955 using the Claymore engine in a lighter chassis. ❏

The first KP71NW had a 39 seat dual entrance body by Scottish Aviation of Prestwick and was handed over to Glasgow Corporation in March 1952, approximately one year after it was built. Consideration was given to exhibiting the chassis at the 1950 Commercial Motor Show at Earls Court, but this was decided against, as it would only invite enquiries for a product which could not be delivered. The EN800 9.76 litre 8 cylinder oil engine was originally set up to run with opposing pairs of cylinders firing together, giving it the characteristics of a 4 cylinder engine. As this did not provide the level of refinement expected in a passenger vehicle, it was converted to run as an eight. FYS 495 lasted in service until 1959 when it was returned to Albion, stripped of its running units, and the shell sold to Glasgow dealers Millburn Motors.

The other KP71NW was BSD 470, which had the last Scottish Aviation p.s.v. body built. It had 30 aircraft style reclining seats, and was used on Western's overnight Glasgow to London service. By March 1953 it had clocked up 33,000 miles at an average fuel consumption of 14.6 mpg., which was said to be a very satisfactory result. However, its performance must have been too good, as its high top speed apparently resulted in drivers being stopped for speeding. The fifth gear was blocked off and the coach transferred to touring duties until withdrawal in 1955. On being returned to Albion it was used as staff transport until its sale to Millburn Motors in 1967. For the next five years it was used as a mobile caravan before its acquisition by collector Iain McKerracher in 1972. BSD 470 is still in his ownership, albeit in unrestored condition.

A rear view of one of the KP71 chassis which shows the complexity of the frame required to house the 8 cylinder engine, and the tubular cross members or stay tubes which were a feature of all Albion chassis. This was the chassis for Western SMT, which was fitted with a special spare wheel carrier mounted on rollers. The carrier was designed to be pulled straight out from below the boot, whereupon the end with the handles was lowered on to the road, and the spare wheel removed. Just behind the nearside front wheel is the oil tank, as the KP engines had dry sumps with scavenge pumps which kept the external oil tanks filled. This arrangement improved ground clearance. The cylindrical object on top of the oil tank is a centrifugal oil filter, which was then newly developed for the KP engines and subsequently patented by Albion. Latterly a compact version was produced under licence by Glacier and used extensively in the FT range in the 1950s, and a larger version was used by three other manufacturers.

Not much is known about the CX based chassis with the 6 cylinder engine. It was the last of the KP types to be finished, and was completed in 1952 some time after the CX range had been discontinued. The type designation is not known, but KD3 would have been an appropriate model name, as it was based on a CX3 chassis. It joined the Albion transport fleet where it also was engaged in long distance haulage as well as local work. What happened to it is not known, but it was certainly gone from Scotstoun by 1955, perhaps finishing its days at some far flung Albion depot.

The model LD1 had a horizontally opposed 2.44 litre two cylinder air cooled engined mounted at the rear and coupled to a Self Changing Gears automatic gearbox, which was later replaced with an Albion constant mesh box on the vehicle shown. It was intended for the mobile shop business where Albion was the market leader in Scotland, but it was not successful. After a period of testing it was decided that the project was not viable and the vehicle was broken up.

How the KP engines worked

The conventional engine. To fully appreciate the novel approach used in the design of the KP crankshaft, it is perhaps useful to understand some of the fundamentals of any four-stroke cycle engine. In such an engine, each cylinder produces a firing or power stroke every second revolution, so that the crankshaft of any 4, 6, 8 or 12 cylinder engine, will receive 2, 3, 4 or 6 power strokes respectively, for each revolution. To even out the effect of these pulses from the pistons via the connecting rods, the crankpins of a conventional engine are positioned in pairs around the 360° revolution of the crankshaft at the following crank angles :

a 4 cylinder has crankpins at multiples of 360° ÷ 2 power strokes   (i.e. 0°, 180°)
a 6 cylinder has crankpins at multiples of 360° ÷ 3 power strokes   (i.e. 0°, 120°, 240°)
an 8 cylinder has crankpins at multiples of 360° ÷ 4 power strokes   (i.e. 0°, 90°, 180°, 270°)
a 12 cylinder has crankpins at multiples of 360° ÷ 6 power strokes   (i.e. 0°, 60°, 120°, 180°, 240°, 300°)

The KP engine. From the above it becomes clear that in most engines the crankpins are positioned around the crankshaft at angles which are multiples of 60°, and it was this common factor which simplified the construction of the built-up crankshaft of the KP series. An individual crank unit had an off-centre crankpin between two circular flange-like webs, each having 6 equally spaced holes machined at 60° intervals. Adjacent crank units could then be rotated relative to each other at the multiples of 60° appropriate to the number of cylinders. The crankshaft was then assembled or 'built-up' with crank units bolted together, and ground outer diameters on the webs formed the location for the main journal roller bearing inner race. As a result, the width taken up by the webs of a conventional crankshaft was reduced, producing a very compact engine with a shorter and stiffer crankshaft for a given capacity and helping to reduce the torsional vibration associated with long crankshafts.

The 4 cylinder EN400 had 2 crankpins at multiples of 180°, and when the piston of one bank was at Top Dead Centre (TDC), the piston of the opposing bank was at Bottom Dead Centre (BDC). With a firing stroke every 180° and only 2 crankpins, it had an additional imbalance which required counter balance weights.

The 6 cylinder EN600 had 3 crankpins at multiples of 120°, giving slightly more even firing pulses than the 4 cylinder, but also required counter balance weights.

The 8 cylinder EN800 was not suited to a 6 hole / 60° divide, as multiples of 60° do not produce the required 90° or 270° crank angles. To overcome this problem but maintain a common 60° crank unit, the 8 cylinder engine was initially assembled as two 'fours' with 0° / 180° crank angles. This meant that 4 pistons were at TDC at the same time and with 2 of these cylinders firing every 180° of crankshaft revolution, this produced the roughness of a 'big four' instead of the smoothness of a conventional 8 cylinder, with its single firing stroke every 90° of crankshaft rotation. Proving to be too rough in service, the 8 cylinder was stripped down and rebuilt using crank units with a 4 hole / 90° divide, resulting in a much smoother engine.

The 12 cylinder EN1200 engine had 6 crankpins at multiples of 120° rather than the 60° that might be expected, but as a result of the opposed piston layout, a firing stroke is achieved every 60° of crankshaft rotation. This was the same crank angle used on the 6 cylinder KP engine and on a conventional in-line 6 cylinder. The 12 cylinder KP had no inherent imbalance and was extremely smooth when running.

Bearings – KP Engine. The main bearings of the KP engine consisted of a large diameter roller bearing positioned between adjacent crankpin units. On the left is the early type of bearing with cage and rollers attached to the inner race. Following engine test bed running, these bearings were replaced by a type which had the roller cage attached to the outer race, resulting in a wider bearing surface and rollers, but within the same overall width. The later type is shown on the right.

Crankpins – KP Engine. A pair of crankshaft units removed from the 12 cylinder engine show the 6-hole circular webs with their ground locating diameters for the roller main bearings. Each crank unit carried two connecting rods with conventional shell bearings, serving cylinders on opposing banks. Since there was no room for balancing weights on the webs they were attached to the crankshaft ends, but were not required on the 12 cylinder engine.

Letter sent to customers in July 1951
regarding takeover by Leyland.

ALBION MOTORS LTD
SCOTSTOUN,
GLASGOW, W.4

MANUFACTURERS OF
REG.
TRADE Albion MARK
MOTOR VEHICLES

BY APPOINTMENT
MOTOR LORRY
MANUFACTURERS

BRANCHES
LONDON
MANCHESTER, LEEDS, SHEFFIELD, BRISTOL.
HULL, NOTTINGHAM, BIRMINGHAM, BELFAST.
EDINBURGH, LINCOLN, CALCUTTA.
TELEPHONES
HEAD OFFICE - SCOTSTOUN 1261 (9 LINES)
LONDON OFFICE - SLOANE 6117, 6118, 6119
WILLESDEN DEPOT - ELGAR 5962/5
TELEGRAMS
"AUTOMOBILE, PHONE." GLASGOW
"KARALBO, WESPHONE." LONDON
"UPKEEP, NORPHONE." LONDON
CABLES
"AUTOMOBILE." GLASGOW

Dear Sirs,

You will no doubt have read in the press of the offer by Leyland Motors Ltd., to acquire the shares of Albion Motors Ltd., which offer the Directors of this Company have recommended the Shareholders to accept. The Directors feel sure that in this proposed amalgamation there will be every opportunity for greater efficiency and reduction of costs.

As an Albion user, you are probably wondering how you will be affected. Your interests were very prominently before the Albion Directors when discussions were taking place and it was felt that by the joint efforts of the two Companies in design, production, etc., you would materially benefit in the supply of vehicles and in service arrangements.

There will be no question of this Company losing its identity - production of Albion Vehicles will continue at Scotstoun in, we hope, even greater quantity - and the operations of the Company will remain under the present management. We shall as before maintain our policy of stressing the importance of the supply of spare parts and service facilities for both new and old models.

We look forward with pleasure to a continuance of our business relationship.

Yours faithfully,
ALBION MOTORS LTD.

W.C. Reid

Director & Sales Manager.

TO THE TERMS AND CONDITIONS OF GUARANTEE AS CONTAINED IN OUR CATALOGUE.
...ly Driven by our Staff at Customers' own Risk and Responsibility.
...s sent to us for Repair, Storage, etc., are held at Owner's Risk, and we
...ss or damage to such goods arising from fire or any unforeseen causes.

ALBION-LEYLAND MERGER

To dispel unfounded rumours arising from the above, I would like to make clear the following points:-

(1) It is the intention of both Companies to maintain their separate individualities.

(2) We intend taking full advantage of exchange of technical information so that both Companies produce the best possible article in their various categories.

(3) The Management of each firm is being left undisturbed, each to manage their own business. Albion will still produce Albion vehicles and Leyland will produce Leylands.

(4) There is no suggestion or intention of altering or stopping the Albion Pension Scheme.

(5) There is no intention to stop the issue of Long Service Certificates.

(6) The amalgamation will not affect distribution of annual bonus which will, as in the past, be determined by the Directors of the Albion Company year by year.

What was said at the announcement of the proposed amalgamation to various representatives of all sections of employees here will bear repeating, namely, that THE FUTURE OF ALBION WILL DEPEND, AS IT HAS DONE IN THE PAST, ON THE EFFORTS OF ALL WHO ARE EMPLOYED THROUGHOUT THE ORGANISATION.

I know of no reason to think that we will be less successful in the future than we have been in the past.

We have plenty of orders and more to come. Material supplies are difficult, but it is up to us to see that we make the best possible use of what we can get.

ALBION MOTORS LIMITED

Jno. Fulton.

Managing Director.

21st September 1951 letter to employees
regarding takeover.

Chapter 7
The Leyland Takeover and its Aftermath
1951 to 1957

At the beginning of 1951 Albion had an impressive range of products. There was a truck model in every significant weight range from petrol-engined 3 tonners to 14½ ton eight wheelers, while on the bus side the small FT3AB was still selling alongside the last of the CX37 double deckers. The AZ series 30 cwt chassis had been withdrawn in 1949 without replacement, because cheaper alternatives were available from mass producers like Ford and Bedford, but the range of commercial vehicles which remained, all with in-house engines (petrol or oil), was not exceeded by any other manufacturer. Leyland was between two and three times the size of Albion, but not so strong at the lower end of the weight range, or in overseas markets.

Perhaps this was the reason which prompted Leyland Chairman, Henry Spurrier, to approach Albion Chairman, Jackson Millar, at the 1950 Commercial Motor Show with the suggestion that there should be an amalgamation of the two companies. Leyland's biggest rival, AEC, had acquired Crossley in 1948 and then Maudslay in 1949, and Spurrier did not want to be left behind. Although sales were still buoyant, Albion felt vulnerable. Much of the bus market had been abandoned to competitors, and the mass producers were making inroads at the lighter end of the commercial range, which had resulted in the withdrawal of the AZ models. The 1948 nationalization of road hauliers operating outside a 25 mile radius of their base had brought about much uncertainty in the industry which led to cancelled orders, as operators switched to short term cheaper models or manufacturers offering short delivery. Despite this the medium weight FT range continued to sell and there was no problem finding buyers

for any cancelled Chieftains, but the newly introduced HD (Heavy Duty) range was not doing so well in this uncertain climate. As Leyland led the market with its heavy range, the attractions of the amalgamation were obvious. Discussions ensued, and despite some opposition from one or two members of the board, the takeover of Albion was completed on 31st July 1951.

Within a month a long term strategy had been worked out. Not surprisingly the new HD range was the first to be affected. By September 1952 the Leyland 0.600 9.8 litre engine had supplanted the Albion EN253 9.9 litre unit in all but the 8 wheeler, which somehow managed to retain the Albion unit, and by September 1954 the whole HD range had been withdrawn. Also, a new smaller 4 cylinder oil engine for both vertical (EN218) and horizontal (EN219) applications, based on the Leyland 0.350, was designed, manufactured and ready for the 1953 Scottish Motor Show in the latest 'Claymore' truck. This engine was produced in two years as against the 10 year gestation period of the EN286, and unfortunately the lack of development time showed in the reliability of the unit, especially in the underfloor version. There were problems with cylinder head gaskets, engine mounts, dynamo brackets, and some engine blocks supplied by Leyland subsidiary West Yorkshire Foundries were prone to cracking. This meant that repeat orders were not forthcoming, which resulted in the model not being made in sufficient numbers to make a profit for the company. Similar if not worse problems existed with the Nimbus, possibly exacerbated by its stop-start operation.

In November 1952 a decision was taken to cease manufacture of petrol engines, after current orders and

HD53. The last new model range to be introduced before the Leyland takeover was the HD series in April 1950, replacing the 6 cylinder CX range. Apart from having a curved dash like the revised Chieftain, it also exhibited a new and imposing radiator, similar to the overseas radiator introduced two years earlier, but with the addition of sun-rays spreading from the 'Albion' script on the top tank. It had the upgraded 9.9 litre engine, now called the EN253, which among other improvements had a heavier timing chain and a more generous crankshaft bearing area. A five speed constant mesh gearbox, much longer than the CX four speed unit, was included in the specification, but no auxiliary box was listed. The chassis was available in four wheelbases, the shortest for tractor work, the next for a tipper, and the two haulage models capable of hauling separate trailers. Herdman's Flour ran this early HD53 six and three quarter tonner, a payload which it could take easily in its stride.

HD55. The six wheeler was the HD55, and these are two 1950 HD55Ls owned by Smiths Potato Estates Ltd., an associate company of Smith's Crisps Ltd, and a faithful Albion customer for many years. Behind the new curved dash Marles cam and double roller steering replaced Albion's own worm and segment steering with its protruding drop arm below the offside headlamp. The new radiator did not have a 'Saltire' badge, as HD trucks did not have model names, and neither did it have an 'Albion Oil Engine' plate, as these were discontinued around the time of the introduction of the HD series. Loads of 12 tons of potatoes were carried on the trucks shown and both trucks survive today.

A 1950 HD55L in the fleet of Robert Deuchar (Duddingston Ales) with a 2204 gallon tank built in Fife by Enamelled Metal Products Ltd. Albions were very popular with brewers, and in the North East alone, they were used by firms like Calders, Federation, Newcastle Breweries, John Rowell, Isaac Tuckers, Vaux, as well as Deuchars. The truck was supplied by Albion concessionaires for the North East, F.W. Cawthorn.

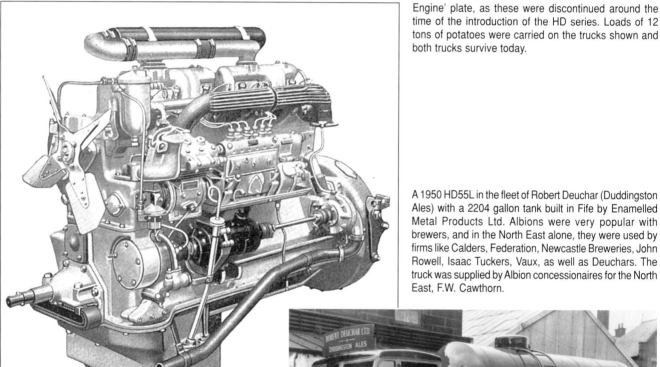

EN253 engine. The EN253 which was installed in the HD range was Albion's last 6 cylinder diesel engine design.

stocks had been cleared. This decision resulted in the termination of development work on a petrol version of the Leyland 0.680, even though one had been built and run successfully on an engine test bed. By August 1953 there were still stocks of parts to build approximately 130 petrol engined FT models, but difficulty was experienced in finding customers for these remaining petrol models. Eventually a contract was drawn up with the SCWS to take most of these chassis at reduced price for delivery early in 1954.

Perhaps as a replacement for the doomed high-powered KP engine, Albion assumed responsibility in 1953 for the design of Leyland's 15.2 litre 0.900 engine, which Albion called the EN900. Leyland built the prototype, but Albion took over the development work, redesigned the block and head gaskets, and changed the design from wet to dry liners. In October 1954 a Büssing 15 litre horizontal diesel engine was acquired and fitted into an HD23 truck so that transmissions could be tested for the new engine, which was due to start production at Scotstoun in 1956. Intended for use mainly as a railcar engine, it saw use in only one Albion model, the 'Royal Scot' HD175, the largest engined bus ever built in Britain. The South African order also called for 6x4 trucks fitted with this engine in vertical configuration, and consideration was given to building a heavy duty Albion to meet these requirements using the same transmission as the HD175. However, this part of the

1953 advertisement for apprentices

contract was eventually fulfilled by Leyland with their Buffalo, while Scammell also utilised the engine in their Super Constructor, also in 1958.

The independent Albion management had pulled the company out of the dropped frame bus market by May 1951, and at takeover only two passenger types remained. These were the heavyweight 'Viking' HD61 and HD63, primarily for overseas markets, and the lighter 'Victor' FT39AN and FT3AB. The HD61 and HD63 were quickly replaced by the Leyland engined HD73, and by the end of 1953 this too was gone leaving only one single model – the FT39.

With one or two notable exceptions, the emphasis was now on everything lightweight, and the new range of Leyland-Albions which was emerging was a far cry from

HD55 (petrol). Supplied to the Public Works Department in Swaziland in 1952, this HD55TRW and low loading trailer are seen loading plant for new road construction in the territory. Although not listed, it nevertheless had a 10.5 litre EN257 petrol engine which was fitted with twin carburettors. It was obviously deemed to require maximum cooling and hence the fitting of a larger than normal tropical radiator of a type similar to those fitted to some of the CX23s of South African Railways. The cab was constructed locally by Wevell Brothers.

the over-engineered products of ten years previously. Throughout the 1950s the FT range continued to make an impression for its reliability and economy, if not for on-the-road performance, but Leyland engines continued to replace Albion designs as the dominance of the parent company made itself felt. In June 1955, Leyland acquired Scammell Lorries Ltd. and claimed to be the largest heavy duty vehicle organization in the world and parent company of 16 subsidiary and associated companies.

Towards the end of 1956 Spurrier requested that two Leyland directors, Stanley Markland and Donald Stokes, be co-opted onto the Albion board. Spurrier, by now Sir Henry, and himself an Albion director since 1953, reasoned that this was required to strengthen joint Leyland-Albion sales. Markland and Stokes were two senior Leyland men with reputations as formidable players in the industry and they effectively replaced two long serving Albion directors, William Pate and Francis Henderson. Six months later, on 5th April 1957, Hugh Fulton, 51 year old Managing Director and son of the co-founder, resigned in apparent disagreement about the direction in which Leyland was taking Albion. ❏

HD57. Topping the range was the HD57, a 14½ ton 8 wheeler like this HD57L tanker owned by the British Dyewood Company of Glasgow. A Harvey cab and Butterfield tank were fitted. The Clayton Dewandre air pressure brakes operated on 3 axles only, the leading axle being unbraked. Like the rest of the HD range a Clayton Dewandre air compressor on the left hand side of the EN253 engine replaced the exhauster of the previous CX models which were vacuum braked. The compressor enabled the fitting of an optional tyre inflator on the right hand chassis frame. The HD57 models retained the Albion engine until the end, being prematurely withdrawn in 1954, a victim of Leyland rationalisation.

The HD57T tipper did not appear until a year after the other models and had a body length which was 6 feet 9 inches shorter than the haulage version on a strengthened chassis with a wheelbase 3 feet 6 inches shorter. Yorkshire operator John Hinchcliffe and Son used a number of Albions including this 8 wheeled tipper which was new in 1953 with Pilot tipping gear.

HD73. After the Leyland takeover, the ranges of the two companies were largely complementary except that the HDs were directly competitive with the 0.600-engined Leylands. The future of the HD range was obviously limited, but to try to ensure that Albion customers switched to Leylands after the HDs were dropped, from September 1952 all two and three axle chassis were fitted with Leyland 0.600 engines in place of the slightly larger Albion EN253 engine. HDs with Leyland engines were then numbered in the 70 series, and this is an HD73TR with Leyland 0.600 engine new to Derbyshire County Council in 1953. Sitting on the low loading semi trailer is a Fowler steam road roller dating from the 1920s which is waiting to be taken to site.

HD75. Externally it was impossible to tell the difference between Albion and the Leyland-engined HDs. However, there was a way to tell them apart. In the driver's cab the Albion-engined models had a gear change lever which was mounted in a position in line with the centre of the steering wheel in the neutral position, whereas the Leyland-engined variants had the gear lever set back nearer the driver. Also the Leyland-engined models had a rear sump compared to the front sump on Albion engines. This is a 1954 HD75N six wheel petrol tanker operated by the Nairobi district of the Shell Company of East Africa Ltd. The 3000 gallon tank and driver's cab were assembled locally.

HD61. The 'Viking' HD61 replaced the 'Viking' CX41 in 1950 and this 1951 example is seen on the Island of Arran in the fleet of Bannatyne, having originally been owned by Dye of Hereford. The differences between the old and new Vikings were not great. Being part of the same family as the 'Heavy Duty' range of commercial vehicles, the HD61 had the upgraded 9.9 litre EN253 engine, five speed constant mesh gearbox and Marles cam and double roller steering. The CX41's straight frame was also retained. This 37 seat coach survived until 1966.

HD63. The date is February 1956 and a five year old SAR.HD63XLW, complete with trailer, is seen on the 50 mile route from Worcester to the Cape. The HD63 was the petrol variant of the Viking, having the EN257 10.5 litre engine, and all 40 were sold to South African Railways. Extra cooling for the petrol engine was provided by an extra (fourth) row of tubes in an otherwise outwardly identical radiator. Neither the HD61 nor the HD63 was listed by September 1952, having been replaced by the Leyland 0.680 engined HD73XLW, and this model too was withdrawn by the end of 1953, leaving the FT39 'Victor' as the only bus chassis offered.

HD23. An order for 230 ten ton 6x4 HD trucks was received from the Ministry of Supply in September 1951, followed by another for 270 in the following year. This early example of the WD.HD23N is seen on test in South Africa in early 1953. They were powered by the EN257 10.5 litre petrol engine, and were of similar specification to the WD.CX23 range supplied to the Ministry 10 years earlier. Indeed, this was the only truck in the HD range to share a model number with a CX type. A number of different bodies were supplied on two wheelbases, with machinery, workshop, cargo, and revolving crane on the longer, and tipper bodies on the shorter. 14.00x20 tyres were fitted and the complete truck was designed for wading to a maximum depth of 2½ feet.

SAR.HD23. South African Railways also ordered a number of HD23 chassis, some of which were bodied as heavy duty buses, such as this impressive looking model SAR.HD23XLW seen here when new in 1954. The Albion 10.5 litre petrol engine was fitted, and it was common practice for SAR to order an additional engine with approximately every ten chassis purchased. Albion developed and built a petrol version of the Leyland 0.680 for this market, but a group decision to abandon petrol engine manufacture was taken soon after, and no more were built.

FT37A. In 1952 certain improvements were introduced to the Chieftain range, the first significant changes since the model was introduced in 1948. These were indicated by the 'A' suffix, and the more important of these were a larger wormwheel assembly on the rear axle, heavier springs, improved braking, flexibly mounted radiator tubes, improved fuel filtration and minor alterations to the wheelbases. The first of eight similar 'Chieftain' FT37AL furniture vans was delivered in 1952 to Westgate Carrying Co., Croydon, New South Wales, for long distance removal work. Bodywork was by Fitch and Sons and totally enclosed the Albion radiator. Six and a half tons of furniture or bulky freight could be carried.

FT39A. The FT39A 'Victor' incorporated similar modifications to the 'A' suffixed Chieftains, and by the end of 1954 was the only passenger chassis offered in the Albion range. In this October 1956 view, a line up of Victors owned by the Keppel Bus Company of Singapore is seen waiting to pick up passengers. The bus at the front is an FT39ALX, the LX suffixes indicating that an extra long wheelbase had been specified.

Autolifts cab. In 1953 a factory cab option became available on the Chieftain, Clydesdale, and vertical engined Claymore, three models which shared the same curved dash and radiator style. The pressed steel cab was made by Autolifts and Engineering Company Ltd. of Blackburn, who were also well known for their tipping gear and bodies. The cabs were bought in by Albion as original equipment, and in contemporary advertising and publicity material the cab was always referred to as the 'factory' cab option without mentioning its Blackburn origins. The Autolifts cab was a well-proportioned and functional design, and was identified by the letter 'A' pressed on the inside panels of the cab doors. Seen delivering a load of concrete for a road construction in the London area in 1954 was this FT37AT 'Chieftain' with Danish Agitator equipment owned by Stirling Ready Mix Concrete Ltd.

FT25/FT27. Announced at the Scottish Motor Show in November 1953 were the vertical engined 'Claymore' FT25 and FT27 3 and 4 tonners, which replaced the FT21 and FT23 petrol engined models. These were the first completely new models introduced under Leyland ownership, and the Leyland influence was evident in the specification which included the new Albion EN218 engine, a four cylinder version of the Leyland 0.350, Leyland clutch and Leyland 4 speed gearbox. Otherwise the rest of the chassis followed the same lines as the petrol-engined models which they replaced, but adopted the curved dash from the Chieftain. Later FT25A and FT27A models used an Albion clutch and gearbox, but the vertical engined Claymore was always intended as a stopgap until the introduction of the underfloor version.

This FT25N 3 ton model with Croft bodywork was delivered in June 1954 to Bilsland's Bakery of Hydepark Street, Glasgow.

A 4 ton FT27N operated by Wm. Crawford and Sons Ltd. of Liverpool, with locally built body by Davidson and Co., new in October 1954.

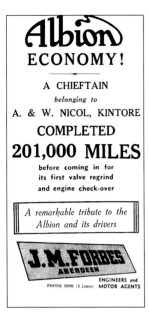

Dealer's advert, July 1954. J.M. Forbes were concessionaries for the shires of Aberdeen, Kincardine, Banff and Moray.

FT107. Introduced at the 1954 Commercial Motor Show at Earls Court was the FT107N, a lightweight six wheeler which was initially sold under the model name 'Chieftain', but was renamed 'Reiver' in 1957. It is believed that Albion sent out 'Albion Reiver' badges to early FT107 customers and invited them to change badges. Somewhat similar to the 'Clansman' FT103 of 1949, it was rated at 10 tons compared with 7½ tons of the Clansman. J.G. Barrack, an Aberdeen haulier, took delivery of this 'Chieftain' FT107N in February 1955. The haulier obviously took pride in his vehicle with the embellishments on the radiator. Note the stag's head on the radiator cap, and the radiator protector bar reminiscent of the 6 ton Model 35 of 1930. Despite being a full 10 tonner, the 4 cylinder 4.88 litre EN286 engine from lighter FT models remained standard.

FT111. The Albion 'Chieftain' FT111TR tractor unit of 1952 had a specially designed frame to take a Scammell coupling, and had an Eaton 2 speed rear axle as standard. The Eaton axle was specified because the usual overhead worm did not allow the low coupling height required for the Scammell equipment, which sat directly above the axle. Three Albion 'Chieftain' FT111TR tractor units delivered to Backhouse and Coppock Ltd. are pictured here, and the trained eye will spot the difference between the hubs of the Eaton axle on the lorry nearest the camera and the standard Albion worm driven unit. Control of the two speed axle was by means of a trigger on the gear lever, which could split any of the five gears on the main Albion gearbox. The Chieftain-Scammell tractors, and in particular later models with the 6 speed overdrive gearbox, earned a reputation as reliable mile eaters on long distance trunk haulage. In 1956 the same combination of Albion 4 cylinder oil engine, Albion 5 speed gearbox and Eaton 2 speed axle was used in an ultra low weight experimental vehicle featuring an aluminium frame, platform and cab. It was assembled by Mann Egerton at their Norwich plant in collaboration with Albion and the British Aluminium Co. Ltd.

MR5. Introduced at Earls Court in 1954 was the underfloor engined Claymore for loads of 3 and 4 tons. Fitted with the horizontal EN219 3.83 litre diesel engine, it shared all the major components of the vertical EN218 from the FT25/27, except that it had a different sump casting and repositioned ancillaries. Taking full advantage of the underfloor configuration, the extended frame dropped down ahead of the front axle allowing a three man cab to be mounted at a low position for particularly easy access. Freedom from engine noise, fumes and heat were other selling points, and the short wheelbase produced a small turning circle ideal for local deliveries in tight loading bays. An Albion 4 speed constant mesh gearbox was fitted with synchromesh on third and top, driving to the usual overhead worm axle. Only tyre equipment differentiated the MR5 and the MR7, although the MR7 was available in a longer wheelbase. On both types, non assisted Lockheed hydraulic brakes were the standard, but vacuum assistance was available as an option, vacuum being generated by the Albion throttle valve on the engine induction system.

It was unusual for Claymores with van bodies to be fitted with separate cabs because the underfloor engine arrangement was particularly suitable for 'walk through' applications. However, W.&R. Jacob specified a body built in Liverpool by the Sandon Motor and Engineering Co. on a 3 ton MR5N chassis with a Scotstoun factory fitted cab.

The Claymore was introduced in Holland in 1956, and became one of Albion's most popular chassis in that market. This early MR7L 4 tonner fitted with attractive Dutch built cab and bodywork is seen operating on furniture delivery round in the old city of Delft, just north of Rotterdam.

MR7. In 1954 when the new underfloor-engined Claymore was introduced, potato merchants W. & A. Graham had a depot at Hunter Street goods yard, Dennistoun, Glasgow, which is now the City Council Car Pound. A short distance away at the corner of Duke Street and Whitefield Street was McRae's Fruiterers and Florist, where the Albion photographer had set up this publicity shot. The potato lorry was the new MR7N 'Claymore' 4 tonner, and the EN219 3.83 litre horizontal engine is clearly visible below the platform. Most Claymores had a trap door in the platform to facilitate maintenance, but if the lorry broke down with a load on it, running repairs to items like the lift pump became almost impossible. The 4 cylinder engine followed closely the design of the 6 cylinder Leyland 0.350, and shared many of its components. It also shared a tendency to blow gaskets due to the use of only 4 studs per cylinder compared to the Albion practice of surrounding the cylinder with 6 slightly smaller diameter studs. The problem was largely resolved with the fitment of a modified gasket, but the engine was never as reliable as the other 4 cylinder unit, the EN286, which was entirely of Albion design. Today the scene is largely unchanged, although the fruit shop closed in the late 1970s and the concrete telephone kiosks are now modern BT units.

MLH3. In 1955 another underfloor engined chassis was introduced, the short lived MLH3 'Cairn' for payloads of 30 to 35 cwts. The mechanical specification was similar to that of the Claymore, except that lighter axles with 6 stud wheels were fitted, the rear axle was an Albion spiral bevel unit and not the usual worm drive arrangement. SGA 572 was one of a batch of 10 Cairns delivered to Glasgow Corporation Education Department in 1956 with Bennett bodywork, joining a large fleet of long lived small Albion buses owned by the authority. It lasted well into the 1970s.

MR9. In November 1955 at the Scottish Motor Show at Kelvin Hall, Glasgow, the line up of small underfloor engined chassis was complete with the introduction of the MR9 'Nimbus'. The design of the Nimbus followed closely that of the Claymore, sharing the identical wheelbase of 11 feet 10 inches of the longer Claymore, but with a wider frame and axles to give an overall width of 8 feet. Other departures from the Claymore were heavier duty rear axles with wider brake shoes, hydraulic shock absorbers front and rear, longer and wider springs, and a sloping radiator to give adequate ground clearance without having to raise the floor. The Nimbus was designed expressly for routes of low traffic density and feeder services, but when it inevitably found itself deputising for larger buses on heavier duties, the lightweight components were found wanting and reliability problems set in. Two buses were shown at the Scottish Show, including this Alexander bodied demonstrator which was tested by Scottish Omnibuses, and which appeared in their livery.

MR11. A big brother for the Nimbus appeared at the Scottish Motor Show in 1957 in the shape of the Aberdonian MR11 which shared many of the design features of the smaller MR9 Nimbus, but in a chassis designed for 30 feet by 8 feet bodywork. Much was made of the lightweight design, performance and fuel economy of the new chassis, these being the same slogans which had been the main selling points of the Nimbus. Documents at the Albion Archive at Biggar indicate that the model was initially called the 'Nimbus-Six' in the period up until launch. The 'Six' referred to the Leyland O.350 six cylinder engine, which drove through an Albion 5 speed gearbox to an overhead worm rear axle, the whole package proving to be slightly underpowered when carrying a full load. The Chieftain clutch was also found to be wanting in this application and a larger Leyland unit was substituted in later production runs.

An early example with lightweight MCW bodywork was this MR11, operated by the North Western Road Car Co. of Stockport, and which is seen on a service between Heath Grove and Buxton in 1957.

Charlie's Cars of Bournemouth was a loyal Albion customer for many years and sent this new Aberdonian to the 1958 British Coach Rally at Brighton in the summer of that year. Coachwork was by Harrington of Hove, and the combination must have been successful as several more were purchased in succeeding years.

WD66. In April 1951 Albion took over design of the FV1300 military vehicle project from Vauxhall, which resulted in an order for 6000 vehicles being obtained from the Ministry of Supply in June 1951. Despite special machines being installed at Yoker to build the vehicles, the order was cancelled in May 1953. However, it was replaced with a new contract, the FV14001, or Model WD66 as it was known at Scotstoun, which became the company's last foray into military vehicle production. It was a semi-forward control 6x6 truck similar to the FT15 of ten years earlier, but with the Rolls Royce B80 Mk.5Q 8 cylinder petrol engine from the FV1300 with the Leyland 0.350 as an alternative. The letters WD were usually used as a prefix to the usual two letter coding, to denote 'War Department', but this was the first time that the letters were used on their own, at least since the 1930s. In fact 'WD' fitted the Albion system where the prefix type letters were based on the first and last letters of the alphabet, so it was reasonable to reserve this coding for a military vehicle. This is one of only nine chassis built, and was delivered to the Ministry of Supply in December 1956.

PF107. The 'Reiver' name was introduced on the FT107 in 1956, and around the same time two new engines were offered in both the Reiver and Clydesdale. The EN286 had grown from 4.88 to 5.47 litres and became the EN287, and as a portent of what was to become standard in later years, the Leyland 0.350 six cylinder 5.76 litre oil engine was also offered. However, Leyland-engined Reivers and Clydesdales were given the new code letters PF, and this is a 'Reiver' PF107L, delivered to Saddlers Transport of Edinburgh in the summer of 1957. Although the Albion five speed gearbox remained standard, 1956 also saw the introduction of the Albion six speed gearbox for all models in the FT/PF range, which increased top speed by 30%, and also effected a useful saving in fuel. This was all for an additional cost of on the chassis price of less than £30.

PF108. Albion largely dropped out of the bonneted truck market after September 1952, but such a model was created by Albatros Automobiel Maatschappij N.V. of Amsterdam, who, from around 1950, imported components in packing cases and produced a number of models which were not available in the UK or elsewhere. The bonneted 6x4 Reiver, which could best be described as a PF108, was a good example. Two locally assembled 'PF108T' tippers are shown here in the service of C.M. Meurs, Haulage Contractors, Kerkrade, Holland, carrying loads of sand. Tipping gear and bodywork were also supplied locally. Also built by Albatros was an overtype Reiver with the front axle moved back to provide a step ahead of the front axle for easy access, an arrangement which pre-dated the LAD cabbed Reiver by two or three years.

24C/1. Announced at the 1957 Scottish Show for the home market only was the Caledonian 8 wheeler, another lightweight chassis, which had a high content of Leyland parts. Behind a Leyland radiator was the Leyland 0.600 engine and Leyland 5 speed gearbox, and an optional Leyland Octopus style cab was also specified. The rest of the chassis was, however, very similar to the HD57 which had ceased production 3 years earlier. Twin Albion overhead worm axles were fitted and, as on the HD, only the three rearmost axles were braked, four axle braking appearing later on. The weight saving came from the use of special steels and light alloys, the low unladen weight allowing a greater payload. The chassis designation 24C/1 did not fit in with normal Albion practice, but was actually a designation borrowed from the Leyland truck range.

This is a 1958 example owned by McKelvie of Barrhead, whose Managing Director, Jim McKelvie, set up Ailsa Trucks, the original importer of Volvo commercial vehicles to Britain.

To further increase the attractiveness of the lightweight Caledonian, Holmes of Preston made the 'Homalloy' glass fibre cab and 'Homalloy' light alloy platform on this 1958 demonstrator. This kept the overall weight of the vehicle down to 6 tons 16 cwt, and allowed a payload of about 17 tons, despite being equipped with optional power steering and third differential. This particular vehicle was a demonstrator at the 1958 Earls Court Motor Show.

24C/3. Six months after the launch of the haulage model came the Caledonian 24C/3T, a tipper version with a shorter wheelbase and chassis strengthened by the use of continuous flitch plates running the full length of the frame. A larger fuel tank and repositioned spare wheel and batteries were the only other differences from the haulage version. Caledon, a haulier based at Broxburn near Edinburgh, had a livery which was obviously based on other Leylands in the fleet with their distinctive cab mouldings, although the Albion version of this cab did not have these extrusions. This cab was designed and built by Leyland, originally in the late 1940s, and was rigidly bolted to the chassis frame. In typical Albion practice the chassis frame was also bolted, unlike the Octopus, which was riveted. In appearance and specification the Albion Caledonian was obviously very similar to the Leyland Octopus, but the Caledonian appeared to have a reputation as a better handling machine than the Octopus.

FT39K. Among the last FT Victors to be built was this FT39KAN, one of 25 supplied to Jersey Motor Transport seen here being loaded for shipment at Portsmouth in April 1958. With 35 seat bodywork by Reading of Portsmouth, the Victor joined a large fleet of similar vehicles already in service on Jersey at that time. The 'K' suffix models had the larger EN287 engine of 5.5 litres capacity and heavier duty front springs.

HD175. Having spent the years since the Leyland takeover producing lightweight vehicles mostly in lower payload sectors, there appeared in 1958 a passenger chassis which broke all records at the other end of the spectrum. The vehicle in question was the mighty 15.2 litre engined 'Royal Scot' HD175, which took to the road for South African Railways in 1958. The very large engine was a horizontal version of the recently introduced Leyland-Albion EN900 oil engine, driving through a ZF AK6 six speed gearbox to twin overhead worm rear axles with no third differential. A concealed front mounted radiator was fitted and power steering was standard. In terms of engine capacity the Royal Scot was the largest bus chassis ever built by a British manufacturer, and has not, nor is it ever likely to be, contested in terms of engine size. The EN900 engine was built at Scotstoun to a basic Leyland design, but with input from both Albion and Leyland engineers. No other Albion chassis was fitted with the engine, although it was used in vertical form in the Scammell Super Constructor and Leyland Buffalo. A total of 20 chassis was made and they lasted in service for about 10 years, which was a long life in that territory. The model name 'Royal Scot' was incorporated into the Albion badge which can be seen above the radiator.

Seen at Queens Dock on the Clyde is the first complete HD 175 chassis to be sent to South Africa, being prepared to be craned aboard the *Tregenna*. Temporary wheels are being fitted for the voyage. A prewar CX3 heads a line up of CX lorries owned by a Paisley contractor about to offload frames and crates which contained a further eight Royal Scot chassis in completely knocked down (ckd) form.

Chapter 8
The Rise and Fall of the Leyland-Albions 1958 to 1980

The traditional Albion radiator disappeared in 1958 with the arrival of the LAD cab, which Motor Panels supplied to Leyland, Albion and Dodge. The Albion version incorporated a number of Scotstoun design features, the most important of which was the access step forward of the front axle, which was not provided on contemporary Leyland and Dodge variants. Albion engineers considered that easy entry to the cab for short haul work and local deliveries was a necessary requirement for the sector of the market in which Albion operated, and it appeared that the Lancashire management took some convincing of this. However the most significant engineering innovation in the new range was the use of a new spiral bevel hub reduction rear axle in place of the long-lived worm axle, making broken half shafts a thing of the past. The new axle was installed in the Chieftain, Clydesdale and Reiver models which were

immediately popular and became the mainstay of the factory until the end of chassis production. Some worm axle models did live on, in chassis like the Aberdonian bus and Caledonian 8 wheel truck. These were both lightweight versions of equivalent Leyland products introduced in 1957, which were to have relatively short life spans.

Stanley Markland, a Leyland director since 1946 and an Albion director for only six months, had replaced Hugh Fulton as Managing Director in 1957, and Sir Henry Spurrier took over as Chairman on the death of Sir Jackson Millar the following year. With Donald Stokes also in place on the Albion board, all links with the founders had gone, and day to day control was now in the hands of men who had not been brought up in the Albion tradition. New markets were found, but increasingly Albions supplied to these markets were badged as Leylands, the first known examples being a batch of Clydesdale buses delivered to Jordan in 1960. Leyland engines were increasingly offered in place of Albion engines, continuing a trend which would eventually lead to the end of engine production in 1967.

During this period new bus models were launched, these being the Lowlander, Clydesdale, Victor VTs, and Viking VKs, which were either variations of Leyland bus designs (The Lowlander) or adaptations of the Albion truck range (Clydesdale, Victor and Viking.) Significant sales to a relatively small number of customers were achieved, but

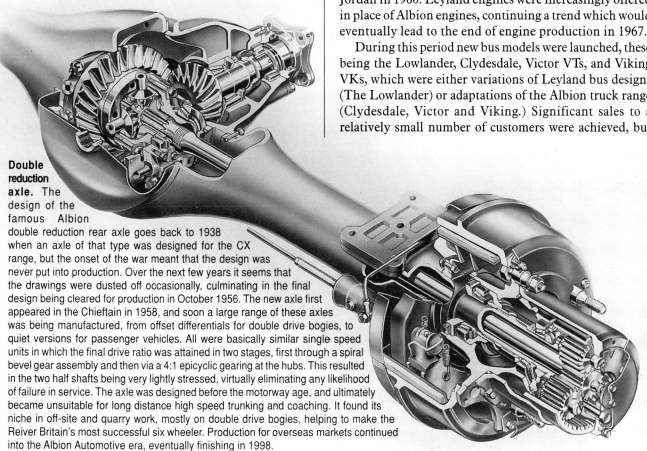

Double reduction axle. The design of the famous Albion double reduction rear axle goes back to 1938 when an axle of that type was designed for the CX range, but the onset of the war meant that the design was never put into production. Over the next few years it seems that the drawings were dusted off occasionally, culminating in the final design being cleared for production in October 1956. The new axle first appeared in the Chieftain in 1958, and soon a large range of these axles was being manufactured, from offset differentials for double drive bogies, to quiet versions for passenger vehicles. All were basically similar single speed units in which the final drive ratio was attained in two stages, first through a spiral bevel gear assembly and then via a 4:1 epicyclic gearing at the hubs. This resulted in the two half shafts being very lightly stressed, virtually eliminating any likelihood of failure in service. The axle was designed before the motorway age, and ultimately became unsuitable for long distance high speed trunking and coaching. It found its niche in off-site and quarry work, mostly on double drive bogies, helping to make the Reiver Britain's most successful six wheeler. Production for overseas markets continued into the Albion Automotive era, eventually finishing in 1998.

the home market for these types had virtually dried up by 1968. However, Albion was still a main player in overseas bus markets, and the Viking and Clydesdale models went on to sell very well in both Australia and Africa.

In 1961 expansion continued under new General Manager A. Craig Macdonald with the purchase of additional adjoining premises. Then in 1969 the former Harland and Wolff premises were acquired, these becoming the South Works and the only buildings now occupied by Albion Automotive at Scotstoun today. But perhaps the most important occasion in those boom years was the opening of a new £2 million extension on 15th February 1966 by Princess Margaret. This new assembly shop was equipped with a conveyor 750 yards long, which was said to be the longest of its kind in Europe.

With these improvements production reached a peak of 7,463 chassis in 1970, but by this time Albion was only one of eight commercial vehicle manufacturers in the new British Leyland Motor Corporation, formed two years earlier. It had lost its limited liability status the same year, and was to lose its identity soon afterwards. No record of when the last Albion came down the conveyor at Scotstoun has been kept, but it is believed to have been towards the end of 1972. From then on Chieftains, Clydesdales and Reivers were badged as Leylands using the G-range cab manufactured at Bathgate, and Vikings and Clydesdale buses were marketed as Leylands in overseas markets. Eight years later, chassis production was moved entirely to Bathgate, leaving the Scotstoun factory as a transmission specialist, which it still is today. ❏

CH3. In addition to the new hub reduction axle, the new CH3 'Chieftain' 7 ton lorry incorporated a revised 4 cylinder 5.5 litre engine, now renamed EN289, which produced more power and better fuel consumption. This was done by employing a higher compression ratio, modified inlet ports and the use of 3 hole injectors. A large oil bath air cleaner, and pneumatic governor were other features of the new engine, which was derated from 100 to 90hp in the CH3. An Albion 5 or 6 speed constant mesh gearbox and Clayton Dewandre vacuum assisted Girling hydraulic brakes completed the specification. This is a 1959 CH3T with 5½ cubic yard end tipping body which was supplied with the new Motor Panels LAD cab minus the optional front bumper.

CD21. The new Clydesdale for 1958 was designated CD21, and could still be differentiated from the Chieftain by the use of 10 stud wheels. Albion engines were no longer available in the Clydesdale, and the Leyland 0.375 of 6.17 litres capacity was now the only engine offered. A new version of the five or six speed constant mesh gearbox was used, taking drive to the hub reduction axle, and air pressure brakes completed the specification. By June 1959 eleven models were offered in the Clydesdale range, which included eight haulage and two tipper models, all available in varying wheelbases, and in widths of 7' 6" or 8'. The exception was the CD21TR tractor unit, the only model available in one width and wheelbase. This is a later CD21ATR, which was approximately 4 years old when it was given the job of hauling this ten ton 70 feet long crane track girder. The detachable rear axle of a King Low Load trailer was fixed to the girder, and the unit was owned by Sheffield contractor Frank Phillips.

CD23. A new bus chassis for export only was the CD23 'Clydesdale' introduced in 1960. Two models were available, the CD23NW and the CD23LW, for normal and long wheelbases. They differed from the haulage model only in wheelbase, load capacity, fuel tank size, and electrical equipment. Seen here in 1967 is a Clydesdale in the service of East African Railways and Harbours, and standing in front of the vehicle is Mr David More, then Head of the Experimental Department at Scotstoun on a visit to Africa to look at operating conditions there. He noted that this well used CD23 was fitted with an unusual radiator overflow outlet which discharged just above the accelerator pedal. If the engine overheated, very hot water would pour on to the driver's right foot. The drivers normally wore sandals and presumably this arrangement was intended to ensure that the vehicle was brought to an immediate halt if the engine overheated! The Clydesdale bus earned a reputation as a

rugged and reliable vehicle with good ground clearance, making it very suitable for operation over unmade roads. It became a big seller, especially in African markets, and developed into a whole range of models with decreasing Scotstoun content, where the engines, gearboxes and rear axles were all bought in.

VT15. The FT39 'Victor', of which some two thousand were built, was replaced in 1958 by two new models, the Albion-engined VT15 and Leyland-engined VT17, also called Victors. The new models followed the same principles of uncomplicated design, the straight frame incorporating the revised EN289 engine, new 5 or 6 speed constant mesh gearbox, and of course, the new spiral bevel hub reduction rear axle.

Here in 1959 is seen a new VT15N delivered to Sarrendar Coach Service of Southern Rhodesia, with a 45 seat bus body built by St. Andrews Coach Builders of Salisbury, who fitted the Leyland Comet style front grill.

The VT15L was designed for bodywork lengths of up to approximately 30 feet, being some 3 feet longer than the VT15N, and this is one delivered to the Foh Hup Bus Company of Kuala Lumpur around the same time. The exposed radiator was not available on the VT15 and this was a dummy radiator supplied by Albion and fitted by the bodybuilder.

VT17/VT23. Chapel End Coaches of Nuneaton operated this 'Victor' VT17L with a Yeates 'Europa' 41 seat coach body new in 1960. It had a Leyland 0.350 engine, Albion 5 speed gearbox and hub reduction axle, but despite this popular specification very few others appear to have made it into the fickle private coach market in Britain. Its replacement, the VT21L did have some success 3 years later with immediate delivery and the substitution of the hub reduction axle for a bought in unit.

For an express service between Kuala Lumpur and Singapore, this 'Victor' VT17L was delivered to Law & Co. of Kuala Lumpur with a coach body built by Lee Kiat Seng Ltd. It featured a full size wash room and toilet, air conditioning and public address system. The Victor on the right has not been identified, but it may be a VT23L model, which had the same specification as the VT17, except that the front axle was set back 14 inches. This allowed the bodybuilder to construct an entrance ahead of the front axle if the customer so desired.

VT19. The Victor VT Range was completed with the addition of two chassis for pantechnicon work or for carrying other loads of a light and bulky nature. They were designated the VT19N and the VT19N(HD), and had wheelbases of 15 feet 6 inches, 2 feet longer than the longest Chieftain. Typical of these duties is SBU 635, a VT19N 1,340 cubic feet pantechnicon for a Lancashire school furniture manufacturer, and NAG 328, a VT19N(HD) for Johnnie Walker Scotch Whisky. HD stood for heavy duty and this chassis incorporated a larger frame section and heavier tyres. The new LAD cab was not standard equipment on the VT range, and the Whisky lorry is fitted with a Homalloy GRP cab which incorporated a step ahead of the front axle as on the LAD cab. NAG 328 survives today and is owned by Ayrshire motor trader Frank MacDougall.

CL3/CL5. The outgoing MR Claymores had failed to make a profit for the company, because a poor reputation for reliablity had resulted in uneconomic volumes. The new CL range, introduced in 1958, incorporated a number of modifications and improvements which were designed to address these problems. The 3.83 litre engine was improved and enlarged to 4.1 litres and renamed EN250H (250 cu.in. capacity), but, more importantly, all the other major components were outsourced in a bid to reduce costs. A David Brown 440/1 four speed gearbox was introduced in place of the Albion unit, and Austin 5 ton axles, front and rear, were employed, the latter being of the spiral bevel type in place of the overhead worm unit. The Albion automatic induction manifold valve provided vacuum for the Lockheed hydraulic brakes, and the platform or body height was reduced by 1½ inches by the use of flatter springs. There were two models in various wheelbases, the CL3 5 tonner and the CL5 4 tonner.

This is a 'Claymore' CL5N with a body by Plested and Son, Uxbridge, which entered service with Callard and Bowser Ltd., who had a fleet of 18 vehicles, sixteen of which were Albions.

For heavier work the CL3 5 tonner could be specified, which may only have differed from the CL5 in tyre and wheel specification. This example was owned by William Sprott Ltd., a coal and fuel oil merchant who had a depot at Partick, Glasgow, about 2 miles from the Albion factory. Motors Panels supplied the factory fitted cab, which was still an option on the Claymore, unlike the new Chieftain, Clydesdale and Reiver where the Motors Panels cab was standard with an allowance for non supply.

NS3. To accompany the new range of Claymores came a new Nimbus model, the NS3, also in 1958. Like the new Claymore, Austin axles front and rear were specified, as was the David Brown gearbox. The larger EN250 engine continued to produce excellent fuel consumption returns, and many, though not all, of the operators' grumbles had been sorted out. Seen here when new in 1960 is a NS3N in the Lawson fleet, by then a subsidiary of W. Alexander and Sons, waiting at Glasgow's Dundas Street bus station to depart on a tour. Joining nine older MR9s, it was one of a fleet of 10 with unusual Alexander bodies, with front and rear styling which took full advantage of that Scottish bodybuilder's enthusiasm for moulded GRP panels. One of these vehicles has so far managed to escape the breaker's torch.

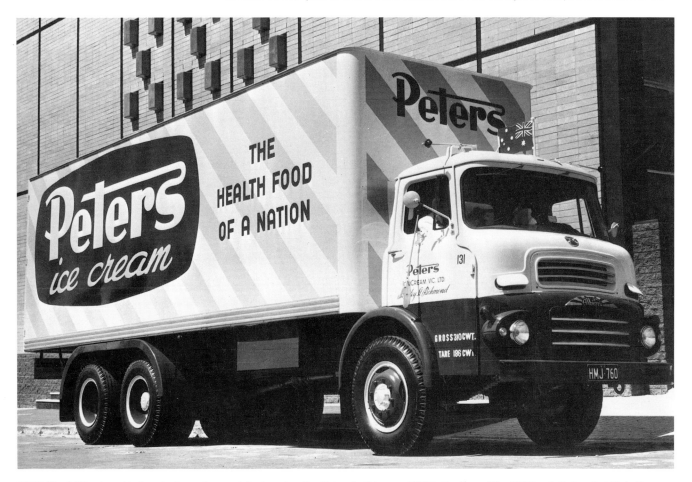

RE27. The LAD cab and hub reduction axle were introduced on the Reiver in February 1959 in the form of the RE27, a 6x2 chassis with trailing rear axle and larger Leyland 0.375 engine. The specification was otherwise similar to the CD21 'Clydesdale' introduced the previous year except that the Reiver used eight stud wheel fixings on the front axle. Delivered in the early 1960s to Peters Ice Cream of Victoria, this was an RE27AL model which had, unsurprisingly, a refrigerated body. Note the hand operated semaphore indicator often used on Australian vehicles at this time.

RE25. By May 1959 the RE25, the 6x4 version of the Reiver was ready, and this RE25T supplied to W.H. Jakeway and Son, a Somerset operator in June/July 1959, was one of the first ones built. In tipper form the Reiver quickly gained a reputation among contractors and quarrymasters as a dependable and useful workhorse which was equally at home on or off-road. Much of this reputation as an off-roader was due to the Albion designed non-reactive suspension on the rear bogie, where a system of bell crank levers and tension rods linked the rear ends of the springs between each rear axle, thereby equalising the forces at these locations at all times. This entirely eliminated the tendency for one of the axles to lift off the ground under full power, braking, or while negotiating difficult tractive conditions.

Another novel feature of the double drive chassis was the way the drive was transmitted to the rear bogie. Since the design of the spiral bevel axle does not permit the propeller shaft to pass straight through the bevel drive unit, the drive from the five or six speed constant mesh gearbox was transmitted to a relay gearbox which is seen situated midway in the chassis. From there the drive was split in two, one output shaft coupled directly to the leading axle of the bogie with the differential offset to the offside. The other shaft, which turned in the opposite direction, passed through the casing of the leading axle as shown to the rearmost axle, which had a differential offset to the opposite side. The relay gearbox could also house a lockable third differential which prevented inter-axle speed variations when cornering, and thereby eliminated mechanical overstressing of the axles and excessive tyre wear. The third differential could be locked by the driver from an air pressure control on the steering column, which would then allow the truck to negotiate site conditions with the minimum of wheel spin.

CH7TR. The full line up of LAD cabbed models was completed in 1960 when the CH7TR 'Chieftain-Scammell' articulated chassis made its appearance and was introduced at a price £40 cheaper than the FT111KTR which it replaced.

This 1960 example hauled a semi-trailer by Carrimore Six Wheelers Ltd., and could accommodate two Riley 4/68 saloons on the top and three on the bottom.

If York 5th wheel coupling gear was required, then the 'Chieftain' CH3 tipper chassis would require to be specified. This heavily loaded CH3AT tractor with Hands semi trailer was owned by timber merchants Hollis Brothers and is seen on the southbound approach to the Blackwall tunnel in East London in June 1962 before the second tunnel was opened.

24C/5. One of the largest orders for the Caledonian came in 1960 from Shell-Mex and BP Ltd. who ordered a batch with 4,000 gallon tanks by Alfred Miles Ltd. of Gloucester. These were 24C/5 models which had Leyland 0.680 engines and a front bogie which was set back to allow an easy entrance cab to be fitted. This meant that the standard Leyland Octopus cab was unsuitable, and the cab order also went to Alfred Miles, with at least one other being supplied by Duramin. Like the tank, the Miles cab was also of lightweight construction, and the forward sloping windscreen design proved to be troublesome after long service. The large cab doors opening forward on the sloping screen pillars created unusual stresses, which, combined with road shocks and general movement of

the vehicle, caused cracks to appear in a number of places. The structure deformed easily, the windscreen glass and surrounds parted company and accident repairs were difficult, all of which led to a number of modifications and rebuilds. One problem which was not resolved was that of reflections at night from the instrument panel on to the sloping windscreen. After retirement, however, the non-rusting cabs found favour with showmen, and many of these Caledonians had extended lives with tanks replaced by a variety of different large capacity bodies. One example survives today in Glasgow. A lightweight Leyland Octopus was announced at the 1962 Earls Court Show, which effectively replaced the Caledonian, and with it the last of the Albion worm drive axles.

CH3A. The date is April 1960 and the first Albion to be purchased by an American operator, at least during Leyland ownership, is handed over to Yale Express Systems Inc. by Mr Robert Hilton (with hat) of Leyland Motors (USA) in a ceremony which included the British Deputy Consul General. The 'Chieftain' CH3AL was fitted with the 5.5 litre Albion EN335 four cylinder oil engine. This was an upgraded EN289 renamed to bring it into line with Leyland nomenclature where the number referred to the cubic capacity in inches, and was the final development of Albion's own EN286 which dated from the 1940s. Among the improvements of the EN335 were a nitrided crankshaft with strip bearings, rearranged auxiliaries, a new fuel pump and a paper air cleaner filter element. Yale was said to be interested in the Chieftain because there were no competitive small and medium range trucks with diesel engines available on the American domestic market. For the USA, 12 volt lighting, cold starting equipment, and semi-tropical cooling were provided. It is believed that only one or two were sold, which did not lead to any significant new orders in America.

CL3A/CL5A. More changes were made to the CL range of Claymores in September 1960, the most important of which was the dropping of the David Brown 4 speed gearbox in favour of the Albion 5 or 6 speed box, although heavier Austin axles were retained. Holmes of Preston built the unusual body on this CL5AN delivered to the Midlands Electricity Board in 1963. The hydraulic platform was made by Simons Engineering, a new feature which was said to reduce time to access lamp standard fittings over conventional tower wagons. They were proved right, because today the tower wagon is virtually extinct. However, the underfloor engine in a lorry or van did not catch on in the same way. It was more successful than its only rival, the similar Dennis Stork, but like the Nimbus, operators claimed that it was never fully developed. Although the Claymore was entirely suitable for unusual applications such as the one shown, or in its more usual role as a local delivery vehicle with its low uncluttered crew cab, the maintenance departments did not like them. The Claymore ceased production in 1965 without replacement and no other manufacturer has dabbled with underfloor engined lorries since. A 'Budgie' scale model was produced based on the vehicle shown.

NS3A. The NS3A 'Nimbus' incorporated similar modifications as the 'A' suffixed Claymores with the Albion five or six speed gearbox replacing the David Brown unit from around September 1960. However, the improvements in the Nimbus did not appear to go far enough as the lightweight chassis could not stand up to the rigours of the stop-start life of a stage service bus. Halifax Corporation operated ten of these Weymann bodied NS3ANs on one man operated services in and out of the city, but reliability problems saw them sold off after only three years. Here, one of the batch, RJX 259, is seen on the road between North Berwick and Dunbar in May 1966, having been sold to Wiles of Port Seton, an East of Scotland operator. Wiles appeared to have more success with Nimbuses on the type of rural operations for which the bus was designed.

LR1/LR3/LR7. Albion announced its return to the double deck bus market in October 1961 when the Lowlander was introduced to the Albion range with three models, the LR1, LR3, and LR7. However, the Lowlander was very much an Albion in name only, as the 0.600 engine, radiator, hydraulic coupling, manual or semi-automatic gearbox, front axle, special drop centre double reduction rear axle and twin fuel tanks were all of Leyland manufacture. Indeed, apart from the first four chassis, all Lowlanders were supplied in ckd form from Leyland and were only assembled at Scotstoun.

From the fibre glass front to the rear of the front springs the Lowlander was almost identical to the Leyland Titan, except that the driving position was some 3 inches lower. Having said all that, there was considerable input by Albion engineers in the rest of the chassis design, which from the bulkhead back was quite different from the Titan, and all the testing was done at Scotstoun. The LR1 had the semi-automatic gearbox, which Leyland called 'Pneumo-cyclic', while the LR3 and 7 had a clutch and 4 speed synchromesh gearbox, the LR7 having air suspension on the rear axle.

UCS 616, a 1963 LR1 with Northern Counties body is seen in service with Alexander (Fife), who acquired it from Western SMT in 1966. It was scrapped in 1978.

7091 HJ was an LR7 with Alexander bodywork, which was new to Southend Corporation Transport in March 1963, and is seen 6 months later at Pier Hill. Lowlanders delivered to English operators were badged and licensed as Leylands, although they retained the Saltire oval plate on the radiator filler cap cover.

Seen outside the factory in 1961 is a prototype LR1, which illustrates the complexity of the frame which was basically the same on all models. The manual or semi-automatic gearbox was positioned amidships in the chassis and well to the nearside to provide a very low central aisle between the seats. To further provide for an uncluttered low floor, an Albion step down gearbox situated at the rear of the engine dropped the propeller shaft to a low position on the nearside of the chassis. Sir Henry Spurrier, by then Chairman of Albion, drove one of the first prototypes (perhaps the chassis shown) for a short run during its first day on the road. He criticised the progression of the brakes at light pedal pressure, which resulted in modifications to the Westinghouse braking system on production models.

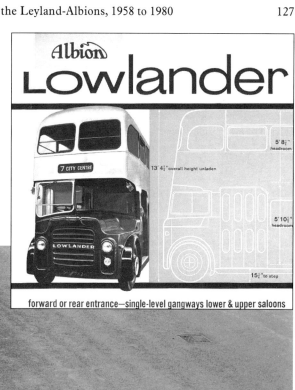

From 1959 the LAD cab became available in front scuttle form only, with or without windscreen, primarily for use with van bodies. However the CWS elected to have their own cab constructed behind an LAD front scuttle for this milk lorry in 1959.

RE29. In September 1961 came the 'Super Reiver' RE29, a heavier duty version of the RE25, with heavier rear springs and axles, chassis frame reinforced with flitch plates, air brakes replacing hydraulics, and lighter steering despite its greater weight. The Leyland 0.400 engine was fitted, having become standard in the Reiver and Clydesdale the previous year. With these improvements the Reiver range became the best selling 6 wheeler chassis in Britain, a dominant position which it held for as long as the Reiver was built at Scotstoun. It was also a very popular chassis in Australia, and J.C. Turner, a Sydney owner-operator, ran this RE29T concrete mixer on contract to Pioneer Ready Mix Concrete. It had the 125hp Leyland 0.400 'Power Plus' engine, and a six speed overdrive gearbox. The equivalent 6x2 model was called the RE31, and the two new models were complementary to existing RE25 and 27 range.

1958 Advertisement. Watts (Factors) Ltd. was an associate company of Red & White, the Welsh bus company which was sold to the British Transport Commission in 1950.

CH13/17. A new £750,000 axle and gearbox facility opened at Scotstoun in early 1963 which had the capability of producing 400 gearboxes a week to cope with chassis production which was twice the 1958 figure. However, gearbox production may have been booming, but the introduction of the Leyland 0.370 six cylinder engine in the Chieftain in April 1962 spelled the beginning of the end for engine production at Scotstoun. At the time three types of engine were being manufactured at Scotstoun, the Claymore's EN250, the Chieftain's EN335, and the big EN900 mostly for railcars and marine use. The Leyland engined Chieftain was called the Chieftain 'Super Six' and there were two basic models, the tipper/haulage CH13, and the CH17 tractor unit. Supplied to Hoveringham in January 1963 was this CH13AT with Edbro tipping gear and substantial 9 cubic yard body. Hoveringham Gravels Ltd. of Nottingham ran a large fleet of tippers which also included many Reivers.

CH13 Fire Chief. The Albion 'Fire Chief', produced in conjunction with Carmichaels of Worcester, was a special version of the CH13 chassis announced in 1964, which differed from the standard chassis in a number of details. Most importantly, the Leyland 0.400S 'power plus' engine, as used in the Clydesdale, was fitted giving an increase in power of 13.6% over the standard unit. Then, between the engine and gearbox a Carmichael power take off was situated, which, on water tender appliances, drove a rear mounted centrifugal pump. Finally, the chassis frame was strengthened with long flitch plates in the form of an inverted 'L', and the suspension was modified with longer springs and telescopic shock absorbers front and rear. Outstanding performance was said to be obtained, and if the highest ratio axle was chosen with the six speed overdrive gearbox, a speed of 67mph was possible. Two wheelbases were available, 3.62m on the CH13AL and 4.08m on the CH13AXL. The vehicle shown was delivered to Derby Fire Brigade in 1965.

VT21. In the late 1940s and early 1950s Albion had some success in the private coach market by making CX39 and FT39 chassis or complete vehicles available for immediate delivery. So in 1963 Albion re-entered this market with the new 'Victor' VT21L, available immediately with Duple Firefly or Plaxton Embassy bodies. As with the rest of the VT range, a basically straight framed chassis with vertical Leyland 0.370 engine and Albion 5 or 6 speed gearbox was standard, but an Eaton single speed rear axle was specified in place of the Albion hub reduction unit.

Climbing a hill in Lanarkshire in 1963 is 825 FVA, an example of the more popular Duple Firefly coachwork, which was owned by Hutchison of Overtown until 1966.

Sold in fewer numbers were the Plaxton variants, and 'Embassy III' coachwork is fitted to 948 JWD, new to Ardenvale Tours of Warwickshire in 1964, and seen in the grounds of Packwood House, near Lapworth. The VT21 was as reliable and durable as anything else in its sector, but had difficulty competing in a market increasingly dominated by mass produced Bedfords and Fords. Production ceased in 1966.

VK41/VK55. Announced at the Scottish Show in November 1963 was the vertical front-engined 'Viking' VK41 which, along with the new VT21, replaced the 'Victor' VT15 and VT17. With a straight frame broadly similar to the VT21, the VK41 differed in that the front axle was set back to accept an entrance ahead of the front axle, and that an Albion hub reduction rear axle was utilised. This was one of three VK41Ls used to transport students from their homes and hostels in Lusaka to various buildings of the University of Zambia. Bodywork was by Bus Bodies (South Africa) which seated 54. Only the Scottish Show prototype VK41 entered service in mainland Britain, although a later higher-powered version, the VK55 found considerable success in export markets. The VK55 had a Leyland 0.401 in place the 0.370, and full air pressure brakes rather than air operated hydraulic. Both models had a special version of the Albion double reduction rear axle which had specially matched gears for silent running.

CD65. In Autumn 1965 came the CD65 'Super Clydesdale' 16 ton gvw, one of two new models using the well known Leyland group Ergomatic cab made by Joseph Sankey and Sons. The Albion version of the Sankey cab was slightly more spartan than that supplied to AEC and Leyland, but items like tachometer, rear central window, additional mirrors and soundproofing could still be specified as extras. A light weight version was also available. The Albion design of the front end of the chassis to accept the Ergomatic cab was adopted by AEC and Leyland. Pictured at a Nuneaton quarrymaster's yard is this 'Super Clydesdale' CD65TW with Homalloy double dropside tipping body, which was owned by local contractors J.C. Walters. Later models CD65A and CD65B were introduced, the latter using the Leyland 0.401 engine.

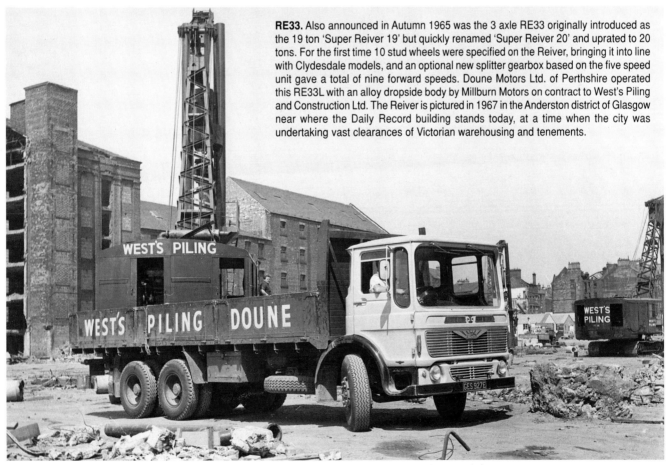

RE33. Also announced in Autumn 1965 was the 3 axle RE33 originally introduced as the 19 ton 'Super Reiver 19' but quickly renamed 'Super Reiver 20' and uprated to 20 tons. For the first time 10 stud wheels were specified on the Reiver, bringing it into line with Clydesdale models, and an optional new splitter gearbox based on the five speed unit gave a total of nine forward speeds. Doune Motors Ltd. of Perthshire operated this RE33L with an alloy dropside body by Millburn Motors on contract to West's Piling and Construction Ltd. The Reiver is pictured in 1967 in the Anderston district of Glasgow near where the Daily Record building stands today, at a time when the city was undertaking vast clearances of Victorian warehousing and tenements.

VK43. Announced at the same time was a new version of the Viking coach chassis, the VK43, a rear engined version of the VK41. The Construction and Use Regulations had recently been amended to increase the rear overhang to 60% of the wheelbase, and this allowed a vertical Leyland 0.400 engine and Albion 5 or 6 speed constant mesh gearbox to be fitted in line behind the hub reduction rear axle with the final drive taken directly to the axle by a single short shaft 1' 11" (584mm) long. The back to front rear axle had the driving head inverted to take what was normally a counterclockwise drive, which meant that when once a Chieftain axle was wrongly fitted on the assembly line a Viking chassis ended up with five reverse and one forward gear! No advantage was taken of the rear engined configuration to provide a dropped frame from the rear axle forward, but as the bus was said to be designed in collaboration with the Scottish Bus Group for work primarily on country bus services, the extra cost of this would not have been justified. The long linkage of light tubular shafts and universal joints which carried the speed change actuation from the gear lever to the gearbox proved to be somewhat troublesome in service. Also the combination of heavy clutch for psv work and constant mesh gearbox made for slow gearchanges, while the inaudible engine note when fully loaded did nothing to help the driver judge changes. On the positive side, the steering was light, the turning circle was good, and the mechanical components were well proven units mostly from the Chieftain truck range. JMS 452E is a VK43AL, new to Alexander (Midland) in 1967 with an Alexander Y-type 40 seat body, and which is now owned by the Albion Vehicle Preservation Trust.

VK49. To address some of the shortcomings of the VK43 for stage carriage work, Albion brought out the VK49 in 1969 with Leyland 'Pneumocyclic' semi-automatic gearbox. The Scottish Bus Group was adopting the growing trend towards one-man operation, and was introducing large numbers of semi-automatic buses to its fleets, accepting that the driver had enough to do without having to deal with a constant mesh gearbox as well. But the tide had turned against the Viking on the domestic market. The vehicle shown, ORS 84H, a VK49L delivered to Alexander (Northern) in June 1970, was the only VK49 to enter service on the home market. It was sold to a Shetland operator in 1981 and was scrapped in 1985. However, the VK49 did find success in Australia, which became the Viking's main market.

VK45/VL3. Later another rear engined model appeared, the VK45 for overseas markets where tropical cooling was required. This differed primarily in the position of the radiator, which was situated beside the engine to its nearside rather than in-line as on the VK43. A pusher type fan was fitted which was designed to blow, rather than draw air through the radiator. This meant that the engine could be positioned at the extreme rear of the chassis, taking up less space in the passenger compartment. For heavier duty work came the 'Valiant' VL3 in 1966, using Clydesdale axles in an otherwise similar chassis. A VL3 chassis is illustrated showing the complicated arrangement of shafts which were required for the pusher type fan.

CH71. In September 1966 the Chieftain CH71 or 'Chieftain 71' arrived, which was a 4x4 version of the Chieftain Super Six CH13C with the normal front axle replaced with a steering version of the Albion double reduction axle. The conversion work on the front axle was carried out by Scammell, who also supplied the 2 speed transfer box mounted amidships. The standard Albion 5 or 6 speed gearbox was coupled to a Leyland 0.370 engine and power steering was standard. This 1968 example was supplied to ICI with a body designed for the carriage of ammonium nitrate.

CH51. A decision had been taken by 1965 to end engine manufacture at Scotstoun, and by 1966 the only engine remaining in production which was fitted to an Albion was the 5.5 litre EN335 unit. To maintain the choice of two engines in the Chieftain range when engine production finally ended in 1967, changes to the specification of the 'Chieftain Super Six' CH13 and CH17 were announced in 1965. The 0.370 engine was replaced by the 0.400 engine in these trucks, but was then reintroduced in November 1967 in an ostensibly new model, the 'Chieftain 51'. This new model, designated CH51, effectively replaced the CH3, the last Albion-engined chassis built at Scotstoun. The last seven of a fleet of 'Chieftain 51' tractor units operated by Circle Cement Transport (a Blue Circle subsidiary) were put up for auction in Zimbabwe in 1996. One of the last, a CH51TR new in 1968, pulled a tandem axle trailer on cement deliveries, and is seen nearing the end of its 28 years of service.

CA81. The fifth and last eight wheel model emerged from Scotstoun in August 1968 in the shape of the 'Cameronian' CA81, which was effectively a Reiver with a 4th axle. Although designed for operation in Australia for use with Dumpmaster bodies of the type shown in the photograph, where extra weight was carried over the front axle, three examples did enter service in Scotland with Russell of Bathgate with bulk grain bodies. However, if the Scottish examples were anything to go by, the Leyland 0.401 six cylinder 6.54 litre diesel engine struggled to haul the 24 ton GVW vehicles.

Commercial Waste Disposal Ltd. of Melbourne operated this 1969 example, which was one of about 100 Cameronians made.

A year before the Cameronian was introduced, Hoveringham Gravels Ltd. took delivery of this 'Special Super Reiver' based on an RE29 chassis. A factory fitted second front axle of Albion manufacture was fitted, and the design may well have been the inspiration for the CA81 which appeared soon afterwards. A 12 cubic yard body by Homalloy was actuated by Edbro tipping gear.

RE129/229. The 'Super Reiver' RE229T introduced in 1969 was the production version of the RE129T prototype which appeared at Earls Court the year before. It was specially designed as a 6 cubic yard concrete mixer and was quite different from the rest of the Reiver range. First of all, the power unit was the AEC AV505 oil engine of 8.2 litres capacity, which drove through a Thornycroft 10 speed gearbox to twin Albion hub reduction axles. Also, the drive to the rear bogie on the RE229 was not the usual Reiver set up of relay box and twin propeller shaft, but was a single shaft layout where the shaft passed through the intermediate axle, immediately to the nearside of the bevel unit, and then to the rear axle. A gear housing

was provided on the front of the intermediate axle which took drive to this axle and also housed the third differential. In addition the gearbox was not of the usual splitter type, but was of the dual range type, where the range of ratios was progressive from 1st to 10th. When 5th gear was reached, the driver would depress the range change switch and return to 1st gear position, whereupon the next five ratios would be available. The modified lower front grill was required to house a hydraulic pump driven by an auxiliary drive coupling at the front of the engine crankshaft. The vehicle shown was one of a large number operated by Ready Mix Concrete and is seen in March 1975 delivering a load of concrete for the construction of the multi-storey car park adjacent to Glasgow's Buchanan Bus Station.

CD40/41 RE40/41. At the 1970 Earls Court Show the last new Albion badged designs were shown. The range shown extended to 4 models, the CD40 and RE40 featuring the Leyland 401 diesel, while the CD41 and RE41 had the turbocharged 410 engine. A Thornycroft 6 speed overdrive gearbox was fitted. A new version of the Ergomatic cab with rectangular grilles sat higher on a straight frame which was not cranked down at the front in the manner of the previous models. But the new models never went into production. The Leyland merger with BMC two years earlier meant closer ties with the Bathgate plant 35 miles to the east, and a reassessment of the model range was inevitable. The show models remained the only ones built, and the vehicle shown, a 'Clydesdale' CD41 24 ton tractor, eventually finished its days in the Albion transport fleet.

2CD4016. From 1972 until 1980 Chieftains, Clydesdales and Reivers were built as Leylands using the G-range cab manufactured at Bathgate. Pictured in June 1979 are a number of Clydesdales in both left hand drive (model E2CD4016N) and right hand drive (model 2CD4016N) form coming down the assembly conveyor which was opened in February 1966. The 750 yard long conveyor was said to be the longest of its kind in Europe, and was moved to Scammell's Watford factory when vehicle production ceased at Scotstoun in 1980. Production of Reivers and Clydesdales continued for another 4 or 5 years at Bathgate before that plant was closed down, marking the end of Albion designed vehicles. The G-range nomenclature was relatively straight forward; E stood for export; 2 meant a radical change in the basic design, CD denoted model name; 40 for naturally aspirated engine; 16 referred to gvw; and N for normal wheelbase. If a turbocharged engine was fitted the model number was 41.

2RE4124. Some long established Albion operators like Doune Motors of Perthshire did not wish to see their Scotstoun built trucks badged as Leylands and went to some trouble to remove the Leyland names and rebadge them as Albions. Around the same time operators were turning away from British Leyland products and trying out foreign makes. Flanked by two Berliets, a relatively uncommon type in Scotland which shared the same cab as the Ford Transcontinental, is GLS 870N, a 1975 G-range cabbed 'Reiver' 2RE4124AL, which was perhaps the last Scotstoun built truck to receive the Albion name. It was the last of twelve Reivers operated by the company since 1960, none of which ever had an axle failure. GLS 870N was scrapped in 1989.

Chapter 9
Back in the Driving Seat Completing the Century

The loss of chassis production in June 1980, followed by gearbox manufacture in 1984, was a considerable blow to the Scotstoun workforce, but by way of compensation Albion gained Bathgate axle production before that plant closed in 1986. Other axle production was transferred from another subsidiary, Alford and Alder, and also from the doomed Guy plant at Wolverhampton soon after. Another significant event occurred in 1987 when the North Works closed. This was the original Scotstoun site where Albion had started making cars and commercials in 1903 and was

by far Scotland's longest lived motor manufacturing site. This left only the South Works supplying axles to Leyland Trucks Ltd.

By now virtually all the companies which Leyland had swallowed up during its years of acquisitions had been closed down, leaving only Albion as the sole survivor of the once famous roll-call of British commercial vehicle manufacturers taken over by Leyland. Since the acquisition of Albion in 1951, Leyland had in the space of 35 years absorbed almost all of the indigenous commercial

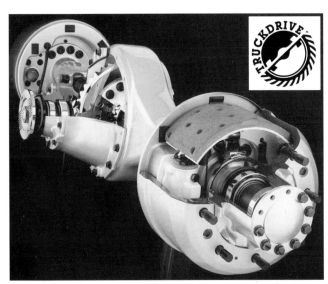

Albion Automotive logo. Albion Automotive is now part of the American Axle and Manufacturing group (AAM).

One of the first results of the company's investment in people and facilities was 'Truckdrive', a new family of light to medium commercial vehicle front and rear axles launched in 1995.

The new DAF 55, made at Leyland, incorporates the new 'Truckdrive' axles. Leyland, like DAF and Foden, is now part of the American Paccar group.

For the heavy range like this DAF 85 eight wheeler, Albion axle components are supplied to DAF in Holland where they are fitted into axle casings supplied by others. An Albion crankshaft made at the Spurrier Plant is also fitted.

vehicle manufacturers in Britain only to see them close one by one; now events had gone full circle – only Leyland and Albion remained.

Despite this savage reduction in size, the hoped for recovery did not come. Commercial vehicle sales were still in the doldrums, and there appeared to be little prospect of Leyland returning to profitability in the near future. Ultimately, in February 1987, Dutch commercial vehicle manufacturer DAF acquired what remained of the Leyland truck empire, including, of course, the Albion plant. But

the security which this merger had promised was short lived as Leyland DAF went into receivership in February 1993 putting the continued existence of the Albion plant in severe doubt.

As things worked out, the collapse of Leyland DAF proved to be Scotstoun's salvation, as it transpired that the parent company had planned to close Albion in 1993 as part of its survival plan. A consortium of names from the industry entered into negotiations with the receiver, which eventually resulted in a management buy-in plan succeeding in November 1993. A new company was born, Albion Automotive, and in a reversal of events of 3 decades earlier, a former Leyland plant fell under Scotstoun control. The Spurrier works at Leyland, which manufactured chassis components and crankshafts, had not found an owner, and was included in the deal. It was certainly ironic that Albion should take over the plant named after the architect of the original takeover of Albion by Leyland, Sir Henry Spurrier.

The revival was now under way. Soon all the Leyland DAF nameplates were removed from the Scotstoun plant and the famous Albion sunrise script was back in place

LDV also fit Albion axles. As with Truckdrive, complete axles are supplied fully assembled with all brake components, and these go straight into the new chassis.

above the main entrance of the South Works. A design and marketing team was hired to replace the people who had been dispersed several years previously. Now everything was in place for Albion Automotive to become a major component supplier to the industry, not just to established customers like the revived Leyland and DAF, but to the whole of the commercial vehicle and motor industry in Britain and abroad. In another significant move, the former Leyland Bus plant at Farington, owned by Volvo since March 1988, was acquired by Albion Automotive in 1995, which gave greater opportunities for that plant to broaden its customer base. The same year a new holding company, Albion Auto Industries Ltd., was formed to provide a group entity for Albion Automotive and for future acquisitions and joint ventures. Thus from 1996 the activities of the company looked like this:

Driveline Division. (Scotstoun plant) Specialising in axles, one of the first results of the company's investment in people and facilities was 'Truckdrive' a new family of light to medium commercial vehicle front and rear axles. The first customer for the new range was Leyland Trucks, who specified 'Truckdrive' in the DAF55. Hypoid gears replaced Albion's traditional spiral bevel system representing a considerable leap forward in technology. A complete range of axles with capacities from 3,200kg to 7,500kg, including 4x4, was now catered for. In 1999 customers for Truckdrive and other components include Leyland Trucks, DAF Trucks, (both taken over by Paccar at different times in 1997/98), LDV, Renault, Optare, Vamco (Iran) and others.

Components Division. (Spurrier and Farington plants). One of the key operations at Spurrier is crankshafts, ranging from those fitted to the Rover 75 car to DAF's all new straight six 12.6 litre 480hp engine. Perkins is another important customer. Albion has also been chosen as the supplier of front and rear suspension components and assemblies for the Rolls Royce Silver Seraph and Bentley Arnage introduced at the 1998 Geneva Motor Show. Half a mile away at Farington, PTOs and driveline flanges are supplied to Volvo, while gearbox, clutch and axle casings are also made. Pipe products are another important activity formed in a variety of materials up to 125mm for fluid carrying and structural applications.

As the centenary approaches, another major development has taken place in the history of Albion. Detroit based American Axle & Manufacturing (AAM) approached the company early in 1998 and talks began which culminated in the takeover of Albion in October 1998. AAM is much bigger than Albion and makes components for cars, light trucks and the four wheel drive market. The future of the Albion is said to be much more secure with more investment and more opportunities for expansion and development. But more importantly, the Albion name is to remain. The new American parent saw the benefit of its historical significance, and also recognised the work that the new company had done in re-establishing the brand since 1993.

So the famous Albion sunrise logo is set to continue to shine as it starts out in its second 100 years, one of the very few British motor manufacturing names from the 19th Century to be still alive and flourishing as it enters the 21st. ❏

The Volvo Olympian is fitted with an Albion drop centre rear axle manufactured at Farington. FirstBus company Midland Bluebird operate R301 LKS, a 1998 Olympian OLY-56 with Alexander Royale 71 seat bodywork, which is seen passing through Dennyloanhead in June 1998.

Front and rear axles on the Leyland built T244 army truck are of Albion manufacture.

Situated beside Yarrow Shipbuilders Ltd. on the banks of the Clyde, Albion Automotive's Scotstoun plant was previously known as the South Works, and was formerly owned by Harland and Wolff for the manufacture of large naval guns. The gap site on the north side of South Street is where the North Works once stood, which incorporated the original 1913 office block and the early reinforced-concrete buildings.

Chapter 10
Trains and Boats and Cranes, etc.
Unusual Applications and Incidents

The success of the A10 model in the First World War meant that the 32hp engine was well tried and tested, and that spares were easily obtained. This reputation led to sales of a number of these engines to other companies, notably Barford and Perkins for use in their road rollers, and reasonable success was also obtained selling a range of marine engines based on the 16 to 32hp petrol engines. The lack of a suitable oil engine in the 1930s meant that there was little demand for Albion engines outside of the Scotstoun factory, but by the early 1950s the reputation of the four cylinder EN286 encouraged Albion to market this engine as a suitable engine for conversion of petrol engined lorries in the under 7 ton category, and also for lightweight buses and coaches.

Industrial applications were also found for the EN286 for uses such as powering compressors, generating sets, and bulldozers. A marinised version was produced called the Albion Albatross, marketed by Ajax Marine Engines of Cheshire. On the back of the success of the EN286 engine, the smaller EN218 based on the Leyland 0.350 also found buyers, and the marinised version marketed by Ajax was called the Albacore. Taking this part of the business further than before, the large EN900 engine of 1956 was built primarily for non-automotive uses, and its two main applications were for railcar and marine usages, the latter being called the Ajax Argosy.

With engine manufacture being scaled down from the late 1950s, gearbox production increased, and many Leyland models were fitted with Albion gearboxes. The 8½ ton Leyland Comet truck, and the Leyland Tiger Cub bus and coach were both offered with Albion 5 speed gearboxes. Later Albion double reduction axles were used extensively throughout the Leyland range, and there was some success in selling these axles to other commercial vehicle manufacturers. ❏

Other Applications of Albion Engines and Components.

Dating from the 1920s, this Barford and Perkins roller acquired an Albion EN286Y engine in the early 1950s. It is very likely that the new engine replaced an Albion 32hp four cylinder petrol engine which was fitted as standard equipment in Barford and Perkins rollers at that time. The 32hp engine was built in large numbers during the first World War and would have been a popular choice for a proprietary engine. Note the 'Albion Oil Engine' plate on the radiator.

British Railways was one of the first customers for the horizontal version of the EN900 engine. In this application it was designated EN901H6, where it provided the motive power for this 2 car set photographed at Lincoln in June 1958. The EN900 15.2 litre engine was based on an original Leyland design, Leyland built the prototype, but Albion did most of the development work on the block, liners and head gaskets.

A Marine version of the EN900 engine was called the 'Ajax Argosy' which was fitted to the 'Lascar' a West Highland Puffer in 1959. The small steam lighter was one of a fleet owned by J & J Hay Ltd. of Glasgow, who used them for the transport of coal, distillery grain, empty herring boxes, building materials, livestock and even removals. They had their maintenance facilities at Kirkintilloch on the Forth and Clyde Canal where the Lascar is seen moored. The vessel was in for a major refit when the opportunity was taken to replace the steam machinery with the diesel power plant.

Glasgow contractors Scottish Land demonstrated a number of items of plant to the press on 10th December 1953 including this Ruston Bucyrus 'Erie' ½ cubic yard excavator which was fitted with an Albion EN286Y4 engine in place of the original American power unit. Also fitted with the same engine was an International TD9 front bladed tractor. The industrial version of the Chieftain engine was also supplied for fitting in compressors and generating sets,

Derbyshire County Council owned this Yorkshire road sweeper with the vertical Claymore EN218 engine new in 1956. The 4 cylinder EN218 was Albion's smallest diesel engine, and since it followed closely the design of the 6 cylinder Leyland 0.350, it shared many of its components.

The Albion-Cuthbertson Water Buffalo tractor was developed and built by James A. Cuthbertson at Biggar with an Albion EN286 engine at the rear driving forward through an Albion 5 speed gearbox. A Cuthbertson designed and patented wire reinforced flexible rubber track enabled the tractor to operate over marshland or soft ground, often on heavy ploughing operations. From 1952 it was marketed by Albion but was assembled by Cuthbertsons with a body manufactured by them. Around 120 were built and virtually all were sold, many to the Forestry Commission. A larger version was also designed with a Leyland 0.600 engine as was a hydrostatic drive model. Around 20 bodies were constructed by the North British Locomotive Co.

A line-up of six of an order for ten generating sets destined for the Sydney Metropolitan Water and Sewerage and Drainage Board with EN286Y engines.

In the early 1950s the continuing trend towards diesels was making itself felt in the lower payload sectors where the mass producers were dominant. The only problem was that Bedford, Ford, Commer, Austin and Morris did not yet have their own compression ignition engine. The solution for operators already running these types was to obtain a suitable conversion. This Bedford SA, or Big Bedford as the type was known, had its Bedford petrol engine removed and replaced with an Albion EN286 engine at the Hull Depot in March 1956.

Unusual Applications and Conversions.

By fitting flanges to the wheels in place of rubber tyres this A10 was used for shunting work in the sidings of Richard Smith, Chemical Manufacturer, Clark Street, Paisley. The tank on the wagon itself was needed to increase traction. A similar conversion was carried out by Adam and Benson Ltd., scrap merchant, West Bromwich.

Albion Concessionaires Millburn Motors replaced the original Albion petrol unit in this ex-army WD.HD23 with a Leyland 0.600 engine removed from a 1949 Alexander (Midland) Leyland PD2 around 1970, and converted it to a recovery vehicle. But the transplanted engine failed to deliver sufficient power for heavy recoveries, and the truck was sold after only a few years. It is seen crossing Albert Bridge over the Clyde in 1972.

Albion's own recovery truck was a former tank transporter WD.CX24 which also had its petrol engine replaced by a diesel, but this time the power unit was the 9.9 litre Albion oil engine. It was sent all over the West of Scotland on recoveries, usually in the capable hands of Albion service engineer Tom McAulay. An HD type radiator was fitted after an accident. It was getting on for 30 years old when seen at Yoker in 1972, not long before the service premises were closed. It was sold to Leyrep Commercials soon after, passing to Doune Motors about 10 years later, and then subsequently to another haulier in Doune where it still resides today.

This 'Clydesdale' CD21CXLW, chassis no. 88114K, started life as a long wheelbase tanker with LAD cab, having been supplied by Albion agents Ford & Slater of Leicester in 1968. By the early 1980s it had found its way to Malta and in 1984 the chassis was delivered to Joseph Brincot Coach and Bodybuilders at Tarxien in Malta, where the engine was brought forward in the chassis and dropped about 8 inches onto modified engine mounts, thus bringing the gearbox just forward of the front axle. A coach body was then built on to the chassis, which produced a floor level where the engine bay protruded by only 5 inches. In 1989 it was converted from a coach to a bus with leather covered seats replacing the coach seats, and the partition behind the driver was done away with. The Albion was snapped in Malta in 1996 by Jim Wilkinson, and it is still in service today.

Bus chassis were often used for demonstration vehicles, and this 'Aberdonian' MR11N was commissioned by the South of Scotland Electricity Board as a mobile showroom in 1959 to help sell electrical appliances. Bodywork was by John Limond, Coachbuilders, of Ayr, using Plaxton parts for the front end to produce a pleasing overall appearance, although no advantage was taken of the set back front axle to provide an entrance at this location. Carrying 2 tons of electrical equipment a fuel consumption of 20.6 miles per gallon was said to be achieved.

This 'Clydesdale' CD21ANW for Israel had a special cab manufactured by Brossel, which took advantage of its fibre glass construction to provide this attractive twin headlamp arrangement. It also differed from the standard product in that an Eaton 2 speed axle was fitted. Israel was a new market for Albion, so an edict from Lancashire dictated these trucks should be badged as Leylands. Also for the Israel market was this locally assembled bonneted version of the LAD cabbed Clydesdale photographed in Jerusalem in 1969.

The Hydrocon Highlander 6 ton mobile crane was based on a specially strengthened CH13 'Chieftain Super Six', and was built in Coatbridge, near Glasgow, by the Lambert Engineering Company. A Hydrocon Highlander is seen in 1963 working at a site in the days when a soft cap was deemed to be adequate head protection. In 1967 the 'Super Reiver' RE29 chassis was used as the basis for the 15 ton Hydrocon Hibernian travelling crane. Both cranes sold well and were said to be especially suitable for working in confined spaces.

A four cylinder Reiver was an unusual platform on which to mount a 3-ton capacity Coles crane. This FT107T was supplied to the Sydney Metropolitan Water and Sewerage and Drainage Board in 1956. The 'T' suffix meant that it was a tipper chassis which would have had a strengthened frame to cope with the unusual stresses such duties involved. A factory cab by Autolifts was fitted.

This Model AM463 started life as an RAF ambulance, and after post-war repurchase by Albion, was re-engined with a 4 cylinder EN285 diesel, the prototype of the EN286 for the FT range. It received a new Rogersons 'shooting brake' body in 1947, with five individual aircraft type seats and a capacious boot. It ran on General Trade Plates, usually 175G, all its subsequent life, which was as staff transport, latterly on Albion's Scotstoun to Yoker inter-works service. Unfortunately It was scrapped by Millburn Motors in 1965, having been replaced by a larger Leyland 2 ton personnel carrier. Rogerson's premises were on the corner of South Street and Balmoral Street, and were otherwise confined by Albion's Scotstoun Works.

The CX range looked old fashioned by the late 1940s and many overseas customers fitted locally made cabs of a much more modern appearance. Compare the Portuguese built cab on this CX5N with the cab on the Moores FT3 on page 68. They are not identical but it certainly looks as if they have been working from the same set of drawings. The local police did not seem to mind being photographed beside the precarious looking load, probably intended for a bridge construction somewhere in Portugal.

A double deck 'Venturer' chassis was used as the basis for this 39 seater with Wevell Bros. bodywork operated in South Africa by Kimberley Bus Service (Pty) Ltd. The chassis was a CX19LW, not a sub-type which was listed, and the large Autovac tank on the front nearside bulkhead was also unusual.

Albion built this trailer chassis for the Lanarkshire Coalmasters' Association for use as a mobile emergency colliery winder with EN236 four cylinder petrol engine. A conventional four speed gearbox was fitted, but with the top gear removed leaving the three lowest ratios. From the gearbox the drive was taken by a short propellor shaft to an underslung worm unit, from which enclosed shafts transmitted the drive to the winding drums.

The end of the road.

Accidents are rare random events which will always continue to happen, but in ever-decreasing numbers thanks to improving safety standards. Nobody was seriously hurt when this Clydesdale from Albion's own transport fleet jack-knifed in South Street on 8th January 1954. The same truck or its identical replacement was sent to Adrolic Engineering of Milngavie to have anti jack-knifing stabilisers fitted in 1956.

Opposite upper: An overheated transmission brake caused this 1931 vintage Model LH27 of Shell-Mex and BP to burst into flames in the Bristol area in 1938. The flammable cargo ensured that the vehicle was completely destroyed.

Opposite lower: Albion chassis with test weights were always a familiar sight in the west end of Glasgow, as vehicles from the Experimental Department were sent out to test some new component or other. However, side impact tests were not usually a feature of these experiments. The runaway wagon had obviously been left unbraked when it got away from the local goods yard in April 1965, and left this Reiver with a badly twisted frame.

Business went on as usual at the Norwood Bar on Wednesday 22nd February 1956 when this Chieftain confectioner's van came through the wall after being in collision with a Corporation bus at the corner of West Street and Gloucester Street, Tradeston, Glasgow. The driver had the presence of mind to jump out of his cab before the Albion entered the pub.

Glasgow Corporation's standardisation on fluid transmissions meant that the later Venturers found their way to the scrapyard long before their time was due. These CX19s dating from 1938 to 1948 all ended their days at Yorkshire scrapyard in 1960.

Some Albions never die, they just slowly return to nature, like this forgotten FT37 somewhere in the south of England.

Dealer's 1954 advertisement for EN286 conversions.

Appendix A
The Albion-Murray Patents

The sound engineering built into every Albion was complemented by a number of inventions by Thomas Murray which were patented by the company and featured as Albion-Murray patents. Although not renowned in later years for being innovative and tending to a more cautious approach, the importance of these patents in establishing Albion's early success should not be underestimated. It is worth describing in some detail how these devices operated, and to understand why they gave Albion an advantage against other products which were often not fully developed.

Albion-Murray Mechanical Lubricator

Albion was one of the first companies to routinely use the forced lubrication of an engine, culminating in the design and development of a mechanical lubricator which was first patented in 1904, and after further development, also in 1905. This device was subsequently used in Albion vehicles and some other applications over the following twenty years.

There were two forms of lubrication common in early engines;

i) *splash lubrication*, where the rotating crankshaft was allowed to dip into the oil bath of a 'wet sump', with the bearings relying on picking up lubricant as they could. Splash lubrication has continued as a very effective method for gearboxes and the differentials of driving axles, where oil levels can be relied upon to vary within a limited range between service intervals.

ii) *gravity lubrication*, where oil slowly drained from a reservoir through a wick or tube, and was allowed to drip onto the bearing. Some manufacturers used heat from the exhaust gas to raise the oil to a certain height or to pressurise a reservoir in an attempt to increase the effectiveness of this method, but any pressure so generated would not have been available until some time after starting up.

This second method was also known as 'total loss' or 'once only' lubrication since the oil was not recovered and usually allowed to drip onto the road, there being no requirement for a sump. In addition, the only filters then available consisted of fine steel mesh able only to trap fairly course particles, and it was therefore desirable for fresh oil to pass through an engine 'once only' from a feed tank, and the lubricant not re-circulated. The commonly used system whereby oil dripped from a feed pipe into a small sight glass for delivery to each bearing was most likely the basis for Murray's device, in which he incorporated a mechanically forced feed. The patent lubricator designed by Murray was fed from an oil reservoir and was sufficient for some 800 miles of running from 1 gallon of oil. It had a metered delivery, with the oil fed to a number of designated lubrication points in turn, and then allowed to drain into a sump for later disposal.

The mechanism had either 6 or 12 ports for 2 or 4 cylinder engines respectively, and was connected to delivery pipes as follows;

2 cylinders / 6 lubricating points: 2 main bearings, 2 big ends, 2 cylinders.
4 cylinders / 12 lubricating points: 3 main bearings, 4 big ends, 4 cylinders and the governor gear.

A fixed steel disc with the appropriate number of ports was pressed against a single rotating gunmetal disc by a central spring, both discs having been carefully ground at the manufacturing stage to form an oil seal when in use. As the disc rotated, it alternately covered and uncovered the inlet and outlet ports, and an attached pump barrel or plunger was given a vertical motion by a fixed face cam ring feeding the outlet ports in turn. Teeth cut on the outside

of the rotating disc were engaged by a ratchet operated by a cam driven from a worm gear on the engine camshaft, and delivery was therefore in proportion to engine speed. The oil delivery rate could be varied externally by adjusting small locking screws mounted on the top of the lubricator for each delivery point. At full engine speed up to 15 drops per minute was available, but after a new engine had been in use for a month or two, 5 drops per minute was recommended for the cranks and 10 drops per minute for the remaining bearings. A 'T' handle projecting from some versions of the lubricator provided extra oil for hill-climbing and also allowed oil to be pumped to the bearings if the vehicle had been out of use for some time. The 'T' handle had one pointed arm which indicated the port being fed as the internal disc rotated, and was not normally touched once the engine was running. Since the moving parts were running in fresh oil, little wear was experienced, and this mechanism proved to be very reliable. It was also claimed to contribute to the smokeless exhaust of the engines so equipped, which was a significant improvement on many engines of the period.

The later Albion-Murray Mechanical Lubricator as fitted to the 24/30hp A6 car, showing the main components and general layout.

Key.
A   Lubricator box
A1 Lubricator cover
B1 Fixed disc
B2 Suction passages
B3 Delivery passages
C   Rotating disc
C1 Rotating disc spring
E2 Pump spring
F   Adjusting screws
F1 Cams
G   Engine drive shaft
G1 Crank
G2 Disc actuating rod
G3 Actuating rod spring
G4 Disc stop spring
H1 Oil sieve

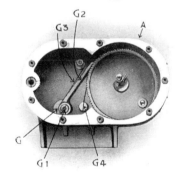

Once only lubrication with its supply of fresh unused oil was considered essential to reduce engine wear, and the lubricator was one of many devices successfully patented by the inventive Murray. It proved essential to the early reputation for long term reliability which soon become an Albion hallmark. In reality, it was common for commercial operators to return the sump oil to the feed tank since there was a reluctance to throw out apparently good oil. This practice may have helped to persuade Albion to accept the inevitable and abandon the mechanical lubricator, which was considerably more expensive to manufacture than a gear type oil pump. The lubricator was eventually replaced by a gear driven pump which re-circulated oil through the engine, despite the lack of efficient filters at that time. However, it was the development of faster vehicles, which finally signalled the end of this important early feature. A gear type oil pump was first used on the 15hp A14 of 1911, the fastest of the Albion models then available with a governed speed of up to 30 mph, dependant on model. The mechanical lubricator was retained on lower speed models and on all marks of the 3-4 ton A10, until its replacement with the Model 27 in 1927. The War Department were so impressed with the very low cylinder wear on the A10, that they encouraged Albion to develop a modified version for aero engines. The aero engine lubricator version is known to have been used very successfully by the All British (Engine) Company on their 360hp, A.B.C. Dragonfly 1A 9 cylinder radial engine for the Sopwith Dragon aircraft of 1919. The lubricator was also manufactured under licence by the Empire Engineering Company of Failsworth, Manchester as the 'Empire-Murray' Patent Valveless Force-Feed Lubricator in 4, 6, 8 and 12 feed standard versions, at prices ranging from £6 up to £14.

Albion-Murray Low Tension Magneto

The ignition systems available to motor manufacturers by the turn of the century, varied in their performance and their reliability. Hot tube ignition was one of the earliest, whereby a tube projected into each combustion chamber and was heated on the outside of the engine by a burner usually fed from the engine fuel supply. The potential for an engine fire is obvious and getting the tubes up to a temperature for starting was hardly an instant affair. Early electrical ignition systems used an accumulator, or battery, to supply ignition plugs via an induction coil, and with no other electrical demands, battery life would be a reasonable three hundred hours or so. The magneto became popular as it is capable of generating sufficient energy for a strong spark at low speeds and since early vehicles were hand started and did not have electric lighting, the battery could be eliminated. By the beginning of the twentieth century, both low tension, and high tension magneto systems had been developed, essentially only differing in the way that the ignition spark was produced. In the low tension system the spark is produced by interrupting a low voltage / higher current circuit within the combustion chamber. In the high tension system, interrupting a primary circuit connected to a coil generates enough voltage in a secondary (low current) ignition circuit to cause a spark to jump between the two fixed points of an ignition plug. Unfortunately, the high voltages generated were just as likely to jump to earth through faulty insulation or dampness and early systems proved unreliable. It was Murray's own development of the low tension magneto which Albion initially chose to adopt as the most reliable ignition method on their early vehicles.

Murray's training as an electrical engineer and his considerable experience in the electrical industry, was put to good use while at Mavor and Coulson in Glasgow, where he worked on an ignition system for the newly established English Daimler Motor Car Company of Coventry. Murray invented a version of the low tension magneto sufficiently different from the mechanism jointly patented by R. Bosch and by F.R. Simms in 1898, to allow it to be also patented. Albion was not unique in using a low tension magneto, but again Murray had been able to design and develop new ideas and improvements in order to gain an advantage in the marketplace. Designed to operate in the opposite manner to normal practice by using a stationary armature and windings, the field magnets constituted the only rotating parts, thus eliminating sliding contacts, commutators or brushes. A single insulated wire led the current to the ignition unit for each cylinder. Mounted to the crankshaft outside the crankcase on the A1, A2 and A3 models, it was moved on the A6 car during its production run to a position between the flywheel and the propshaft. Subsequent new models used the front of the crankshaft for the Albion-Murray patent governor, except for the A6 which continued with a governor mounted on the side of the engine. The Murray low tension magneto which was first patented in 1899, served the early models well and contributed greatly to their reliability, a fact which was recognised by the award of a Silver Medal in 1903, the only award given for ignition devices in the 1,000 mile reliability trials organised by the Automobile Club of Great Britain & Ireland.

Having redesigned the magneto, Murray turned his attention to the ignition device itself, which also incorporated ignition advance and retard gear at the base of a column arrangement. A low tension magneto uses 'make and break' contacts inside the combustion chamber which allow the current to build up when closed, and create an ignition spark as they are opened. Using an almost identical arrangement to the Bosch & Simms' patent, the

contacts were operated externally by a small hammer supported by a rod resting on a cam driven by the engine. A lip on the cam caused the platinum tipped points to open rapidly at the moment of maximum current. This action did create a clicking noise when the engine was running, but Murray's patented spring loaded buffers incorporated within the ignition column virtually eliminated this noise and contributed to the quiet running of these engines. Each cylinder had its own ignition column and the moving arm, or 'wyper spindle', which protruded into the combustion chamber was a possible source of sealing problems. The necessary adjustments to the mechanism were considered reasonable on 2 cylinder engines, but with the introduction of the 4 cylinder A10 in 1910, the low tension magneto was replaced with the high tension magneto which used a non-moving ignition ('sparking') plug.

The simplicity of the current generator of the Murray Low Tension Magneto is shown in this view of the early type fitted to the 24/30hp A6 car.

Key
J   Armature winding
L   Output to bus bar
M   Semi-circular magnets
N   Phosphor bronze drum
P   Pole pieces
Q   Armature carrier

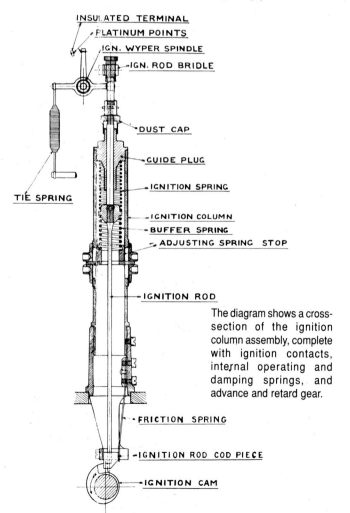

The diagram shows a cross-section of the ignition column assembly, complete with ignition contacts, internal operating and damping springs, and advance and retard gear.

It was considered by Albion that the greater the number of cylinders, the more difficult and less likely that adjustments would be made on a regular basis to the low tension mechanism. Although this maintenance work was perhaps more likely to be omitted on commercial vehicles than on private cars, all future new models from the A10 on with magneto ignition used the high tension type. The magneto was eventually replaced on motor vehicles by the introduction of the dynamo as additional demands from electrical equipment became common, and there was no point in having two electrical generators. Magnetos continued to be popular on motor cycles and aircraft for many years, and as with the patent mechanical lubricator, Murray's low tension magneto found an aviation application. The specially designed Murray Polar Induction Magneto was used as the basis for the majority of aero engine magnetos until the advent of the jet engine.

Albion-Murray Engine Speed Governor

Murray had first patented a governor in 1891, just one year after his graduation, and long before his involvement with Albion. The speed related governor was well established from the early days of steam, but it was the manner in which it was applied to the Albion petrol engines that made their early models stand out from the competition. Albion proudly claimed in their brochures that they were the first manufacturers of petrol engines to fit a governor which was correct under all conditions of engine speed. On Albions fitted with the low tension magneto ignition system, the throttle lever was also connected to a Murray patent engine speed governor, and not solely to the throttle valve as may be expected. The throttle lever formed an interconnection between the governor, the carburettor and the ignition system, and was so arranged to ensure that the ignition timing and the air flow was always in the correct relationship to the engine speed. At whatever position the lever was set, the car would ascend or descend a hill at constant speed, assuming of course that the car was in the correct gear for the gradient. The simplicity of this control allowed the driver to concentrate on the road ahead, and was sensitive enough to prevent the tendency of the engine to race when the clutch pedal was depressed.

From the model A10 onwards, the governor was fitted to an extension of the crankshaft forward of the timing gear, sealed in an oil tight tapered cast housing bolted to the engine crankcase, and supported by an extended sump. Thus rendering it tamper-proof at least from the driver's point of view, it was of special interest to commercial operators since driver abuse from overspeeding of the engine was eliminated. The vehicle could be relied upon to be operated within the recommended limits of the manufacturers, thus extending the working life of the engine. However, its ease of use and contribution to smooth running was also popular with the new breed of motor car owners and drivers, with the driveability and smoothness of the early Albion vehicles often remarked upon in road tests of the period. Although an early selling point, Albion's continued use of strictly governed engines was later to cause some pressure on sales as the demand for higher average speeds increased in the 1930s, especially from coach operators.

After the introduction of the Bosch Z4 high tension magneto on the 4 cylinder A10, the throttle lever only controlled the governor, which in turn operated a throttle valve at the top of the induction pipe. A separate timing lever mounted just below the throttle lever and connected directly to the magneto, enabled the timing point, or advance and retard, to be adjusted independently. ❑

The governor formed the basis of a more complex integrated control for the engine as shown in this schematic diagram of its operation.

Key
A   Albion patent carburettor
A5   Carburettor operating lever
A7   Extra air valve operating lever
B   Bob weights
B2/3   Operating rods
C   Throttle lever
C1/2   Operating rods
D5   Advance/retard connection

The governor consisted of bob weights which moved outwards against spring pressure as engine speed increased, moving a forked operating rod in a grooved sleeve.

This offside view of the 24/30hp engine from the A6 car, shows how the three patents described are positioned on this model. The mechanical lubricator was attached to the front of no. 1 cylinder and fed 12 locations with oil, and the magneto ignition columns are visible to the right of each cylinder. Fed from a carburettor mounted out of sight on the nearside, the inlet manifold and throttle valve are also prominent, the latter operated by the linkage from the governor, which on this engine is contained within the housing at the lower right hand side.

Appendix B
Model and Chassis Numbering Systems

In Albion parlance chassis were either 'bonnet type' or 'overtype', never 'normal control' or 'forward control'. A chassis was never designated as a Type, always as a Model; Model 24, Model 41, Model 127, etc., these being examples of the system which was introduced after 1924 when the original A prefix was dropped. Models were sometimes abbreviated to M24, M41, M127, etc., but later in the 1920s special prefix letters were introduced to identify sub types of models.

Taking as examples passenger models PKB26 and PM28, the prefix system for buses was as follows:

- The first letter prefix of P stood for 'Passenger'.
- The second letter, K or M in these examples, was related to carrying or seating capacity.
- The third letter, B in our example PKB26, was used only if a wheelbase, frame length or other feature was not the normal or standard type.

Later with increasing standardisation the third prefix letter was dropped, while the second letter continued to be related to chassis differences which affected seating capacity, e.g. the 38 seat PV141 and 40 seat PW141. There may have been variations of these rules, and it should be noted that the Models 80 and 81 double deckers were not allocated prefix codes.

For commercials the system was similar, as exemplified by Models LB41 and LHA473:

- The first prefix letter L stood for 'Lorry' (sometimes replaced with S for 'Subsidy' Scheme model).
- The second letter, B or H in these examples, was related to the weight range.
- The third letter was again used only if items like wheelbase, frame length or perhaps tyre specification (i.e. solids or pneumatics), were other than the normal or most common type, e.g. A in our example LHA473 (denoting in this case a wheelbase variation).

Later the letter L was dropped, and the first prefix letter became the weight range letter. Starting at B for the 30 cwt B118, the series continued through to T for the T561 15 ton 8 wheeler. The letters which were used in this system were B,C,J,H,K,L,M,N,P,R and T, each letter usually denoting a progressive increase in weight range. In this system the letter M was not an abbreviation for 'Model' and P did not mean 'Passenger'. For wheelbase variations the letters A, B and C gave way to S, N and L. An example of the final pre-1937 system was the KL127, this being a 6 ton (K) weight range, long (L) wheelbase Model 127.

For military vehicles the standard prefixes were dropped in favour of WD (War Department), e.g. WD131, or AM (Air Ministry), e.g. AM463. The same applied to fire engines, e.g. FE43, while an additional prefix Sp (Special) was used to highlight major differences from standard build, e.g. Sp.LB40. Some time later WD also became an additional prefix, and also SAR (South African Railways), and these additional prefixes continued to be used for special orders for many years to come.

In addition to prefixes, model numbers themselves were also manipulated to indicate improvements or variations. In the mid 1930s some models numbered in the 400 series or higher were developed from models which shared the first two numbers. The models affected could be identified by

their similar chassis number groupings. Examples were the Model 473 which was a development of the Model 47, and the M557 which was based on the M55.

For new models introduced after 1937, an entirely new system of model code letters was used in front of type numbers which were now no longer unique to each model. The system was simply based on the first and last letters of the alphabet, the second and the second-last, and so on; AZ, BY, CX, DW, EV, KP and WD were all taken up, but WD was not used in this later system until 1955 when the mainly Rolls Royce engined WD66 military prototypes were built. However, there were two main exceptions to this rule – the FT range, introduced in 1939, and the HD range, which started production in 1950. The T in FT was one letter out because it was felt imprudent to use the letter U in conjunction with F, while the letters HD were chosen to emphasise the Heavy Duty nature of these larger chassis.

There were other exceptions. No explanation has been found for KD, but it was probably a Drawing Office allocation of K for the emerging family of underfloor engined chassis, and D for the diesel version of the EN1200 engine. The experimental Light Delivery chassis was dubbed, appropriately enough, LD, but the underfloor engined chassis introduced in the 1954-1957 period had code letters MR (Mid-engined or Medium Range) and MLH (Mid-engined or Medium Light Horizontal). One other code which has defied explanation was PF, which was used to identify Leyland-engined alternatives in the then-current FT range.

Individual suffix letters adopted after 1936 included T (Tipper), TR (Tractor unit), W (8 ft. Wide), X (Extra) and S, N, and L (Short, Normal, and Long wheelbases). Other suffixes starting with A (e.g. FT3A) meant a major improvement in a particular model, and this might be followed by B, C, etc. for subsequent improvements.

From 1958, a new system of type letters more closely identified with model names was introduced – CA (Cameronian), CH (Chieftain), CD (Clydesdale), LR (Lowlander), NS (Nimbus), RE (Reiver), TA (Talisman), VA (Valiant), VT (Victor) and VK (Viking). Later this system was adopted by Leyland itself for its own Lancashire built products.

The only chassis of this period which did not use a letter code prefix was the 24 ton gvw Caledonian 24C/1, 24C/3 and 24C/5, a range of lightweight 8 wheelers which had a high content of Leyland parts. These models had much in common with the 8 wheeled Leyland Octopus which had similar codings.

From the early days of the Albion Motor Car Company a series of chassis numbers was allocated to each new model. Each batch of twelve chassis (ten from 1938 onwards) was given one multi-digit number, and each individual chassis in that batch received a unique letter suffix between A and L (with I and G omitted from 1938). As an example the new overtype model CX1 was allocated the series 54000 to 54100. The first ten chassis produced were 54000.A, 54000.B, 54000.C, then D, E, F, etc. up to 54000.L, with 54001.A following on.

The major advantages were that a chassis number on its own could identify the model, and therefore the major components that it had, and the system would last twelve or ten times longer before it started to run out of numbers. The chassis type and chassis number were carried on a plate mounted in the driver's cab. This plate was always referred to as the 'Caution Plate', because it contained a caution that overloading would cancel the maker's guarantee, and it also carried the unit numbers of the gearbox(es) and axles. ❑

Appendix C
Model List
1899 to 1972

Model	Chassis Nos. From	Dates of Production	Engines	Layout	Final Drive	Notes	No. of Preserved / Surviving.
A1		1899-1903	(8hp)	R	OC	Dog Cart; 2/4 seats, tiller steering up to 1902.	3
A2		1901-1903	(8/10hp)	R	OC	Dog Cart; similar to A1; 4 seats; steering wheel & 10hp from 1902.	6
A3	1-199	1903-1915	(12hp)	B	OC	2 seat car; 4 seat rear entrance / 5 seat side entrance cars.	13
A3	1-199	1903-1915	(12hp)	B	OC	7-11 seat wagonette; all 12hp models have 12 sloping bonnet louvres.	"
A3	213-228/247	1904-1915	(16hp)	B	EC	4-7 seat rear & side entrance cars; model identified by 10 sloping bonnet louvres.	"
A3	213-228/247	1904-1915	(16hp)	B	OC	15-40 cwt lorry/van; identified by 10 sloping (also 9 vertical) bonnet louvres.	"
A3	213-228/247	1904-1915	(16hp)	B	EC	7-15 seat wagonettes & charabancs; identified by 10 sloping bonnet louvres.	"
A6	200-212	1907-1911	(24/30hp)	B	EC	4-5 seat side entrance car; (no bonnet louvres).	2
A10	248-399	1910-1926	(32hp)	B	OC	3 ton lorry & 72 cwt pantechnicon; identified by 14 vertical bonnet louvres.	–
A10	248-399	1910-1926	(32hp)	B	OC	19-29 passenger charabancs, 34 passenger double deck bus; 14 bonnet louvres.	–
A10	248-399	1910-1926	(32hp)	B	OC	4 ton; identified by 14 vertical bonnet louvres.	–
A10 Mk.ll	1500-2080	1923-1926	(32hp)	B	OC	3 / 4 ton; tapered bonnet & 2 pairs of 5 horizontal louvres.	14
A10 Mk.lll	2800-2810	1925-1926	(32hp)	O	OC	3 / 4 ton; first overtype.	–
A12	600-620	1913-1916	(25hp)	B	EC	40 cwt lorry/van; 10 bonnet louvres.	1
A12	600-620	1913-1916	(25hp)	B	EC	19-25 passenger bus, also 25 seat torpedo charabanc; 10 bonnet louvres.	"
A14	400-430	1911-1915	(15hp)	B	OW	10-20 cwt; 9 vertical bonnet louvres (all versions).	3
A14	400-430	1911-1915	(15hp)	B	OW	2 seater coupe up to de-luxe 6 seater.	"
A14	400-430	1911-1915	(15hp)	B	OW	8 / 10 passenger wagonette.	"
A16	900-1010	1914,1918-20	(20hp)	B	OW	20 / 30 cwt; 11 (also 9) vertical bonnet louvres.	1
A16	900-1010	1914,1918-20	(20hp)	B	OW	12 / 15 passenger bus.	"
A20	3000-3100	1920-1925	EN20 (20hp)	B	OW	25-40 cwt lorry/van; 15 seat charabanc; with 9 bonnet louvres.	7
24	4000.A	1923-1932	EN24 (24hp)	B	OW	20-40 cwt lorry/van; 2 pairs of 5 horizontal louvres.	29
24	4000.A	1923-1932	EN24 (24hp)	B	OW	'Viking' 18 passenger coach, also 14-22 passenger bus; 6 bonnet louvres.	"
26	5000.A	1926-1933	EN50(30/60hp)	B	UW	'Viking' 14-29 passenger, dropped frame; 6 bonnet louvres.	1
26	5500.A	1928-1933	EN53(30/90hp)	B	UW	'Viking Six' 14-29 passenger, dropped frame; 6 bonnet louvres.	–
27	6000.A	1926-1933	EN50(30/60hp)	B	OW	2.5-4 ton, first 3 ton with live axle; 6 bonnet louvres.	8
28	7000.A	1926-1932	EN50(30/60hp)	O	UW	'Viking' (from 1929) 32 passenger half cab.	5
28	7500.A	1926-1932	EN53(30/90hp)	O	UW	'Viking Six' (from 1929) 32 passenger.	–
31	12000.A	1927-1931	EN50/57/59	B	OW	3-4 ton, first 6 wheel (6x4); 6 bonnet louvres.	–
32	12500.A	1928-1933	EN53/57/62	O	OW	3 / 4 ton; 6 wheel (6x4).	–
33	13000.A					No details available.	–
34	10000.A	1927-1933	EN51(35/55hp)	B	OW	4 / 5 ton; 6 bonnet louvres.	2
35	8000.A	1927-1932	EN51(35/55hp)	O	OW	4, 5 / 6 ton; first model designed as overtype.	3
36	10100.A	1933	EN65(35/70hp)	B	OW	5 / 6 ton; Merryweather fire engine.	–
37	8100.A	1932-1933	EN65(35/70hp)	O	OW	5 / 6 ton.	–
38	13500.A					No details available.	–
40	9000.A	1928-1929	EN52(20/36hp)	B	UW	30 cwt lorry / van; 17 passenger bus; with 5 bonnet louvres.	1
41	14000.A	1928-1935	EN52/58/63/64/68	BO	OW	35 cwt; 17 passenger; Merryweather f/e, also Perkins Wolf, Dorman 4DS.	23
42	14500.A			B	OW	Prototype 40 cwt	–
43	14500.A	1931-1936	EN58/63/64/68	B	OW	40 / 45 cwt; Merryweather fire engine. Also Perkins Wolf, Dorman 4DS.	1
44	15500.A	1931-1935	EN58/64/68	O	OW	40 / 45 cwt. Also Perkins Wolf, Dorman 4DS.	–
45	17000.A	1931	EN50(30/60hp)	B	OW	4 ton.	–
46	14500.A	1931-1936	EN58(20/42hp)	B	OW	50 cwt	1
47	15500.A	1932-1935	EN64(20/42hp)	O	OW	50 cwt	1
48	15000.A/B	1929-1930	EN224	B	UW	'Victor' 20 passenger, dropped frame, (2 only).	–

Model	Chassis Nos. From	Dates of Production	Engines	Layout	Final Drive	Notes	No. of Preserved / Surviving.
49	15000.C	1930-1933	EN61/68/230	B	UW	'Victor' 20 passenger, dropped frame.	–
50	17100.A	1931-1934	EN60(30/60hp)	B	OW	4 ton.	2
51	17500.A	1931-1933	EN60(30/60hp)	O	OW	4.5 / 5 ton.	2
52	6200.A	1934-1935	EN205(30/65hp)	B	OW	4 ton. Also Gardner 4LW, Beardmore HOE4, Dorman 4JUR/4HW.	–
53	6600.A	1933-1935	EN205(30/65hp)	O	OW	Also Gardner 4LW, Beardmore HOE4, Dorman 4JUR/4HW.	–
54	17200.A	1933-1935	EN200(30/65hp)	B	OW	4.5 / 5 ton.Also Gardner 4,5,6LW, Beardmore HOE 5/6.	–
55	17600.A	1933-1935	EN200(30/65hp)	O	OW	4.5 / 5 ton.Also Gardner 4,5,6LW, Beardmore HOE 5/6.	3
56	10200.A	1933-1935	EN70/80/85	O	OW	6 ton. Also Gardner 5,6LW, Beardmore HOE 5/6.	–
57	8200.A	1933-1935	EN70/80/85	O	OW	6 ton. Also Gardner 5,6LW, Beardmore HOE 5/6.	–
58	10900.A	1934-1935	EN85(49/110hp)	B	OW	10 ton, 6 wheel (6x4).Also Gardner 4,5,6LW, Beardmore HOE 5/6.	–
59	8900.A	1933-1935	EN85(49/110hp)	O	OW	10 ton, 6 wheel trailing axle (6x2). Also Gardner 5,6LW, Beardmore HOE 5/6	–
65	16000.A	1930-1933	EN60/232	O	UW	'Valkyrie' 38 pass. 'for economy operation', dropped frame. Also 4LW, HOE5	4
66	16200.A	1933-1934	EN70/200	B	UW?	Merryweather fire engine (8 only).	2
67	16200.A	1933-1934	EN70/75/200	O	UW	'Valkyrie' 36 pass dropped frame. Also 4,5LW, B'more HOE 5, Dorman 4HW	1
68	16400.A					No details available (See model 69).	–
69	16401.A	1934-1936	EN75/76/200	O	UW	'Valkyrie' 32 / 36 passenger, dropped frame. Also Gardner 4,5LW.	–
70	11500.A	1931-1934	EN70/75/85	O	UW	'Valiant' 32 / 36 pass, wide dropped frame. Also 5,6LW, Beardmore HOE 5.	1
71	11601.A	1934-1935	EN75/76/80/85	O	UW	'Valiant' 32 / 36 passenger with wide dropped ftrame. Also Gardner 5,6LW.	–
72	11601.E	1935	Gardner 6LW	B	UW	'Valiant' 28 / 32 passenger with wide dropped frame; (1 only).	–
80	18000.A	1932-1934	EN80/85	O	UW	'Venturer' 56 passenger double deck. Also Gard. 5,6LW, Beardmore HOE 6.	2
81	18101.A	1935-1938	Gardner 6LW	O	UW	'Venturer' 48 / 56 passenger double deck. Also Beardmore HOE 6.	–
85	18500.A	1933	EN85	O	UW	'Valorous' experimental 60 passenger 6 wheel (6x4) double deck.	–
111	21000.A-C	1933	EN210	O	UW	'Victor' 24 / 26 passenger with dropped frame (3 only).	–
114	24001.A	1934-1940	EN211/212	B	UW	'Victor' 24 / 28 passenger with dropped frame. Also Gardner 4LK.	1
115	25001.A	1934-1940	EN211,212	O	UW	'Victor' 24 / 32 pass d/frame. Also Gard. 4LK, Dorman 4DS, P'kins Panther.	2
118	28000.A	1935-1940	EN211/216	B	OW	30 / 40 cwt Also Gardner 4LK.	9
119	30000.A	1935-1939	EN211/216	O	OW	30 / 40 cwt Also Gardner 4LK, Dorman 4DS.	1
122	28000.A	1935-1940	EN211/216	B	OW	40 / 50 cwt Also Gardner 4LK, Dorman 4DS.	11
123	30000.A	1935-1939	EN211/216	O	OW	40 / 50 cwt Also Gardner 4LK.	4
124	28000.A	1937-1938	Perkins Leopard	B	OW	3 ton.	–
125	30000.A	1936-1939	EN211/216	O	OW	3 ton. Also Gardner 4LK.	3
126	36000.A	1935-1940	EN212	B	OW	3.5 / 4.5(?) ton, 'H' prefix series. Also Gardner 4LK.	4
126	36101.A	1935-1940	EN212	B	OW	3.5 / 5 ton, 'K' prefix series. Also Gardner 4LK.	4
127	37000.A	1935-1941	EN211/212	O	OW	3.5 / 5 ton, 'J' prefix series. Also Gardner 4LK.	4
127	37101.A	1935-1941	EN211/212	O	OW	3.5 / 6 ton, 'K' prefix series. Also Gardner 4LK.	26
128	38000.A	1936	EN211	B	OW	4 ton, 6 wheel (6x2).	–
129	39000.A	1936-1940	EN212	O	OW	6 ton, 6 wheel (6x2).	–
131	41000.A	1933-1937	EN206	O	OW	3 ton, 6 wheel for War Dept. Also Gardner 5LW.	–
133	41100.A/B	1936	Gardner 6LW	O	OW	3 ton, 6 wheel for War Dept; (2 only.)	–
136	41200.A	1935-1936	EN85	B	OW	6 wheel goods (6x4).	–
137	41300.A	1937-1938	EN85	O	OW	6 wheel goods (6x4).	–
141	44001.A	1935-1937	EN76/80/85/200	O	UW	'Valkyrie' 35 / 40 passenger with dropped frame. Also Gardner 4/5/6LW.	1
145	45000.A	1936-1938	EN76/77/85	O	UW	'Valkyrie' 37 / 42 pass. dropped frame, 6 wheel (6x4 or 6x2). Also 4/5/6/LW.	–
188			Perkins Wolf			No further details.	–
463	14750.A	1936	EN68	B	OW	3 ton bonnet type based on model 46. Also Dorman 4DS.	5
463 (AM463)	14800.A	1935-1939	EN213/217	B	OW	3 ton ambulance, refueller, tractor, etc. for Air Ministry c/w Gruss air susp.	3
473	15750.A	1932-1935	EN64/68	O	OW	3 / 5 ton based on model 47. Also Dorman 4DS.	5
520	6300.A	1935-1937	EN200/205	B	OW	4 / 5 ton based on model 52. Also Gardner 4/5LW.	–
525	6400.A	1933-1934	EN205	B	OW	5 ton.	–
530	6700.A	1935-1937	EN80/200/205	O	OW	4 / 5 ton based on model 53; Merryweather f/e. Also Gardner 4/5LW.	1
535	6800.A	1933-1935	EN205	O	OW	5 ton.	–
540	17300.A	1935-1937	EN75/200	B	OW	6 ton based on model 54. Also Gardner 4/5LW.	1
546	17200.A					No details available, see model 54.	–
547	17400.A	1935-1938	EN80/85	B	OW	6 ton. Also Gardner 5/6LW.	–
549	10921.A	1935-1938	EN80/85	B	OW	12 ton, 6 wheel (6x4 or 6x2). Also Gardner 5/6LW. (Approximately 12 only.)	–
550	17700.A	1935-1937	EN75/76/200	O	OW	6 ton based on model 55. Also Gardner 4LW.	5
553	3200.A	1936-1938	EN75/76/80/85	O	OW	9 / 10 ton, 6 wheel (6x4). Also Gardner 5LW.	–

Model	Chassis Nos. From	Dates of Production	Engines	Layout	Final Drive	Notes	No. of Preserved / Surviving.
556	17600.A					No details available see model 55.	–
557	17800.A	1935-1938	EN76/80/85	O	OW	6 / 7.5 ton. Also Gardner 5/6LW.	3
559	8920.A	1935-1938	EN80/85	O	OW	12 / 13 ton, 6 wheel(6x4 or 6x2).Also Gardner 5/6LW.	–
561	33000.A	1935-1938	EN85	O	OW	15 ton, 8 wheel (8x4). Also Gardner 6LW.	–
563	33001.K	1937	Gardner 5LW	O	OW	9 ton, 6 wheel twin steer (6x2) (1 only).	–
AZ1	50000.A/B	1937	EN270	O	SB	30 / 40 cwt (2 only).	1
AZ2	50500.A	1937	EN270	B	SB	30 / 40 cwt (1 only).	–
AZ3	50010.A	1938	EN275	O	SB	3 ton (1 only).	–
AZ5	50020.A	1939, 1945-49	EN271/272	O	SB	30 / 45 cwt	9
AZ7	50260.A	1940, 1945-46	EN275	O	SB	57 cwt	–
AZ8	50760.A	1940	EN275	B	SB	3 ton (1 only).	–
AZ9	50036.A	1946-1949	EN271/272	O	SB	58 cwt	3
BY1	52000.A	1937-1940	EN214/215	O	OW	3 ton, 6 wheel (6x4) for War Dept.	–
BY3	52200.A	1940-1941	EN278	O	OW	3 ton, 6 wheel (6x4) for War Dept.	–
BY5	52450.A	1941-1945	EN280	O	OW	3 ton, 6 wheel (6x4) for War Dept.	1
BY7	52600.A					1 only; no further details.	–
CX1	54000.A	1936-39, 44-49	EN233/234/236	O	OW	6 / 7.5 ton. Also Gardner 4LW pre-1940.	7
CX2	54700.A	1938-39, 44-49	EN233/234/236/237	B	OW	7.5 ton. Also Gardner 4LW pre-1940.	–
CX3	55000.A	1937-39, 44-49	EN242/243/245	O	OW	6 / 7.25 ton. Also Gardner 5/6LW pre-1940.	6
CX4	55700.A	1938-39, 44-49	EN242/245	B	OW	7.25 ton. Also Gardner 5/6LW pre-1940.	2
CX5	56000.A	1937-39, 47-49	EN242/243/245	O	OW	11 / 13 ton, 6 wheel (6x4 or 6x2). Also Gardner 6LW pre-1940.	1
WD.CX6	56700.A	1940-1941	EN244	B	OW	10 ton, 6 wheel (6x4) general service truck for War Dept.	1
CX7	57000.A	1938-39, 46-49	EN242/243/245	O	OW	14.5 / 15 ton, 8 wheel (8x4). Also Gardner 6LW pre-1940.	2
CX8	57000.A					No details available (see CX7).	–
CX9	58000.A	1938-40, 45-50	EN233/234/236	O	UW	'Valkyrie' 32 / 39 pass. dropped frame s/deck. Also Gardner 4LW pre-1940.	2
CX10	58500.A					No details available (see CX12/14).	–
CX11	58000.A	1937-1940	Gardner 5LW	O	UW	'Valkyrie' 32 / 39 passenger single deck with dropped frame.	–
CX12	58500.A					No details available (see CX10/14).	–
CX13	58000.A	1938-42, 45-48	EN242/245/246/256	O	UW	'Valkyrie' 32 / 39 pass. dropped frame s/deck. Also Gardner 6LW pre-1940.	2
CX14	58500.A	1939	EN245	B	UW	Fire appliance based on CX13.	–
CX15	59000.A					Reserved for 5 cylinder 6 wheel single deck bus/coach chassis, none built.	–
CX17	59000.A					Reserved for 6 cylinder 6 wheel single deck bus/coach chassis, none built.	–
CX19	60000.A	1938-42, 45-49	EN242/247	O	UW	'Venturer' 50 / 60 passenger double deck. Also Gardner 6LW pre-1940.	12
CX20	60002.K	1939	EN245	B	UW	Fire appliance based on CX19 (1 only).	–
CX21.SAR	60500.A	1939-1941	EN246	O	OW	7 / 8 ton, 6 wheel (6x4) for South African Railways.	–
CX21	60520.A	1938-1940	EN242/245/248	O	OW	7 / 8 ton, 6 wheel (6x4). Also Gardner 6LW.	–
CX22	60850.A	1939	EN242	B	OW	6 wheel (6x4).	–
WD.CX22	63700.A	1943-1945	EN244	B	OW	6 wheel (6x4) heavy artillery tractor for War Dept.	21
CX23	60520.A	1939-1941	EN242/248	O	OW	9 / 10 ton, 6 wheel (6x4).	–
CX23.SAR	61000.A	1939, 1947-49	EN243/246/256	O	OW	9.5 / 10 ton, 6 wheel (6x4) for South African Railways.	–
WD.CX23	61050.A	1941-1944	EN244	O	OW	10 ton, 6 wheel (6x4) general service truck for War Dept.	–
WD.CX24	61400.A	1941-1944	EN248	B	OW	6 wheel (6x4) tank transporter tractor c/w Albion 2 axle semi-trailer for WD.	2
CX25	61500.A	1938-1939	EN242/246	O	UW	'Valkyrie' passenger single deck with wide dropped frame.	–
CX27	62000.A	1938-1939	EN234/242/245	O	OW	10 ton, 6 wheel twin steer (6x2). Also Gardner 5LW.	–
CX29	62500.A	1938-1940	EN242/245	O	OW	10 ton, 6 wheel (6x4). Also Gardner 5LW.	–
CX31	63000.A					No details available.	–
WD.CX33	63500.A/B	1943-1944	EN248 twin engined		OW	8 wheel (8x8/8x6) tank transporter heavy tractor c/w trailer for WD (2 only).	–
CX37	60101.A	1949-1951	EN243/256	O	UW	'Venturer' 56 / 66 passenger double deck.	1
CX39	60301.A	1948-1950	EN243/256	O	UW	'Valiant' 29 / 41 passenger single deck with wide dropped frame.	4
CX41	60860.A	1948-1949	EN243/256	O	OW	'Viking' 34 / 57 passenger single deck with straight frame.	–
DW1	39100.A	1939	EN212	O	OW	2 / 3 ton; designed for overseas. Also Gardner 4LK.	–
DW2	38100.A	1938-1939	EN212	B	OW	2 / 3 ton; designed for overseas.	–
DW3	39500.A	1938-1940	EN212	O	OW	3 / 5.5 ton; designed for overseas.	–
DW4	38500.A	1938-1940	EN212	B	OW	3 / 5.5 ton; designed for overseas.	–
WD.EV1	34000.A	1938	EN236	O	OW	3 ton, four wheel drive (4x4) general service truck fro WD (1 only).	–
FT1	70000.A	1939				Special version of FT3 for Air Ministry. No further details available.	–
FT3	70500.A	1940-1947	EN277	O	OW	4.5 / 6.5 ton.	6

Model	Chassis Nos. From	Dates of Production	Engines	Layout	Final Drive	Notes	No. of Preserved / Surviving.
FT3A	70729.J	1947-1954	EN277/282	O	OW	5 / 6.5 ton; revised model with new axles.	16
FT3AB	70729.J	1947-1951	EN277/282	O	OW	'Victor' 27 / 31 passenger single deck with straight frame.	"
FT3A6W		1948-1951	EN277/282	O	OW	7.5 ton, 6 wheel (6x4); petrol engined equivalent of 'Clansman' FT103.	–
FT5	71500.A	1947	EN271	O	OW	3 ton.	–
FT7	71500.A	1947	EN271	O	OW	4 ton.	–
WD.FT11	72000.A	1942-1944	EN280	O	OW	3 ton four wheel drive (4x4) machinery truck for War Dept.	4
WD.FT15	72700.A	1945-1946	EN281	B	OW	6 wheeled (6x6) field artillery tractor for War Dept.	3
FT17	72800.A	1947	EN286	O	OW	5 / 6 ton.	–
FT19	72100.A	1947	EN277	O	OW	5 / 6 ton.	–
FT21	71530.A	1949-1954	EN271/272	O	OW	3 ton.	15
FT23	71530.A	1950-1954	EN271/272	O	OW	4 ton.	3
FT25	71700.A	1954-1957	EN218	O	OW	'Claymore' 2.5 / 3 ton with Leyland gearbox; 'A' suffix had Albion gearbox.	1
FT27	71700.A	1954-1957	EN218	O	OW	'Claymore' 3 / 5 ton with Leyland gearbox; 'A' suffix had Albion gearbox.	10
FT35	72801.A	1948-1952	EN286	O	OW	'Clansman' 5 ton.	11
FT36	70150.A	1948-1952	EN286	B	OW	'Clansman' 5 ton.	1
FT37	72801.A	1948-1951	EN286	O	OW	'Chieftain' 6.5 ton.	33
FT37A	73200.A	1952-1953	EN286	O	OW	'Chieftain' 5 / 6.5 ton.	6
FT37C	74000.A	1953-1957	EN286	O	OW	'Chieftain' 5 / 6.5 ton.	26
FT37E/H	74500.A	1953-1957	EN286	O	OW	'Chieftain' 4.5 / 6.5 ton.	9
FT37K	74208.F	1957-1958	EN287	O	OW	'Chieftain' 6.5 ton.	21
FT38	70150.A	1948-1950	EN286	B	OW	'Chieftain' 6.5 ton.	–
FT39	72801.A	1948-1952	EN286	O	OW	'Victor' 27 / 31 passenger single deck with straight frame.	12
FT39A	73700.A	1952-1956	EN286	O	OW	'Victor' 27 / 31 passenger single deck with straight frame.	22
FT39KA	73824.D	1956-1958	EN287	O	OW	'Victor' 27 / 31 passenger single deck with straight frame.	7
FT39(K)ALF	73824.D	1951-1958	EN286/287	O	OW	'Chieftain' 4 ton pantechnicon; EN287 in FT39KALF.	–
FT101	70050.A	1949-1957	EN286	O	OW	'Clydesdale' 7.5 ton.	6
FT101K	72429.C	1957-1959	EN287	O	OW	'Clydesdale' 7.5 ton.	5
PF101	64500.A	1955-1959	Leyland 0.350	O	OW	'Clydesdale' 7.5 / 9.5 ton.	3
FT102	71000.A	1949-1951	EN286	B	OW	'Clydesdale' 7.5 ton.	1
PF102	66500.A	1956	Leyland 0.350	B	OW	'Clydesdale' 7.5 ton, LHD only.	–
FT103	71100.A	1949-1951	EN286	O	OW	'Clansman' 7.5 ton, 6 wheel (6x4).	11
FT104	71200.A	1949-1951	EN286	B	OW	'Clansman' 7.5 ton, 6 wheel (6x4).	–
FT105						No details available.	–
FT107	79000.A	1954-1957	EN286	O	OW	'Chieftain' 10 ton, 6 wheel (6x4).	–
FT107K	79029.F	1957-1959	EN287	O	OW	'Reiver' 8 / 10 ton, 6 wheel (6x4).	1
PF107	66000.A	1956-1959	Leyland 0.350/0.375	O	OW	'Chieftain' 8 / 10 ton, 6 wheel (6x4); renamed 'Reiver' from 1957.	4
FT111TR	70300.A	1952-1957	EN286	O	SB	'Chieftain' 15 ton gtw tractor, Scammell coupling, Eaton 2 speed axle.	2
FT111KTR	70334.A	1957-1959	EN287	O	SB	'Chieftain' 15 ton gtw tractor, Scammell coupling, Eaton 2 speed axle.	3
FT121	72150.A					No details available.	–
HD23	61510.A	1953	EN253	O	OW	10 ton, 6 wheel (6x4) fully articulated rear bogie.	–
WD.HD23N	61100.A	1953-1954	EN257	O	OW	10 ton (6x4), GS truck, workshop, machinery & crane (War Dept FV11102).	5
WD.HD23S	61200.A	1953-1954	EN257	O	OW	10 ton (6x4), GS truck, tipper, cargo (WD FV11105).	–
SAR.HD23	61200.A	1953-1954	EN257	O	OW	10 ton, 6 wheel (6x4) for South African Railways.	–
HD53	55100.A	1950-1952	EN253	O	OW	6.75 ton.	1
HD55	56100.A	1950-1952	EN253	O	OW	12 ton, 6 wheel (6x4).	3
HD57	57100.A	1950-1954	EN253	O	OW	14.5 ton, 8 wheel (8x4).	9
HD61	60870.A	1950-1952	EN253	O	OW	'Viking' 39 / 43 passenger single deck oil engine, straight frame.	–
SAR.HD63	60870.A	1950-1952	EN257	O	OW	'Viking' 39 / 43 passenger single deck for SAR, petrol engine, straight frame.	–
HD73	55300.A	1953-1954	Leyland 0.600	O	OW	6.75 ton.	2
HD73XLW	56720.A	1952-1953	Leyland 0.680	O	OW	39 / 43 passenger single deck for SAR, straight frame.	–
HD75	56300.A	1953-1954	Leyland 0.600	O	OW	12 ton, 6 wheel (6x4).	–
SAR.HD175	56400.A	1957	EN901	U	OW	'Royal Scot' very heavy duty passenger 6 wheel (6x4) single deck for SAR.	–
KD23	64100.A	1951	EN1200/2	U	OW	Experimental goods 6 wheel (6x4), hor. opposed underfloor engine (1 only).	–
KP71	64000.A/B	1951	EN800	U	OW	Experimental pass. single deck, hor. opposed underfloor engine (2 only).	1
LD1	50800.A/B	1953	EN301	UR	SB?	Experimental lightweight goods, hor. opp. air cooled u/floor engine (2 only).	–
WD66	52700.A	1955	Rolls Royce B80	O	OW	5 ton 6 wheel (6x6) cargo truck (War Dept. FV14001). Also Leyland 0.375.	–
24C/1	57200.A	1957-1961	Leyland 0.600/0.680	O	OW	'Caledonian' 24 ton gvw 8 wheel (8x4) haulage, Leyland Octopus cab.	–

Model	Chassis Nos. From	Dates of Production	Engines	Layout	Final Drive	Notes	No. of Preserved / Surviving.
24C/3	57200.A	1957-1961	Leyland 0.600/0.680	O	OW	'Caledonian' 24 ton gvw 8 wheel (8x4) tipper, Leyland Octopus cab.	–
24C/5	57200.A	1959-1961	Leyland 0.680	O	OW	'Caledonian' 24 ton gvw 8 wheel, set back front axles, Miles or Holmes cab.	1
MLH3	51100.A	1955-1957	EN219	U	SB	'Cairn' 30 / 35 cwt	2
MR5	80000.A	1954-1957	EN219	U	OW	'Claymore' 3 ton.	–
MR7	80000.A	1954-1957	EN219	U	OW	'Claymore' 3.5 ton.	4
MR9	82000.A	1955-1959	EN219	U	OW	'Nimbus' 30 / 36 passenger single deck.	1
MR11	82500.A	1957-1960	Leyland 0.350/0.375	U	OW	'Aberdonian' 39 / 45 passenger single deck.	5
CA81	80200.A	1967-1972	Leyland 0.400/0.401	O	SBDR	'Cameronian' 22 ton gvw, 8 wheeler (8x4) LAD cab, mainly for Australia.	–
CD21	64700.A	1958-1972	Leyland 0.375/0.400	O	SBDR	'Clydesdale' 11.5 ton LAD cab.Leyland 0.401 replaced 0.400 from 1969.	1
CD23	64700.A	1960-1972	Leyland 0.375	O	SBDR	'Clydesdale' 47 passenger single deck, straight frame, for overseas.	–
CD65	57300.A	1965-1972	Leyland 0.400/0.401	O	SBDR	'Super Clydesdale' 16 ton gvw, Ergomatic cab; Leyland 0.401 from 1969.	4
CH3	75000.A	1958-1967	EN289/335	O	SBDR	'Chieftain' 10.25 / 11 ton gvw LAD cab.EN335 in CH3A from 1959.	5
CH7	73300.A	1960-1967	EN335	O	SBDR	'Chieftain-Scammell' 16 ton gtw, Scammell coupling and LAD cab.	–
CH13	76700.A	1962-1970	Leyland 0.370	O	SBDR	'Chieftain' Super Six' 11 ton gvw LAD cab.	7
CH17	74270.A	1962-1972	Leyland 0.400/0.401	O	SBDR	'Chieftain Super Six–Scammell' 18 ton gtw, Scammell coupling and LAD cab	1
CH51	83500.A	1967-1969	Leyland 0.370/0.400	O	SBDR	'Chieftain 51' 13 ton gvw / 20 ton gtw LAD cab.	3
CH53	84900.A	1967-1969	Leyland 0.400	O	SBDR	'Chieftain 53' 18 ton gtw tractor with Scammell coupling.	–
CH71	84500.A	1966-1970	Leyland 0.370	O	SBDR	'Chieftain 71' 12 ton gvw on road, 10 ton gvw off road; 4 wheel drive (4x4).	–
CL3	51200.A	1958-1965	EN250	U	SB	'Claymore' 7 ton, Austin axles, David Brown 'box. 'A' suffix had Albion 'box.	20
CL5	51200.A	1958-1965	EN250	U	SB	'Claymore' 5.7 ton, Austin axles, David Brown gearbox. 'A' suffix-Albion box	"
LR1	62100.A	1961-1966	Leyland 0.600	O	SBDR	'Lowlander' 72 / 74 pass. lowheight d/deck, semi-auto box, leaf springs.	10
LR3	62100.A	1961-1966	Leyland 0.600	O	SBDR	'Lowlander' 72 / 74 pass lowheight d/deck, synchro box, leaf springs.	"
LR7	62100.A	1961-1966	Leyland 0.600	O	SBDR	'Lowlander' 72 / 74 pass lowheight d/deck, synchro box, rear air suspension.	"
NS3	82050.A	1958-1963	EN250	U	SB	'Nimbus' 30 / 36 pass. s/deck, David Brown 'box; 'A' suffix had Albion 'box.	21
RE25	66600.A	1958-1965	Leyland 0.375	O	SBDR	'Reiver' 15.5 ton gvw, 6 wheel (6x4), LAD cab.	–
RE27	66200.A	1959-1967	Leyland 0.375	O	SBDR	'Reiver' 15.5 ton gvw, 6 wheel trailing axle (6x2), LAD cab.	1
RE29	67000.A	1961-1972	Leyland 0.400/0.401	O	SBDR	'Super Reiver' 18 ton gvw, 6 wheel (6x4), LAD cab.	4
RE31	67000.A	1962-1972	Leyland 0.400/0.401	O	SBDR	'Super Reiver' 16 / 18 ton gvw, 6 wheel trailing axle (6x2), LAD cab.	–
RE33	69000.A	1966-1972	Leyland 0.400/0.401	O	SBDR	'Super Reiver 20' 20 ton gvw, 6 wheel (6x4) Ergomatic cab. 0.401 after 1969	2
RE35	69000.A	1966-1972	Leyland 0.400/0.401	O	SBDR	'Super Reiver 20' 20 ton gvw, 6 wheel trailing axle (6x2) Ergomatic cab.	–
RE129	?	1967	AEC AV505	O	SBDR	Prototype of RE229, but with usual Reiver relay box and twin propshaft.	–
RE229	87500.A	1968-1972	AEC AV505	O	SBDR	'Super Reiver' 20 ton gvw, (6x4), LAD, conc mixer chassis; single propshaft.	1
TA3	56500.A	1958	Leyland 0.600	O	OW	'Talisman' heavy duty 6 wheel (6x4) 58/65 passenger for Rhodesia. (5 only).	–
VK41	53000.A	1964-1972	Leyland 0.370	F	SBDR	'Viking' 41 / 42 passenger single deck front entrance; air/hydraulic brakes.	1
VK43	53401.A	1965-1970	Leyland 0.400/0.401	R	SBDR	'Viking' 41 / 43 pass s/deck front ent; air/hydraulic brakes. 0.401 after 1969.	8
VK45	53600.A	1965-1972	Leyland 0.400/0.401	R	SBDR	'Viking' 41 / 43 pass s/deck with tropical cooling; air/hydraulic brakes.	–
VK49	?	1968-19?	Leyland 0.400	R	SBDR	'Viking' 41 / 43 pass s/deck front ent., semi-auto 'box; air/hydraulic brakes.	–
VK55	?	1968-1972	Leyland 0.400/0.401	F	SBDR	'Viking' 41 / 42 passenger single deck front entrance; air pressure brakes.	–
VL3	51500.A	1966-19?	Leyland 0.400	R	SBDR	'Valiant' passenger single deck with tropical cooling and Clydesdale axles.	–
VT15	79100.A	1958-1963	EN289/335	O	SBDR	'Victor' passenger single deck forward entrance.	–
VT17	79600.A	1958-1963	Leyland 0.350	O	SBDR	'Victor' passenger single deck forward entrance.	–
VT19	79100.A	1958-1966	EN289/335	O	SBDR	'Victor' 4.7 ton pantechnicon. Also heavy duty VT19(HD) 6.6 ton.	1
VT21	78110.A	1963-1966	Leyland 0.370	O	SB	'Victor' 41 passenger single deck forward entrance, Eaton rear axle.	1
VT23	78400.A	1963-19?	Leyland 0.370	F	SBDR	'Victor' passenger single deck front entrance.	–

Note: a small number of models have been omitted due to incomplete data.

Key:

Layout:
(i.e. Driving Control / Engine Position)

B: Bonnet type (Normal Control).
O: Overtype (Forward Control).
F: Front engine (ahead of front axle).
R: Rear engine.
U: Underfloor engine.

Final Drive:

EC: Enclosed Chain
OC: Open Chain
OW: Overhead Worm
UW: Underslung Worm.
SB: Spiral Bevel
SBDR: Spiral Bevel Double Reduction.

Other Abbreviations:

Cwt   Hundredweight (1/20th of a ton.)
GTW: Gross Train Weight (Tractor Unit plus trailer).
GVW: Gross Vehicle Weight.
LAD: Steel cab made by Motor Panels Ltd., Coventry, for and with design and tooling costs paid by Leyland, Albion and Dodge. The Albion version had a step ahead of the front axle.
SAR: South African Railways.
WD: War Department.

Appendix D
Engine List
1899 to 1972

ALBION ENGINES

Type	Fuel/ Cyls.	Format	H.P.	Bore Inches	Stroke Inches	Swept Vol/ Ltrs	Offered in Models / (Notes)
8hp	P2	HO		4	5	2.05	A1.
10hp	P2	HO		4	5	2.05	A1, A2.
12hp	P2	V		4 $^1/_2$	5	2.61	A3.
15hp	P4	V		3 $^1/_8$	5	2.51	A14.
16hp	P2	V		4 $^7/_8$	5	3.06	A3.
20hp	P4	V		3 $^1/_2$	5	3.47	A16.
24/30hp	P4	V		4 $^1/_4$	4 $^1/_2$	4.19	A6.
25hp	P4	V		4 $^1/_2$	5 $^1/_2$	5.74	A12.
32hp	P4	V		4 $^1/_2$	5	5.21	A10.
EN20	P4	V	20	3 $^1/_2$	5	3.15	A20.
EN24	P4	V	24	3 $^7/_8$	5	3.86	M24.
EN50	P4	V	30/60	4 $^5/_{16}$	4 $^3/_4$	4.54	M26, 27, 28, 31, 45.
EN51	P4	V	35/55	4 $^5/_8$	5 $^1/_2$	6.05	M34, 35.
EN52	P4	V	20/36	3 $^1/_2$	4 $^3/_8$	2.76	M40, 41.
EN53	P6	V	36/90	3 $^7/_8$	5	5.80	M26, 28, 32.
EN57	P4	V	30/45	4 $^5/_{16}$	4 $^3/_4$	4.54	M31, 32.
EN58	P4	V	20/42	3 $^1/_2$	5	3.15	M41, 43, 44, 46.
EN59	P4	V	30/60	4 $^5/_{16}$	4 $^3/_4$	4.54	M31.
EN60	P4	V	30/60	4 $^5/_{16}$	5 $^1/_4$	5.02	M50, 51, 65.
EN61	P4	V	30/60	4 $^5/_{16}$	5 $^1/_4$	5.02	M49.
EN62	P4	V	30/45	4 $^5/_{16}$	5 $^1/_4$	5.02	M32.
EN63	P4	V		?	?	?	M41.
EN64	P4	V	20/42	3 $^1/_2$	5	3.15	M41, 43, 44, 47, 473.
EN65	P4	V	35/70	?	?	?	M36, 37.
EN68	P4	V	23/60	3 $^3/_4$	5	3.62	M41, 43, 44, 49, 463, 473.
EN70	P6	V	38/85	4	4 $^7/_8$	6.02	M56, 57, 66, 67, 70.
EN73		V		?	?	?	
EN75	O6	V	38/75	4	4 $^7/_8$	6.02	M67, 69, 70, 71, 540, 550, 553.
EN76	O6	V	43/90	4 $^1/_4$	5 $^1/_4$	7.32	M69, 71, 141, 145, 550, 553, 557.
EN77	O6	V	43/90	4 $^1/_4$	5 $^1/_4$	7.32	M145.
EN80	O6	V	43/100	4 $^1/_4$	5	6.97	M56, 57, 71, 80, 141, 530, 547, 553, 557, 559.
EN85	P6	V	49/110	4 $^1/_2$	5	7.81	M56, 57, 58, 59, 70, 71, 80, 85, 136, 137, 141, 145, 547, 553, 557, 559, 561.
EN200	P4	V	35/80	4 $^5/_8$	5 $^1/_2$	6.05	M54, 55, 66, 67, 69, 141, 520, 530, 540, 550.
EN205	P4	V	30/65	4 $^5/_{16}$	5 $^1/_4$	5.02	M52, 53, 520, 525, 530, 535.
EN206	P4	V	30/68	4 $^5/_{16}$	5 $^1/_4$	5.02	M131.
EN210	P4	V	23/60	3 $^3/_4$	5	3.62	M111.
EN211	P4	V	23/65	3 $^3/_4$	5 $^3/_8$	3.89	M114, 115, 118, 119, 122, 123, 125, 127, 128.
EN212	P4	V	23/65	3 $^3/_4$	5 $^3/_8$	3.89	M114, 115, 126, 127, 129, DW1, 2, 3, 4.
EN213	P4	V	26/65	4	5 $^3/_8$	4.42	M463 (AM463).
EN214	P4?	V		?	?	?	BY1.
EN215	P4	V	23/60	3 $^3/_4$	5 $^3/_8$	3.89	BY1.

ALBION ENGINES

Type	Fuel/ Cyls.	Format	H.P.	Bore Inches	Stroke Inches	Swept Vol/ Ltrs	Offered in Models / (Notes)
EN216	P4	V	20/45	3 ½	5 ⅜	3.89	M118, 119, 122, 123, 125.
EN217	P4	V	23/60	3 ¾	5 ⅜	3.89	M463 (AM463).
EN218	P4	V	-/60	3.96	4.75	3.83	FT25, 27. (Derived from Leyland 0.350.)
EN219	P4	H	-/55-60	3.96	4.75	3.83	MLH3, MR5, 7, 9. (Derived from Leyland 0.350.)
EN224	P4	V		3 ½	5	3.15	M48. (Experimental engine.)
EN230	P4	V		3 ½	5	3.15	M49. (Experimental engine.)
EN232	P4	V		4 ⁵⁄₁₆	5 ¼	5.02	M65. (Experimental engine.)
EN233	O4	V	35/70	4 ⅝	5 ½	6.05	CX1, 2, 9.
EN234	O4	V	35/78	4 ⅝	6	6.61	CX1, 2, 9, 27.
EN236	P4	V	35/85	4 ⅝	5 ½	6.05	CX1, 2, 9, EV1.
EN237	P4	V	36/80	4 ¾	6	6.96	CX2
EN240	O6	V					(Experimental bus engine circa 1936, probably 9.08 litres.)
EN242	O6	V	52/105	4 ⅝	5 ½	9.08	CX3, 4, 5, 7, 13, 19, 21, 22, 23, 25, 27, 29.
EN243	O6	V	52/120	4 ⅝	6	9.91	CX3, 5, 7, 23, 37, 39, 41.
EN244	O6	V	52/100	4 ⅝	5 ½	9.08	CX6, 22, 23.
EN245	P6	V	52/120	4 ⅝	5 ½	9.08	CX3, 4, 5, 7, 13, 14, 20, 21, 27, 29.
EN246	P6	V	54/144	4 ¾	6	10.46	CX13, 23, 25.
EN247	P6	V	52/105-120	4 ⅝	5 ½	9.08	CX19.
EN248	P6	V	54/140	4 ¾	6	10.46	CX21, 23, 24, 33.
EN250	P4	H	-/72	4.10	4.75	4.10	CL3, 5, NS3. (Derived from Leyland 0.375.)
EN253	O6	V	52/120	4 ⅝	6	9.91	HD23, 53, 55, 57, 61.
EN256	P6	V	54/144-155	4 ¾	6	10.46	CX13, 23, 37, 39, 41.
EN257	P6	V	54/165	4 ¾	6	10.46	HD23, 63.
EN270	P4	V	?	?	?	?	AZ1, 2.
EN271	P4	V	20/45-48	3 ½	4 ½	2.84	AZ5, 9, FT5, 7, 21, 23.
EN272	P4	V	21/53	3 ⅝	4 ½	3.04	AZ5, 9, FT21, 23.
EN275	P6	V	25/65	3 ¼	4 ½	3.67	AZ3, 7, 8.
EN277	P6	V	30/80-85	3 ½	4 ½	4.26	FT3, 19.
EN278	P6	V	30/80	3 ½	4 ½	4.26	BY3.
EN280	P6	V	32/95	3 ⅝	4 ½	4.57	BY5, FT11.
EN281	P6	V	32/95	3 ⅝	4 ½	4.57	FT15.
EN282	P6	V	32/80	3 ⅝	4 ½	4.57	FT3.
EN285	O4	V					(Experimental prototype of EN286 1939 to 1947.)
EN286	O4	V	-/75-85	4 ¼	5 ¼	4.88	FT17, 35, 36, 37, 38, 39, 101, 103, 102, 104, 107, 111.
EN287	O4	V	-/93	4 ½	5 ¼	5.50	FT37, 39, 101, 107, 111.
EN289	O4	V	-/90	4 ½	5 ¼	5.50	CH3, VT15, 19.
EN301	O2	HO	-/35	4 ¼	5 ¼	2.44	LD1. (Experimental air cooled engine.)
EN335	O4	V	-/94	4 ½	5 ¼	5.50	CH3, 7, VT15, 19.
EN400	O4	HO	-/75	4 ¼	5 ¼	4.88	(Experimental 'KP' engine circa 1950 – not used in vehicle)
EN600	O6	HO	-/115	4 ¼	5 ¼	7.32	(Experimental 'KP' engine circa 1950 fitted in CX3 type chassis.)
EN800	O8	HO	-/150	4 ¼	5 ¼	9.76	KP71. (Experimental engine.)
EN901	O6	H	-/200	5 ½	6 ½	15.20	HD175. (Developed from Leyland 0.900 design.)
EN1200/1	P12	HO	-/240	4 ¼	5 ¼	14.64	(Experimental 'KP' engine circa 1950 – not used in vehicle.)
EN1200/2	O12	HO	-/240	4 ¼	5 ¼	14.64	KD23. (Experimental 'KP' engine.)

OTHER ENGINES

Type	Fuel/ Cyls.	Format	H.P.	Bore Inches	Stroke Inches	Swept Vol/ Ltrs	Offered in Models / (Notes)
AEC							
AV505	O6	V	154	4.56	5.12	8.21	RE129, 229.
BEARDMORE							
HOE	O4	V	54	4 1/4	6	5.58	M52, 53.
HOE	O5	V	85	4 1/4	6	6.97	M54, 55, 56, 57, 58, 59, 65, 67, 70. (85 bhp at 2000 rpm.)
HOE	O6	V	84	4 1/4	6	8.36	M54, 55, 56, 57, 58, 59, 80, 81. (84 bhp at 1800 rpm.)
DORMAN							
4DS	O4	V	51	3.54	4.72	3.05	M41, 43, 44, 115, 119, 122.
4JUR	O4	V	60	4.0	5.12	4.21	M52, 53.
4HW	O4	V	73	4.53	5.12	5.40	M52, 53, 67.
GARDNER							
4LK	O4	V	53	3 3/4	5 5/16	3.80	M114, 115, 118, 119, 122, 123, 125, 126, 127, DW1.
4LW	O4	V	68-75	4 1/4	6	5.60	M52, 53, 54, 55, 58, 65, 67, 69, 145, 520, 530, 540, 550, CX1, 2, 9.
5LW	O5	V	85-94	4 1/4	6	6.97	M54, 55, 56, 57, 58, 59, 67, 69, 70, 71, 80, 131, 141, 145, 520, 530, 540, 547, 553, 557, 563, 559, CX3, 4, 11, 27,29.
6LW	O6	V	102-112	4 1/4	6	8.37	M54, 55, 56, 57, 58, 59, 70, 71, 72, 80, 81, 133, 141, 145, 547, 557, 559, 561, CX3, 4, 5, 7, 13, 19, 21.
LEYLAND							
0.350	O6	V/H	94, 100, 105	3.96	4.75	5.76	MR11, PF101, 102, 107, VT17.
0.370	O6	V	106, 110	4.07	4.75	6.08	CH13, CH51, 71, VK41, VT21, 23.
0.375	O6	V/H	105	4.10	4.75	6.17	CD21, 23, MR11, PF107, RE25, 27.
0.400	O6	V	125	4.22	4.75	6.54	CA81, CD21, 65, CH17, 51, 53, RE29, 31, 33, 35, VK43, 45, 49, 55, VL3.
0.401	O6	V	138	4.22	4.75	6.54	CA81, CD65, CH17, RE29, 31, 33, 35, VK43, 45, 55.
0.600	O6	V	125, 130	4.80	5.50	9.80	24C/1, 3, HD73, 75, LR1, 3, 7, TA3. (LRs had 140bhp 'Power Plus'.)
0.680	O6	V	150	5.00	5.75	11.10	24C/1, 3, 5, HD73.
PERKINS							
WOLF	O4	V	45	3.35	4.75	2.80	M41, 43, 44, 188.
LEOPARD	O4	V	60	3.94	5.0	3.99	M124.
PANTHER	O6	V	85	3.50	5.0	4.73	M115.
ROLLS-ROYCE							
B80.Mk5Q	P8	V	164	3 1/2	4 1/2	5.67	WD66.

Key:

Fuel:

O: Oil ('heavy oil', i.e. diesel)
P: Petrol

Format:

H: Horizontal
HO: Horizontally Opposed
V: Vertical

H.P:

HP. Horse Power; shown as RAC (or Treasury Rating) / Brake Horse Power.
BHP: Brake Horse Power.

Appendix E
Chassis Output, Staff and Workforce Graphs

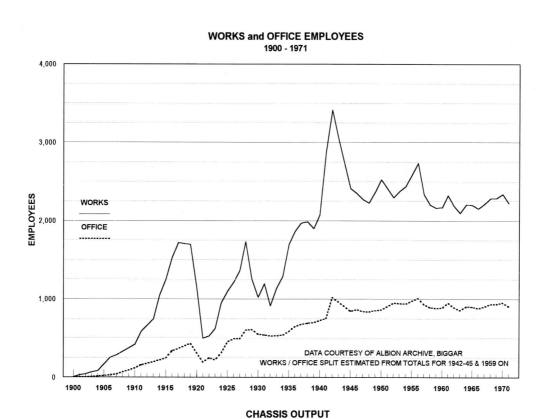

WORKS and OFFICE EMPLOYEES
1900 - 1971

DATA COURTESY OF ALBION ARCHIVE, BIGGAR
WORKS / OFFICE SPLIT ESTIMATED FROM TOTALS FOR 1942-45 & 1959 ON

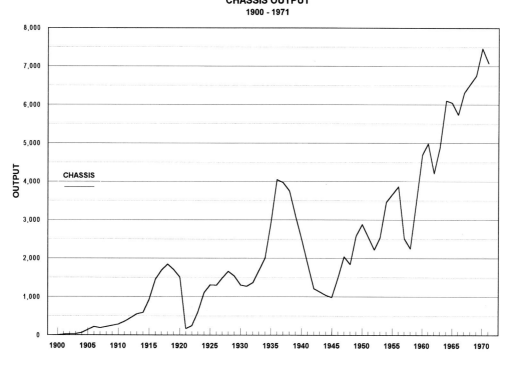

CHASSIS OUTPUT
1900 - 1971

Bibliography

Unpublished material:
Albion Directors General Minute Books, 1925-1958. (Unpublished documents Albion Archive.)

Trade Journals:
Commercial Motor
Commercial Transport (South Africa)
Modern Transport
Leyland Journal
World's Carriers

Other Publications:
Albion Service Manuals, Handbooks & Spares List. (Albion Motor Car Co. Ltd. & Albion Motors Ltd., 1905-1975.)
G.G. Hilditch, *A further Look at Buses* (Ian Allan, 1981.)
Albion Chassis List, All Double Deck Models. (PSV Circle 2CXB391, 1997.)
E. Molloy, *Automobile Diesel Engines* (George Newnes Ltd.,1955.)
Catalogue of the Sword Collection (Historic Cars Ltd., Irvine.)
Chassis List, Albion Motors Ltd., Single Deck Passenger Models 1931-1952 (PSV Circle CXB39, 1998)
Commercial Motor Index (Autopress Ltd., Brighton, reprinted 1964.)
Bart Vanderveen, *Historic Military Vehicles Directory* (Battle of Britain Prints International Ltd. 1989.)
G.G. Hilditch, *Looking at Buses* (Ian Allan, 1979.)
Sam McKinstry, *Sure As the Sunrise* (John Donald Publishers Ltd., 1997.)
The Automobile Engineer Yearbook for 1920 (Iliffe & Sons Ltd., 1920.)
Doug Jack, *The Leyland Bus* (Transport Publishing Company, Derbyshire, 1977.)
The Modern Diesel (Iliffe & Sons Ltd., 1941.)
Anthony Bird & Francis Hutton-Stott, *The Veteran Motor Car Pocketbook* (B.T.Batsford Ltd., London, 1963.)
Pat Ware, *Tugs of War* (Warehouse Publications, 1995.)

Acknowledgements

The authors would like to thank the following people who have provided great assistance in the compilation of this book:- (in alphabetical order.)

Jim Anderson *(Formerly Industrial Engineering Manager, Albion Motors.)*
Colin Bent *(Military Vehicle Historian.)*
Alex Brown *(Formerly Albion Motors Chassis Assembly.)*
Peter Burt *(Albion Motors & Albion Automotive Engineer.)*
Jimmy Cairns *(Formerly Edinburgh Depot Manager Albion Motors.)*
Jimmy Carmichael *(Formerly Albion Motors Engineer & Highland Bus Service of Glenboig.)*
Bill Clark *(Vintage Car Owner & Enthusiast.)*
Graham Ewing *(Motor Vehicle Historian.)*
Allan Galt *(Formerly Experimental Department, Albion Motors.)*
Charlie Gibb *(Formerly of Millburn Motors Ltd. Glasgow, Albion Concessionaires.)*
Andy Gibbs *(Vehicle Restorer & Owner.)*
Robert Grieves *(Motor Vehicle Historian.)*
Mick Hayton *(Haulage Contractor and Albion Archivist, Dumfries)*
Christopher Hogan *(Honorary Editor, Post Office Vehicle Club.)*
George Heaney *(Motor Vehicle Historian.)*
Tim Henderson *(Grandson of the co-founder of the 1902 Limited Company.)*
Brian Lambie, MBE *(Keeper, The Albion Archive, Biggar Museum Trust.)*
Tom McAulay *(Formerly of Repair Shop, Albion Motors, Yoker Works.)*
Andrew McCance *(Formerly Plant & Production Manager, Albion Motors.)*
May MacDonald *(Formerly of Albion Motors Publicity Department.)*
Frank MacDougall *(Farmer & Vintage Commercial Vehicle Collector.)*
Iain MacGregor *(PSV Circle Sub-Editor; AVPT Chairman.)*
Iain McKerracher *(Engineer & Vintage Commercial Vehicle Collector.)*
Prof. Sam McKinstry *(Reader, Paisley University & Former Albion Accountant.)*
Ian Maclean *(Formerly Field Service Engineer, Albion Motors; AVPT Registrar.)*
David More *(Formerly Head of Experimental Department, Albion Motors.)*
Jimmy Murdoch *(Formerly of Albion Motors Engine Assembly.)*
Rob Blackwood Murray *(Managing Director, SA Roadcarriers [Pty.] Ltd. & Grandson of the Co-founder.)*
Willie Newbigging *(Formerly Progress Dept. Albion Motors.)*
Charlie Ramsay *(Formerly Chief Buyer Albion Motors.)*
John Rentoul *(Formerly Proprietor, Doune Motors Ltd., Haulage Contractors.)*
Bill Struthers *(Coachbuilder & Motor Engineer, Jackton.)*
Richard Toft *(Military Vehicle Historian.)*
Brian Veale *(Formerly Shell-mex & BP & Chief Engineer, Motor Transport.)*
Maurice White *(Motor Engineer and Commercial Vehicle Restorer)*
Jim Wilkinson *(Motor Vehicle Historian & Vintage Vehicle Collector)*
Jim Wilson *(Formerly Chief Draughtsman, Albion Motors.)*
Jim Wilson *(Conservation Technician, Glasgow City Council Museum of Transport.)*

Of the above we would particularly like to give special mention to the following; Tom McAulay, who entrusted us with his significant collection of technical and other material; Brian Lambie, who gave us unlimited access to the archive at Biggar and searched out many elusive photographs and particulars; Ian Maclean, who gave much help with technical details, and also with the appendices relating to model and engine lists, including the information on surviving Albions; Iain MacGregor, for help with PSV matters; David More, who supplied technical details relating to the KP models; Peter Burt, for his help on our behalf at Albion Automotive; Jim Wilkinson, for supplying information on FT and 127 models; John Rentoul, who loaned us his large collection of Albion service manuals; Charlie Gibb, for answering questions relating to aspects of vehicle maintenance; Colin Bent, for all his help on military matters; and, last, but not least, Iain McKerracher, for practical support. Ian Maclean, Iain MacGregor, Evelyn Adams and Helen McPherson checked various parts of the drafts and proofs.

The photographs in this book are largely from the former Albion Motors publicity department, supplied by those mentioned above. Other photographs were taken by, or supplied from the private collections of Dave Fawcett, Robert Grieves, Willie Guthrie, George Heaney, Bryan McAinsh, Frank McDougall, Iain MacGregor, Ian Maclean, Roy Marshall, Norman Miller, Tom Thomson, John Ward, S.N.J. White, Jim Wilkinson, British Telecom Archives, The Imperial War Museum, and our own collections. We have been unable to trace the source of a small number of photographs, and we apologise if anyone has been missed out. ❑

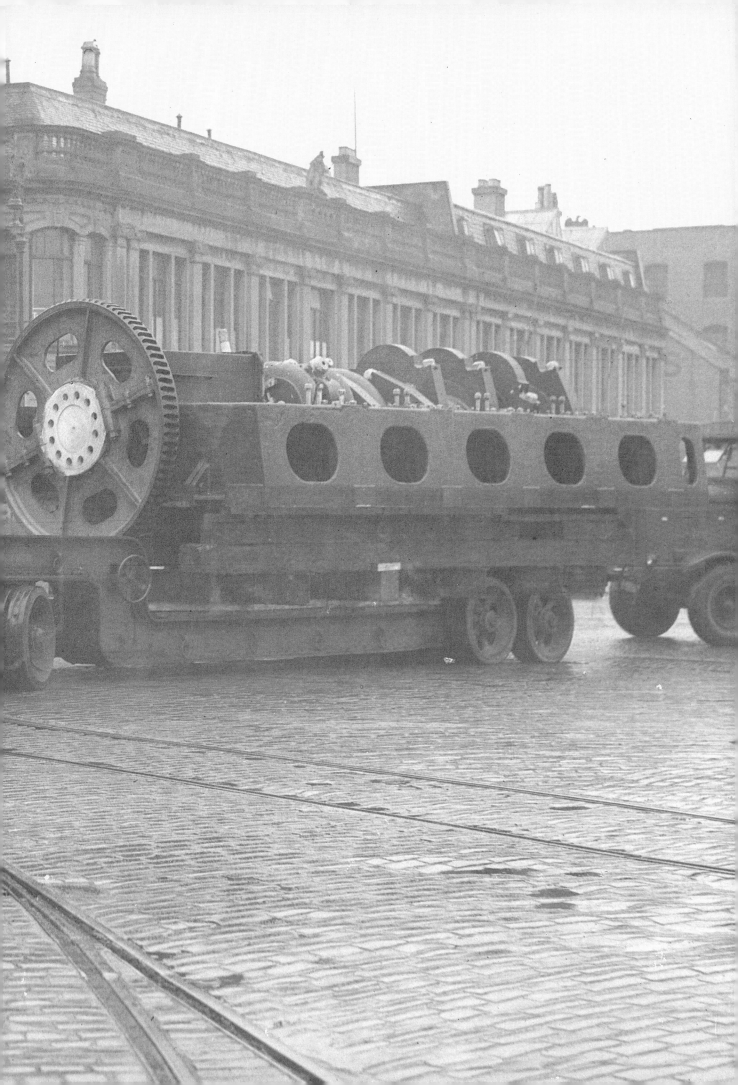